Campaign Reform

Campaign Reform

Insights and Evidence

Edited by
Larry M. Bartels
and
Lynn Vavreck

Ann Arbor

THE UNIVERSITY OF MICHIGAN PRESS

Copyright © by the University of Michigan 2000
All rights reserved
Published in the United States of America by
The University of Michigan Press
Manufactured in the United States of America
♾ Printed on acid-free paper

2003 2002 2001 2000   4 3 2 1

No part of this publication may be reproduced, stored in a
retrieval system, or transmitted in any form or by any means,
electronic, mechanical, or otherwise, without the written
permission of the publisher.

A CIP catalog record for this book is available from the British Library.

Library of Congress Cataloging-in-Publication Data

Campaign reform : insights and evidence / edited by Larry M. Bartels and
   Lynn Vavreck.
      p. cm.
   Includes bibliographical references and index.
   ISBN 0-472-09731-8 (cloth : alk. paper) — ISBN 0-472-06731-1
(pbk. : alk. paper)
    1. Political campaigns—United States.   2. Elections—United States.
I. Bartels, Larry M., 1956–   II. Vavreck, Lynn, 1968–

JK2281 .C29 2000
324.7'0973—dc21   00-044313

Contents

Preface	vii
Chapter 1. Campaign Quality: Standards for Evaluation, Benchmarks for Reform *Larry M. Bartels*	1
Chapter 2. Assessing Attack Advertising: A Silver Lining *John G. Geer*	62
Chapter 3. How Does It All "Turnout"? Exposure to Attack Advertising, Campaign Interest, and Participation in American Presidential Elections *Lynn Vavreck*	79
Chapter 4. Watching the Adwatches *Kathleen Hall Jamieson and Paul A. Waldman*	106
Chapter 5. Shifting the Balance: Journalist versus Candidate Communication in the 1996 Presidential Campaign *Marion Just, Tami Buhr, and Ann Crigler*	122
Chapter 6. Is Reform Really Necessary? A Closer Look at News Media Coverage, Candidate Events, and Presidential Votes *Daron R. Shaw*	145
Chapter 7. Regime Support and Campaign Reform *Bruce Buchanan*	173
Chapter 8. Campaign Reform: Insights and Evidence Report of the Task Force on Campaign Reform	201
Task Force Members	249
Index	253

Preface

The Task Force on Campaign Reform was commissioned by The Pew Charitable Trusts to contribute the scholarly expertise of leading political scientists to the public debate on campaign reform. The task force gathered periodically over a fifteen-month period in Chicago, Washington, and Princeton to deliberate about the state of the political process, the practical implications of academic research on campaigns and elections, and the likely consequences and prospects of proposed reforms of the campaign process. This volume presents the fruits of those efforts.

Larry Bartels's introductory chapter on campaign quality provides a theoretical and historical overview of the issues at stake in campaign reform. Bartels develops a variety of normative standards for evaluating campaign discourse and systematically applies those standards to data on the content of campaigns and media coverage, citizens' attitudes, and voters' behavior in presidential elections of the past five decades. This chapter was originally presented at a roundtable session at the 1997 annual meeting of the American Political Science Association, with stimulating commentaries by E. J. Dionne Jr., Shanto Iyengar, Stanley Kelley Jr., and Thomas Mann.

The subsequent chapters by John Geer; Lynn Vavreck; Kathleen Jamieson and Paul Waldman; Marion Just, Tami Buhr, and Ann Crigler; Daron Shaw; and Bruce Buchanan explore a variety of more specific issues relevant to the reform agenda. All of these chapters were originally presented and critiqued at a conference on campaign reform convened in Princeton in June 1998.

Geer's chapter presents an ambitious, systematic examination of the content of campaign advertising, finding a silver lining in the significant issue content of attack ads, which many campaign observers have dismissed as vacuous and corrosive. Vavreck estimates the impact of campaign negativity on public interest and electoral turnout in recent presidential elections, concluding that "attacks are not causing voters to stay away from the polls, nor are they the roots of declining interest in campaigns." Jamieson and Waldman evaluate the impact of campaign adwatches, providing strong circumstantial evidence from recent presidential campaigns and from the campaign surrounding President Clinton's proposed health care reform that such adwatches deter campaigners from making false or unfair claims. Each of these chapters poses an important challenge to conventional wisdom about the nature and impact of campaign advertising and helps to buttress the task force's rather unconventional views regarding the role of advertising in contemporary campaigns and what to do about it.

Just, Buhr, and Crigler's and Shaw's chapters focus more broadly on media coverage and campaign events. Just and her colleagues contrast the "candidate agenda" in the 1996 presidential election with the "media agenda": the authors' extensive content analysis demonstrates that "old" and "new" media alike focused most of their attention on campaign strategy and process, whereas candidate-controlled communications (speeches, ads, debates, and free airtime) were generally more substantive. Conversely, Shaw examines the interaction between candidates' actions and how the media report them, tracing changes in vote intentions in the 1992 and 1996 presidential campaigns to favorable media coverage of significant campaign events. Together, these two analyses highlight what is at stake in the struggle between candidates and journalists for control of the campaign agenda as well as the limitations of what either side alone can accomplish in a strategic environment marked by both conflict and cooperation.

Buchanan's chapter takes up some of the broad institutional and cultural issues raised in Bartels's opening chapter. Buchanan argues that declining turnout, trust in government, and faith in the electoral process represent long-term threats to American democracy but that campaign reform could contribute to effective political socialization by promoting "civic investment" by citizens. He emphasizes the positive association between investment behavior—learning and voting—on one hand and regime-supportive attitudes on the other and advocates specific reforms that show some promise of mobilizing citizens despite weak individual incentives for participation and variable situational stimuli.

The capstone of our efforts, and of the present volume, is the collective report of the Task Force on Campaign Reform. It draws on the research of task force members presented in the preceding chapters but also (and more importantly) on a much broader range of research by scholars of electoral politics, voting behavior, and political communication. It reflects the task force members' shared understanding of how well contemporary political campaigns satisfy the needs of American democracy—and how they might do better. The task force report was released in September 1998 and has been circulated widely among reformers, political activists, journalists, and political scientists.

We are doubly grateful—first as the task force's chair and executive director, respectively, and again as the editors of this volume—for the willingness of our distinguished colleagues to contribute so much time and expertise to this long and multifaceted collective effort. The enthusiasm and professionalism with which they applied themselves to the campaign reform agenda and to the scholarly issues it raised will be evident to readers of the task force report and of the background papers collected here.

The task force was aided in its work by the students in a policy workshop on campaign reform directed by the two of us in the fall of 1997 in Princeton University's Woodrow Wilson School of Public and International Affairs. The workshop was composed of eight master's degree candidates in the Woodrow Wilson School: Wendy C. Berry, DeAngela J. Burns, Jennifer Kim, José Quiñones, Richard S. Sheres, Daniel S. Volchok, Christopher Walker, and Robert Witajewski. These students sampled the academic literature on campaigns and elections; met with scholars, politicians, journalists, and political activists; produced background papers addressing several key issues in the reform debate; and issued a collective report summarizing their own conclusions and proposals. We are grateful for their assistance and salute their energy, intelligence, and idealism.

We are also grateful to the many scholars, campaigners, journalists, and political reformers who contributed to the task force's efforts by sharing ideas or evidence, pointing out flaws in our arguments, or pushing us to consider new problems or proposed solutions. E. J. Dionne Jr. of the *Washington Post,* Paul Taylor of the Alliance for Better Campaigns, and Amy Gutmann of Princeton University's Center for Human Values deserve special notes of thanks. Also at Princeton, Reggie Feiner Cohen, Patricia Trinity, Patricia Cohen, and Dean Michael Rothschild of the Woodrow Wilson School provided invaluable logistical support. And at Dartmouth, Evan S. Greenbaum provided editing and indexing assistance.

Finally, we wish to record our heartfelt gratitude to The Pew Charitable Trusts—and especially to Paul C. Light, the former director of the trusts' Public Policy Program, and his staff—for the enthusiasm with which they initiated our work and the generosity with which they supported it. The Pew Charitable Trusts have recently sponsored a variety of innovative projects in the general area of campaign discourse and civic culture, ranging from direct political activism to data collection and evaluation projects to training seminars and outreach programs. We are pleased and proud to contribute to their important efforts.

As social scientists, we especially commend the willingness of The Pew Charitable Trusts to fund careful evaluations of the impact of campaign reform efforts. Too often, well-meaning foundations scurry restlessly from one promising initiative to another, never pausing long enough to assess the impact of the activities they support. By contrast, The Pew Charitable Trusts have funded serious independent evaluations of their own projects and others in a variety of areas, including free airtime, civic journalism, and deliberative opinion polls. Those evaluations have made an important contribution to our own efforts to assess the likely consequences of actual and proposed campaign reforms. They should stand as models to be emulated by any private or public funding agency that is more interested in positive results than in good intentions.

LMB, Princeton, New Jersey
LV, Hanover, New Hampshire

Chapter 1

Campaign Quality: Standards for Evaluation, Benchmarks for Reform

Larry M. Bartels

Political campaigns are at the center of American democracy and of the ordinary citizen's connection with the democratic process. They should be our primary occasions for political education, collective choice, elite accountability, and democratic legitimation. Instead, the ordinary citizen's perception of the electoral process is marked by cynicism and dissatisfaction with the nature and tone of contemporary campaign discourse.

The symptoms are various and familiar. The proportion of citizens who say elections make the government responsive to their concerns has declined sharply over the past three decades. So has the proportion of people who bother to turn out to vote. Prospective voters say they are dissatisfied with the candidates offered by the two major parties, and many people claim that they would prefer a multiparty system or no parties at all. Politicians are held in low esteem (with most parents saying they would not want their children to grow up to be president), and the journalists who cover politics are held in even lower esteem. Campaigns are routinely criticized for being too negative and insubstantial—or, when they are less negative and insubstantial, for being too boring to engage ordinary citizens.

These symptoms are of a piece with disturbing trends in the broader civic culture of the contemporary United States: increasing dislocation and social isolation, declining trust and confidence in a wide variety of political and social institutions, and increasing pessimism regarding the prospects for economic and social progress. Thus, it is understandable and appropriate that the electoral process has become a primary focus of the broader public debate about what is wrong with American civic culture and how to fix it.

In recent years, this increasingly vibrant public debate has spawned a variety of creative ideas about how to improve the quality of political campaigns. Advocates of "civic journalism" have proposed that press coverage of campaigns should focus on the issues prospective voters say are important rather than on what the competing candidates choose to emphasize. Others have argued that the press should pay more attention to what the candidates say and do, downplaying the role of journalists as umpires and interpreters (Patterson 1993). Critics of political advertising have instituted "adwatches" that attempt to identify and neutralize unfair or misleading ads (Broder 1990; Jamieson 1992). Meanwhile, broadcasters have been urged, with some success, to provide free television time for unmediated appeals by the candidates, absent the imagery and gimmicks of paid advertisements (Taylor 1996; Adasiewicz et al. 1997). Changes have been proposed in the nature and format of public debates among the candidates. Even public opinion polls have come in for a good deal of scrutiny, including a creative attempt to cross them with civics seminars and focus groups to produce a hybrid "deliberative opinion poll" (Fishkin 1995).

The energy and interest evident in the current public debate about the nature and tone of political campaigns is certainly heartening. But the intellectual level of the debate is rather less heartening; the various diagnoses and prescriptions reflect a good deal of righteous indignation but relatively little grounding in any sophisticated understanding of relevant campaign processes. As a result, would-be reformers risk squandering their attention on trivial aspects of the problem of campaign quality and on potential "improvements" in the campaign process that would, in fact, have little or no effect—or even, unintentionally, make things worse.

This is one point at which scholars of electoral politics can make a significant contribution to the debate. While political scientists certainly have no monopoly on either normative or empirical insights regarding the problem of campaign quality, they do have professional expertise that is highly relevant to the development and evaluation of potential campaign reforms. Their systematic understanding of the American electoral process should undergird any serious diagnosis of the strengths and weaknesses of that process, and their more detailed research on campaign strategy, media effects, political information processing, and voting behavior should provide a scientific basis for assessing the likely consequences of proposed reforms.

In this chapter, I seek to clarify the stakes in the public debate over campaign reform by developing and applying systematic standards for evaluating campaign discourse. My analysis stops short of evaluating specific proposed campaign reforms. Would different formats increase or decrease the educational value of campaign debates? Would concentrated blocks of free television time in the last two weeks before the election have more or less impact than the same amount of time distributed more evenly over the whole election year? Should journalists be encouraged to provide more unfiltered reports of what candidates say and do on the campaign trail? I don't know. Nevertheless, it seems to me that an important first step toward answering specific practical questions like these is to develop and apply clearer and more systematic standards for evaluating campaign quality.

Measuring Campaign Quality: Standards and Evidence

To claim that any proposed reform would or would not improve the campaign process, some more or less explicit standards for evaluation are needed. As Kelley (1960, 8) put it almost forty years ago, "A set of standards for evaluating campaign discussion is logically prior to useful criticism of it or suggestions for reforming it."

What do we want campaigns to be, or to do? Kelley's own answer to this question was that campaigns should help to educate prospective voters:

> Campaign discussion should help voters make rational voting decisions. It has an informing function. . . . To state it another way, the voter would have to know what it is that distinguishes the candidates for a particular office, one from another; and he would need sufficient information to predict the future consequences of these differences for the realization of the purposes he holds to be most important. (1960, 8, 10)

This standard for evaluation in turn suggested a variety of more or less specific "qualitative tests" of campaign quality:

> Are voters exposed to the arguments of both sides? Does the discussion facilitate the identification of distortions and of false statements of fact? Are the candidates' statements of their views and intentions clear? Do candidates define their points of disagreement? Do campaigners offer evidence for their assertions and give reasons for favoring (or for having favored) particular policies? Are the sources of information clearly identified? If the answers to all these questions are "no," it is difficult to see how such a discussion could be expected to favor rational electoral action. If they are "yes," the probability that it will should be considerably increased. (Kelley 1960, 16)

Other scholars and political observers have suggested a variety of other standards for evaluating campaigns, including some closely related to Kelley's and others reflecting rather different normative conceptions. For example, Just et al. (1996, 242–43) argued, "There are several indicators that tell us how well a campaign has succeeded as a democratic instrument: whether the candidates and the news media structured the debate so as to address the issues the people wanted discussed; the amount of information and number of considerations the people take into account in their vote choices; and the degree of satisfaction that the people have with the campaign and the candidates." Jamieson focused even more on procedural issues, arguing that

> how we elect is as important as who we elect. The process of election . . . either provides or denies citizens the opportunity to ratify their own futures by participating in a discussion of the challenges facing the country and the ways and means of addressing them. Out of open discussion of the ends and means of national policy, a campaign can forge a consensus. In the clash of alternatives will emerge a stronger final plan and a better president. (1992, 237)

Here, I propose three general categories of standards reflecting some of the diversity of normative perspectives in the existing literature on campaign quality. In each case, I also identify some specific indicators that might serve as useful benchmarks for evaluating the quality of campaign discourse. These specific indicators figure in my attempts to measure and account for variations in campaign quality in recent U.S. presidential elections.

Campaign Tone

One obvious general standard of campaign quality involves what might be called the tone of the campaign. Do candidates and their surrogates and supporters debate the important issues of the day, or do they engage in evasion and character assassination? Do the news media convey a clear sense of what is at stake in the electoral process, or are they obsessed with campaign tactics and hoopla and constrained by the "fundamental view that politics is more image than substance" (Greenfield 1982, 15)?

For some observers, these concerns about the behavior of campaigners are motivated, implicitly or explicitly, by concerns about the effects of that behavior on prospective voters. To that extent, campaign tone may be a means to an end rather than an end in itself. However, the behavior of campaigners may also serve in its own right as a basis for evaluating campaign quality. For example, we might value the availability of relevant information even if prospective voters choose not to avail themselves of that information, or deplore misleading or trivial campaign communications independent of any effect they may have on campaign learning or public satisfaction with the electoral process. Campaign tone may also be significant for instrumental reasons that do not stem (at least not directly) from its presumed effects on prospective voters; this seems to me to be the import of Jamieson's (1992, 237) argument that "how we elect is as important as who we elect."

To better evaluate "how we elect," Jamieson has organized an ambitious collection of data relevant to evaluating the tone of political campaigns—the Campaign Discourse Mapping Project based at the University of Pennsylvania's Annenberg School for Communication (Campaign Discourse Mapping Project 1996). The project staff collected and analyzed news coverage, speeches, televised ads, and debates from the 1960, 1980, 1988, 1992, and 1996 presidential campaigns. These materials were coded to provide detailed characterizations of the content and structure of campaign rhetoric, including measures of the sophistication of campaign assertions, the extent to which they were supported with relevant evidence, and the extent to which they offered explicit comparisons between the candidates rather than pure attacks or self-promotion.

My own temporal reach is even wider, encompassing every presidential election since 1952. Thus, I rely here on somewhat less detailed measures of potentially relevant campaign behavior for which data are available over longer spans of time. In particular, I employ in the analysis that follows an indicator of "Advertising Tone" measuring the extent to which candidates' television ads were predominantly positive or negative (coded by John Geer for elections from 1960 through 1992), an indicator of "Network News" measuring the total volume of campaign coverage on the network evening news programs (coded by John Zaller for elections from 1968 through 1996), an indicator of "Bad News" measuring whether press characterizations of the presidential candidates were predominantly positive or negative (coded by Thomas Patterson for elections from 1960 through 1992), and an indicator of "Policy Schema" measuring whether news stories about each campaign were framed primarily in terms of "policy schema" or "game schema" (also coded by Patterson from 1960 through 1992).

Public Attitudes toward the Electoral Process

A second general standard of evaluation is that successful campaigns should enhance public attitudes toward the electoral process. Much of the current interest in campaign reform seems to stem from the perception that citizens are bored, cynical, and dissatisfied with political campaigns. As I will subsequently show, public satisfaction with campaigns and elections—as with the political system more generally—has been declining almost steadily for more than three decades, reaching new lows in 1996. Buchanan nicely captures the potential consequences of this decline:

> [P]reponderantly bad campaigns . . . diminish system capacity in precisely the areas good campaigns serve: problem solving and support. Another kind of cost is reckoned in normative terms: the widely perceived dilution of democracy, which occurs when those whose consent is required for legitimate government increasingly exit in disgust. A short step away lurk additional problems. Electorates that feel marginalized or chronically disaffected, for example, are potential threats not only to the legitimacy but also to the stability of any regime that fosters democratic expectations. And an estranged citizenry cannot but weaken, via a more fragile and contingent brand of support, a presidency that traditionally draws much of its strength from its link to the people. (1996, xi)

I focus here on three specific aspects of public attitudes toward the electoral process. First, I measure public interest in each presidential campaign since 1952 using data from public opinion surveys conducted in the two months before each election. This measure taps public engagement with the ongoing campaign as it happens and thus provides some opportunity to gauge how successfully each campaign captured the citizenry's interest.

Second, I measure the favorability of public evaluations of the candidates. Regardless of which candidate prospective voters end up supporting, we would prefer that they come away from the campaign esteeming both contenders. To the extent that they do so, we might credit the campaign process for replenishing the reservoir of public support on which successful political leadership depends.

Finally, I measure public attitudes toward the electoral process itself, using data from a survey question asking how much "having elections makes the government pay attention to what the people think." This measure taps more abstract and, presumably, long-term faith in the electoral process rather than direct engagement with a specific campaign. Nevertheless, we might expect good campaigns to foster faith in the electoral process and bad campaigns to erode that faith.

Voter Learning

If we think of an election primarily as a public spectacle or a democratic ritual, the attitudes of citizens toward the candidates and the campaign process may loom large in evaluations of campaign quality. However, if we think of an election primarily as a mechanism for political choice, the bottom line of how campaigns affect (or fail to affect) voting behavior and election outcomes may be more important. The attempt to specify whether and how campaigns "matter" has, of course, been a vibrant cottage industry in academic political science (Finkel 1993; Holbrook 1996; Bartels 1997), while the conviction that they do matter motivates the prodigious efforts of candidates, campaign consultants, and other political actors.

Unfortunately, academic studies of electoral politics have done relatively little to specify the normative implications of observed campaign effects. Is the tendency of campaigns to prime the state of the economy as an electoral consideration a testament to the substantive connection between governing and campaigning or an invitation to what Tufte (1978, 143) referred to as "myopic policies for myopic voters" (Bartels 1992, 252–55, 264–65)? Should the tendency of campaigns to reinforce preexisting partisan loyalties be derided as a source of "divisiveness" or applauded on the grounds that it "facilitates voters' 'normal' or expected choice of candidates" (Ansolabehere and Iyengar 1995, 96, 10)? The answers to these questions are by no means clear.

Conversely, some potential campaign effects are clearly relevant to any evaluation of campaign quality. Most obviously, we are likely to consider a campaign successful to the extent that it teaches prospective voters about the "attitudes, temperaments, and competence of candidates; their policy commitments and intentions; their past actions in both public and private life; [and] their party and other affiliations" (Kelley 1960, 12).

My analysis focuses on three distinct aspects of voter learning. First, I examine the extent to which prospective voters recognized the relative positions of the competing candidates on important political issues. Issue placements provide one straightforward and relatively objective indicator of the extent to which prospective voters "know what it is that distinguishes the candidates for a particular office, one from another" (Kelley 1960, 10). Indeed, issue placements have often been employed (for example, by Zaller 1992) as objective indicators of general political awareness.

Since issue stands by no means exhaust the range of potentially relevant bases of candidate evaluation, I also examine the richness of more general candidate considerations, as measured by the number of responses prospective voters provided to open-ended survey questions tapping potential reasons to vote for or against each presidential candidate. Since these open-ended questions allow survey respondents to focus on whatever considerations they consider most relevant rather than requiring specific bits of political information specified by the analyst, such questions have the twin virtues of flexibility and generality. The impressions citizens report in response to these questions may, of course, vary greatly in their accuracy and cogency. Nevertheless, the extent to which citizens have anything to say, good or bad, about either candidate may provide another useful indicator of campaign learning.

Finally, since prospective voters may not want or need detailed information about candidates' specific issue positions and may be led astray as well as informed by the impressions they report in response to open-ended survey questions, I propose a third measure of campaign learning derived from actual voting behavior. This measure is based on the notion that even relatively uninformed voters may succeed in voting as if they are well-informed if they can use party labels, endorsements, and other cues in the campaign environment to mimic the behavior of better-informed voters who are, in other respects, similar. In effect, such uninformed voters may succeed in learning how they should vote without ever learning, much less recalling, all the steps in the chain of reasoning leading to a "correct" vote choice. We might count campaigns as successful to the extent that they contribute to such "low-information rationality" (Popkin 1991), even if they do not produce significant increases in objective knowledge of specific issue positions or in the apparent richness of subjective candidate considerations.

Data and Analysis

The primary data analyzed here are from the most comprehensive body of surveys on the political attitudes and behavior of the American electorate, the National Election Studies (NES). My data set consists of 22,839 observations from twelve separate NES studies covering every presidential election from 1952 through 1996.[1] Some questions relevant to an evaluation of campaign quality have been asked consistently in each of these twelve elections, providing a good deal of historical perspective and considerable scope for analyses of the impact of changing campaign practices on the attitudes and behavior of the electorate.

Comparisons of survey responses over time—either across campaigns or within a single campaign—may be complicated by extraneous variation in the demographic characteristics of the survey sample at any given point in time. To minimize such complications, all of my analyses include statistical controls for individual survey respondents' age, education, income, race, and sex. The quantities reported in all of the tables and figures are for a "typical" respondent—a forty-five-year-old white female with a high school diploma and median family income.

The corresponding quantities for respondents with different demographic characteristics often differ, but patterns of change over time across or within campaigns are usually very similar for different demographic groups. Moreover, all of the demographic groups remain roughly similar in size over the four and a half decades covered by the NES surveys, with one important exception: in recent election years, respondents without high school diplomas are much less numerous and those with at least some college education are much more numerous. Thus, the primary effect of my convention of reporting results for a "typical" respondent with a specific set of fixed demographic characteristics is to control away any changes over time in attitudes, knowledge, or campaign effects that result from the electorate's increasing education rather than from changes in campaign practices.

To maximize the visual clarity of the figures, they all include the entire period from 1952 through 1996, even when data for some of those years are unavailable. I have routinely recoded ordinal survey responses to range from zero to one hundred, with equal spacing of categories. Thus, for example, responses to the NES question on interest in the campaign are coded as zero for "not much interested," fifty for "somewhat interested," and one hundred for "very much interested." However, my analysis of candidate considerations employs the actual number of "likes" and "dislikes" mentioned by each respondent, which ranges from zero to twenty (since NES recorded up to five "likes" and up to five "dislikes" for each of the major party candidates).

Some of the figures include, in addition to the main trend line, separate trend lines for respondents who said they follow government and public affairs "most of the time" and for those who said they follow government and public affairs "only now and then" or "not at all." Average responses from the former group (usually but not always above the main trend line) are denoted by upward-pointing triangles; average responses from the latter group (usually but not always below the main trend line) are denoted by downward-pointing triangles.

Some of the questions analyzed here were asked in NES pre-election surveys conducted in the two months before each election; others were asked in post-election surveys. All of my analyses of pre-election questions include a date-of-interview variable to allow for linear trends in responses over the two months of the fall campaign; the quantities reported in the tables and figures represent the estimated average values of the corresponding variables as of Election Day. All of my analyses of post-election questions omit the 10 percent or so of pre-election respondents for whom no post-election interview was obtained. In addition, all of my analyses of pre- and post-election questions include a variable identifying panel respondents (in 1960, 1976, 1992, and 1996) to minimize potential effects of panel attrition or panel conditioning on the mean values reported in the tables and figures.

Campaigners' Behavior

I begin my assessment of campaign quality by focusing on the behavior of campaigners—candidates and their supporters and the news media who report their activities to readers and viewers. Do candidates address issues of public concern clearly and honestly, or do they obfuscate and evade public debate? Do they campaign by promoting their own accomplishments and plans or by denigrating those of their opponents? Do the news media report the substance of the campaign thoroughly and engagingly to their audiences, or do they portray the campaign as a "game" in which campaign tactics, hoopla, and verbal gaffes are more important than programs, promises, and performance? Do they convey balanced portrayals of the competing candidates to the public or focus only on criticisms and conflicts?

Some of these questions are obviously more amenable than others to systematic investigation. Any attempt to measure campaign behavior over substantial periods of time, especially in ways that facilitate comparison across election years, must be a complex and labor-intensive process. Thus, I will focus on a few potentially significant aspects of campaign behavior that have already been extensively examined by other scholars. The result will be an assessment of campaign quality that is far from exhaustive in scope but a good deal more extensive and systematic than would otherwise be the case.

Negative Ads

Political scientists have paid a good deal of attention in recent years to the phenomenon of negative campaign advertising. The most vigorous and well-supported argument for the significance of negative political ads in the academic literature was presented in Ansolabehere and Iyengar's (1995) experimental study of advertising effects. According to Ansolabehere and Iyengar, "the tone of political campaigning contributes mightily to the public's dwindling participation and growing cynicism" (105) and "the single biggest cause of the new, ugly regime is the proliferation of negative political advertising on tv" (10).

In particular, these authors argued that negative advertising shrinks the electorate by turning off political independents and polarizes the electorate by reinforcing the preexisting views of partisan loyalists. The second of these claims is relatively familiar, and its normative significance is, as I have already suggested, unclear. However, the claim that "the tone of political campaigning contributes mightily to the public's dwindling participation and growing cynicism" has clear and quite significant implications for any assessment of campaign quality.

In support of these claims, Ansolabehere and Iyengar (1995; Ansolabehere et al. 1994) mustered extensive evidence from a series of experiments in which subjects watched doctored videotapes of news programs containing positive and negative campaign ads from statewide races in California, including some ads with the same topics, themes, and visuals but alternative positive and negative voice-overs. They found that both sets of ads reinforced the partisan consistency of reported vote intentions among Democratic and Republican subjects—especially those least attentive to politics. They also found that subjects exposed to negative messages were less likely to express any intention to vote—especially those who considered themselves political independents.

The concerns about negative advertising raised by Ansolabehere and Iyengar and many other campaign observers have been questioned on both normative and empirical grounds. Mayer (1996) argued "In Defense of Negative Campaigning" on the grounds that it helps to clarify differences among candidates. Adasiewicz, Rivlin, and Stanger (1997, 9) reasoned along similar lines that "as a research item, 'negativity' is problematic because it conflates concepts, among them the difference between legitimate differentiation and illegitimate, or dirty, attack." Jamieson (1992) likewise argued that distortion is more troublesome than mere negativity and that self-promoting ads are more likely than negative ads to contain false claims.

At the same time, Lau, Pomper, and Mazeika (1995) have questioned the empirical premise that negative advertising is a potent weapon in the arsenal of contemporary campaigners; if, as Lau and his coauthors asserted flatly, "negative campaigning doesn't work" (18), then it seems likely to reflect a temporary fad in campaign tactics rather than a permanent blight on the electoral process. Ansolabehere and Iyengar's specific experimental finding that negative advertising depresses voter turnout has also been challenged on empirical grounds by Finkel and Geer (1998): their analysis of survey data from real campaigns rather than laboratory experiments turned up no systematic relationship between advertising tone and turnout over a series of presidential elections.

The data on advertising tone employed (and reported) in Finkel and Geer's (1998) analysis are presented in figure 1. The data are derived from Geer's content analysis of spot ads (sixty seconds or less) in the Kanter Political Commercial Archive at the University of Oklahoma; the broader content analysis project of which they are a part is described by Geer (1998).[2] Geer's measure of advertising tone represents the difference between positive and negative appeals, each expressed as a percentage of all the issue and trait appeals coded in each campaign's television spots.[3] The theoretical maximum value is 100 when all appeals are positive, and the

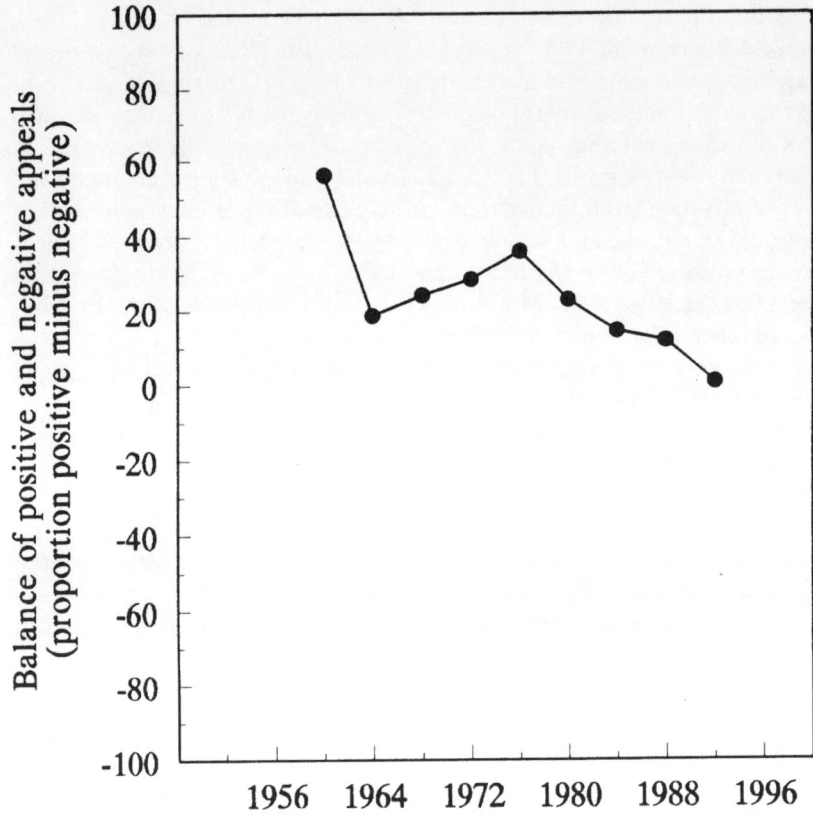

Fig. 1. Advertising tone.
Balance of positive and negative issue and trait appeals in presidential candidates' spot television ads, as coded by Geer.

theoretical minimum value is –100 when all appeals are negative; a value of zero reflects an even balance between positive and negative appeals.

Geer's analysis indicates that the tone of spot ads declined markedly between 1960 and 1964—the year of the famous "Daisy" spot evoking the danger of nuclear warfare—before rebounding in the next few election cycles. However, the 1980s were marked by a steady decline in advertising tone, from a balance of roughly two to one between positive and negative appeals in 1976 to almost exact parity in 1992.[4]

The overall balance between positive and negative appeals in Geer's data does not support the most alarmist views regarding the prevalence of negative political advertising. Even in the current hostile, negative climate, presidential candidates have apparently been making as many positive as negative appeals. Moreover, Ansolabehere and Iyengar's (1995) experimental results suggest that positive ads probably do as much or more to mobilize prospective voters as negative ads do to demobilize them. If that is the case, the increasing negativity of campaign ads may be significant not for having added a new, negative element to the campaign environment but for having eroded an old, albeit little-noticed, positive element of political campaigning.

Ambiguity and Distortion

While negative advertising has received a good deal of attention in the political science literature, other aspects of campaign behavior have been relatively less studied. Page's (1978) pioneering study of issue ambiguity and distortion provided a useful model of how to relate variations in attitudes and perceptions of citizens as reflected in opinion surveys to variations in observable candidate behavior. More recently, Franklin (1991) has exploited the much greater variation in campaign behavior observable in Senate elections to explore the impact of "obfuscation" on the clarity of public perceptions of candidates' issue stands.

Using data from the 1988 NES Senate Election Study, Franklin found that the variance of citizens' perceptions of incumbent senators' ideological positions was not much smaller for senators seeking reelection in 1988 than for those whose terms were not up. In that most direct sense, election campaigns did not seem to contribute significantly to issue clarity. However, his more detailed analysis relating the variance of ideological perceptions to the behavior of the competing candidates showed that incumbents who emphasized issues in their campaigns significantly reduced the variance of voters' ideological perceptions, especially when the incumbents emphasized a small number of issue themes. Conversely, challengers who emphasized issues significantly increased the variance of prospective voters' ideological perceptions of the incumbent, presumably by contradicting the incumbent's own ideological assertions. As Franklin put it, "the net effect of elections is dwarfed by the variation due to campaign strategy. The import of this is that while elections do not produce a statistically significant reduction in perceptual variance, the dominant elements in determining the clarity of candidate perception rest with the candidates themselves" (1991, 1209).

Of course, the clarity with which the candidates present their ideologies and issue positions is only one of several aspects of campaign behavior that have been or might be subjected to critical scrutiny. For example, the controversial "Willie Horton" ads in the 1988 presidential campaign—which sought to link candidate Michael Dukakis with a kidnapping and rape committed by an African-American convict furloughed from the Massachusetts prison system—generated renewed interest in the electoral uses of implicit appeals to racial prejudice. Jamieson (1992, chap. 1) examined the rhetoric and imagery of the Horton ads; Kinder et al. (1989) used survey data from the 1988 presidential campaign to examine their effect; and Mendelberg (1997) conducted a series of experiments designed to explore the psychology and political impact of implicit and explicit racial appeals.

Media Coverage

Campaign advertising reaches prospective voters more or less directly; but most other forms of campaign behavior are filtered through the news media. Candidates may give speeches explaining and justifying their policy proposals from sunrise to sunset, but if the journalists covering the candidates choose not to report and interpret those proposals for their listeners and readers, the speeches themselves can only affect the relatively small number of citizens who hear them firsthand. Thus, the nature of the filter interposed between candidates and the public by the news media is a crucial variable in contemporary campaigns and a potentially crucial determinant of campaign quality.

One obviously important aspect of this filtering process is the extent to which the news media provide any information at all about the campaign. If newspapers, television news programs, and other media consider the electoral process newsworthy, prospective voters may have ample opportunity to follow campaign developments; if the news media do not pay attention, even interested, motivated citizens will find it difficult to do so—and citizens may be less likely to become interested and motivated in the first place.

The most important news outlets in modern American society are the half-hour evening news programs broadcast by each of the three major television networks. These programs provide authoritative summaries of each day's important events for tens of millions of viewers. Thus, the single best indicator of the extent to which the news media as a whole pay attention to a given campaign is the amount of campaign coverage provided by the network evening news programs.

John Zaller has organized an extensive content analysis of presidential election coverage by the television networks and other news media for his forthcoming book entitled *A Theory of Media Politics.* Figure 2 presents his data on the volume of presidential campaign coverage in each election year since 1968 as measured by the average number of minutes of campaign coverage on the three networks' half-hour evening news programs on weekdays in October. Since a half-hour news program contains about twenty-two minutes of programming sandwiched between the

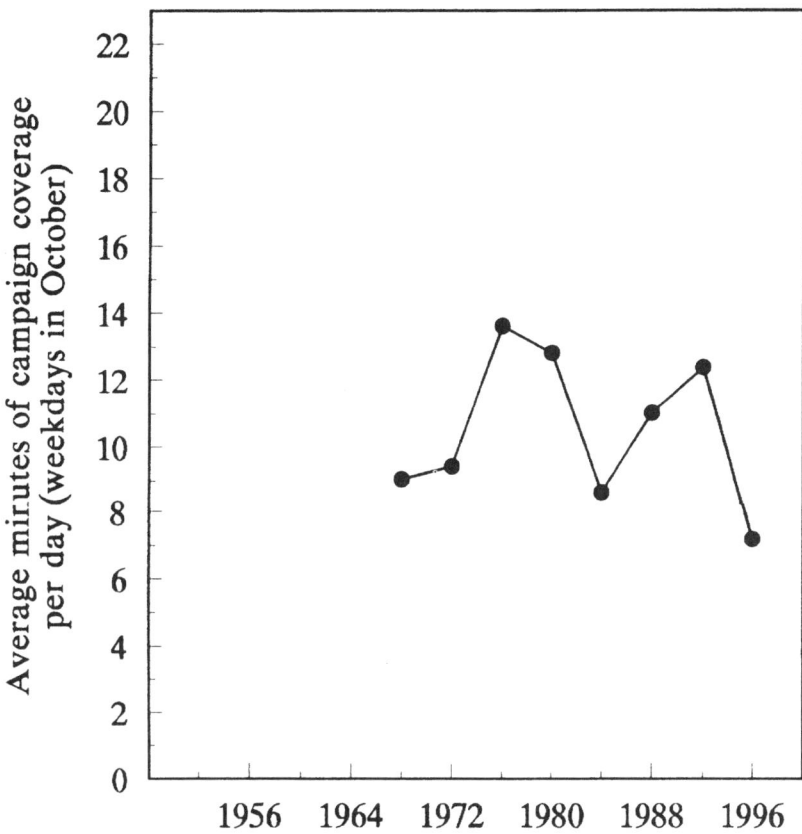

Fig. 2. Network television news coverage.
Volume of presidential campaign coverage on network evening news programs, as coded by Zaller.

advertisements, the theoretical range of this measure is from zero to about twenty-two. The actual range in figure 2 is from seven to fourteen minutes, which indicates that the amount of coverage devoted to the presidential campaign at its peak ranged from about one-third to a little less than two-thirds of the total network television news hole.

This substantial variation across election years in the amount of network news coverage devoted to the presidential campaign may be surprising. It is unclear to what extent the variation is attributable to the varying press of other news during these periods and to what extent it reflects judgments by television journalists about the newsworthiness of the campaigns themselves. Whatever the reason, the most intensely covered campaigns—in 1976, 1980, and 1992—received about five minutes' more network news coverage each evening than the least-covered campaigns—in 1984 and 1996. The figure of 7.2 minutes for 1996 is especially striking, representing a decline in coverage of about one-third from the previous historical average and of more than 40 percent from the relatively high figure for 1992.[5]

While the sheer volume of media coverage is one potentially important aspect of campaigns, the nature of that coverage may also be important. Sophisticated, highly substantive reporting may elevate the level of campaign discourse, while inaccurate, sensational, or trivial coverage may demean the candidates and the electoral process. Unfortunately, most campaign observers seem to consider the latter possibility more plausible than the former. For example, data from the Campaign Discourse Mapping Project (1996) suggest that campaign discourse in candidates' speeches and debates is richer in detail, more positive in tone, and better supported by evidence than would appear from media coverage of that discourse. While candidates rarely attack their opponents in debates or ads without offering evidence relevant to their claims, the news media usually report the attacks without the evidence. And while 40 to 45 percent of the content of debates, ads, and free television time in 1996 provided direct comparisons between the candidates, less than 10 percent of news content did so (Adasiewicz, Rivlin, and Stanger 1997, 10).

The most ambitious attempt to describe and evaluate the news media's behavior in presidential campaigns is Patterson's (1993) book, *Out of Order*. Patterson argued that the press has evolved over the past forty years from a neutral observer and reporter of campaign events into a major independent actor in the electoral process—a cynical and sometimes arbitrary filter intruding itself between politicians and the public. "If this pattern were found in another institution," Patterson wrote,

> it would be described by the press as an abuse of power. It *is* an abuse of power—and it goes largely unchecked. The press has become more assertive and judgmental, and yet it has no real accountability. . . . The press is in the news business, and the news is simply not an adequate guide to political choice. (202, 206)

The "acid bath" of press negativity criticized by Patterson (1993, 201) does not stop with the candidates but extends to the electoral process itself. According to a content analysis of television coverage of the 1992 general election campaign by the Center for Media and Public Affairs cited by Patterson, "on-the-air sources were deeply critical of the election: 100 percent of those quoted said the choices were bad, and 93 percent said the quality of the campaign was bad." And this in a campaign rated by most observers as unusually elevated and efficacious!

Patterson's argument regarding the role of the press in presidential campaigns is supported by an especially useful example of consistent media content analysis over a series of elections. For every presidential election from 1960 through 1992, Patterson analyzed campaign coverage in the *New York Times* and *Time* and *Newsweek* magazines to assess the extent to which the press conveyed "bad news" rather than "good news" about the candidates; the extent to which the press framed election stories in terms of strategy, the "horse race," and "campaign controversies" rather than policy issues; the extent to which reporters interpreted campaign events rather than simply describing them; and the extent to which the tone of campaign coverage was set by journalists rather than by the candidates or other political actors. Two examples of his results are shown in figures 3 and 4, which reproduce, respectively, Patterson's estimates of the proportion of "bad news" in newsmagazine coverage of each campaign and the percentage of *New York Times* front-page campaign stories in each election year organized in terms of "policy schema" rather than "game schema" (Patterson 1993, 20, 74).

Both of these measures show fairly consistent trends over the thirty-two-year period covered by Patterson's content analysis: the proportion of bad news nearly tripled, from a little more than 20 percent to about 60 percent, while the proportion of policy schema declined from about half to about 20 percent. Comparable trends appear in all of the content analyses reported by Patterson, and all of these trends are broadly consistent with his argument that press coverage of political campaigns has become increasingly judgmental, cynical in tone, and obsessed with campaign strategy and tactics rather than policy issues.

One implication of this fact is that his various indicators are all strongly correlated across campaigns. For example, the correlation between the "Bad News" measure in figure 3 and the "Policy Schema" measure in Figure 4 is −.84, and the average (positive or negative) correlations between these and other measures of press behavior Patterson reported range from .75 to .96. Patterson's measures of press behavior are also strongly correlated with Geer's measure of "Advertising Tone" presented in figure 1. The correlation between "Bad News" and "Advertising Tone" is −.83, while the correlation between "Policy Schema" and "Advertising Tone" is +.63.

If our aim is to evaluate campaign quality on the basis of these various measures of campaign behavior, the fact that they share a strong common trend may simplify the task considerably. Any relative weighting of positive advertising tone, positive news coverage, candidate-centered

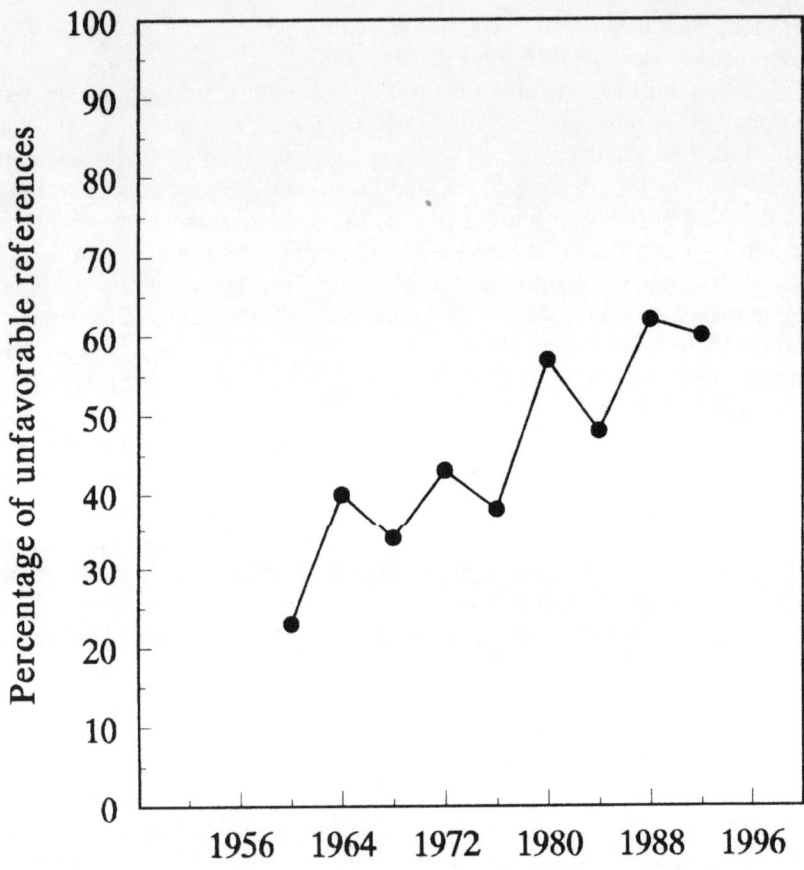

Fig. 3. "Bad News" media coverage.
Prevalence of unfavorable references to major-party candidates in *Time* and *Newsweek* (excluding "horse race" references), as coded by Patterson.

reporting, and policy focus will produce a broadly similar evaluation: by any of these criteria, the quality of presidential campaigns has declined considerably and fairly steadily since 1960.

Unfortunately, if our aim is to assess the specific effects of these various aspects of campaign behavior, the fact that they are so strongly intercorrelated may be a significant nuisance. For example, if we care about negative press coverage because we believe it makes citizens less interested and more cynical, our ability to test that belief will be significantly hampered by the fact that the same campaigns featuring large amounts of neg-

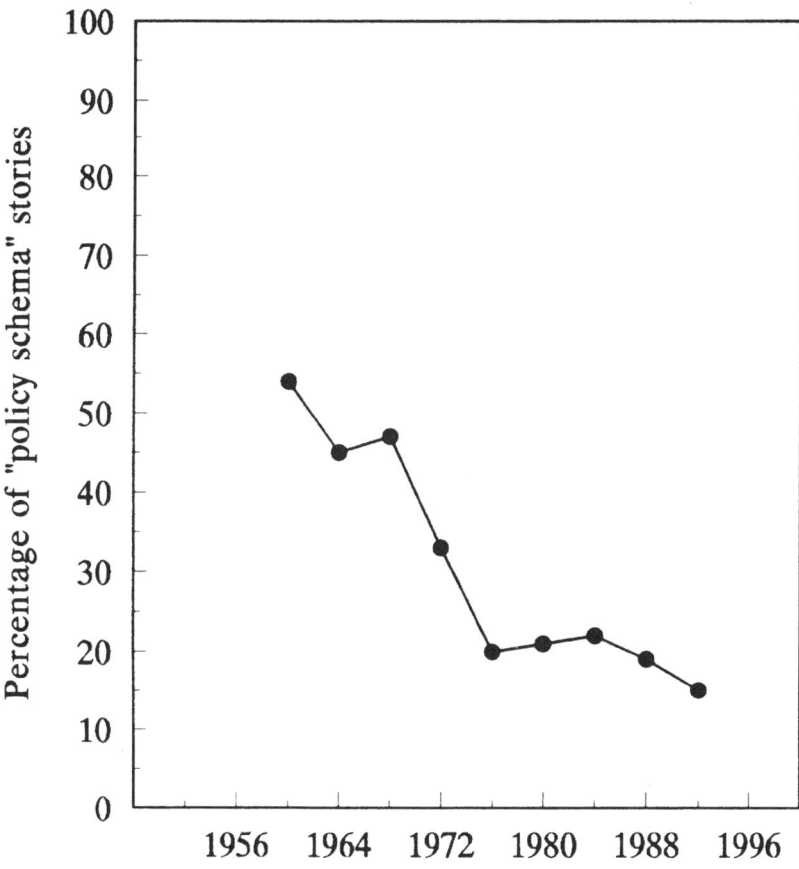

Fig. 4. "Policy Schema" in media coverage.
Prevalence of policy schema versus game schema in *New York Times* front-page campaign stories, as coded by Patterson.

ative press coverage have also featured large amounts of negative advertising, focused disproportionally on game schema, and so on. Which—if any—of these factors really matters? Controlled experiments of the sort pursued by Ansolabehere and Iyengar (1995) may help to answer that question but have their own limitations with respect to external validity. Field studies focusing on specific campaign settings with unusual configurations of campaign behavior may also be helpful. For now, however, we must sort out the relevant causal possibilities as best we can, using the data that recent political history happens to provide, making appropriate allowances for the resulting uncertainties in our inferences about the political consequences of campaign behavior.

Attitudes toward the Process

If we evaluate the quality of presidential campaigns by judging the behavior of candidates and journalists, the indictments of negative advertising by Ansolabehere and Iyengar (1995) and others and of media coverage by Patterson (1993) and others suggest that things are bad and getting worse. However, it is at least arguable that the behavior of candidates and journalists is less relevant than the effect of that behavior on the public. I have argued that two kinds of potential effects are especially relevant: how campaigns contribute (or fail to contribute) to prospective voters' learning about the candidates and issues, and how campaigns affect public attitudes toward the electoral process more generally.

Before addressing learning about the candidates and issues, this section focuses on public attitudes toward the electoral process. In particular, I examine three aspects of public attitudes toward the electoral process that happen to be relatively well-measured in the NES survey data: interest in the campaign, evaluations of the candidates, and faith in elections as a mechanism for ensuring political responsiveness. These three attitudes provide a fortuitous mix of concrete and abstract elements and of immediate and long-term evaluations. Thus, they touch on much of what has concerned observers of the American electoral process over the past forty years.

Interest in the Campaign

In every presidential election campaign since 1952, NES has asked a random sample of citizens how interested they are in the ongoing campaign. Their responses are summarized in figure 5, which shows the average level of interest for a "typical" survey respondent (a forty-five-year-old white female with a high school diploma and median family income) at the end of each of the twelve campaigns. Beginning in 1964, the figure also shows average levels of interest for the third or so of each year's sample who said they followed government and public affairs "most of the time" (denoted by upward-pointing triangles) and for the third or so who said they followed government and public affairs "only now and then" or "not at all" (denoted by downward-pointing triangles).

The question on following government and public affairs is distanced from the question on interest in the campaign in two different senses: it

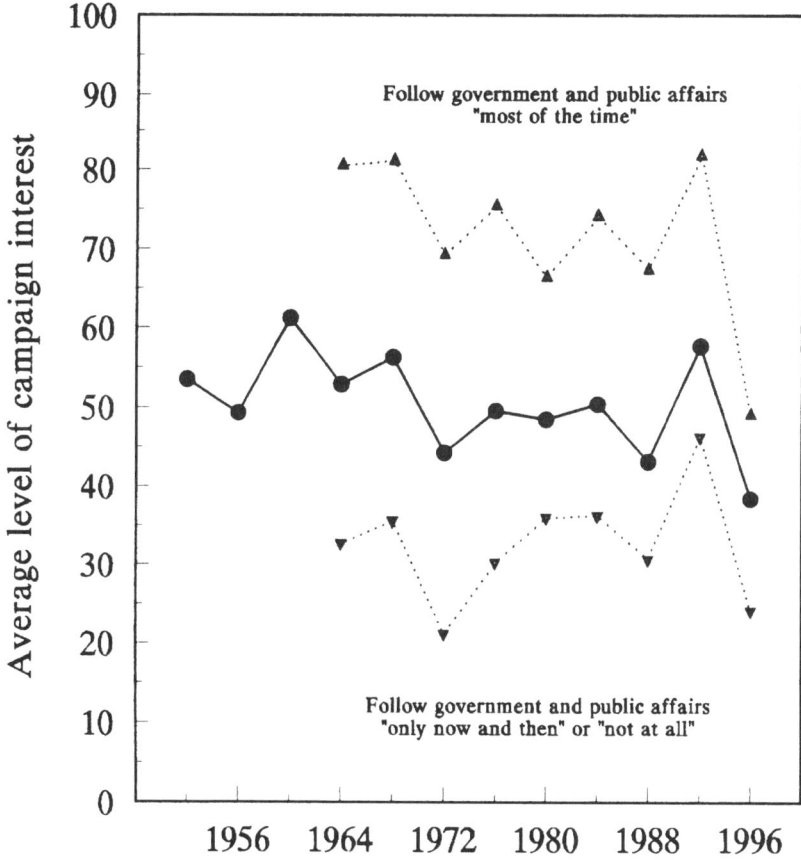

Fig. 5. Interest in the campaign.
"Some people don't pay much attention to political campaigns. How about you? Would you say that you have been very much interested, somewhat interested, or not much interested in the political campaigns so far this year?"

refers to long-term behavior "whether there's an election going on or not," and it is asked in a separate post-election interview. Still, it should not be surprising that the two subgroup trend lines in figure 5 are widely separated, with those who followed public affairs "most of the time" being much more interested in the current campaign as well.

Perhaps surprisingly, interest in the campaign peaked in 1992 not only among the third or so of the electorate least used to following government and public affairs but also among the third or so who did so most regularly. This pattern of change seems to cast some doubt on the hypothesis that additional interest in 1992 was generated primarily by the candidates' appearances on MTV, the Phil Donahue and Arsenio Hall shows, and other unconventional media outlets. While talk-show appearances may have appealed to citizens unused to following mainstream political discourse, the unusually high interest among those most attuned to politics and public affairs might more plausibly be attributed to the fact that the mainstream news media also devoted unusually heavy attention to the 1992 campaign.

The main trend line in figure 5 shows a gradual decline in campaign interest in the public as a whole amounting to about ten points on the hundred-point scale but with significant fluctuations in particular election years. The campaigns of 1960 and 1992 mark high points in public interest, while those of 1972, 1988, and 1996 mark low points. Thus, to the extent that public interest in the campaign is relevant to an evaluation of campaign quality, there does appear to be meaningful variation both in the long-term trend and in specific elections.

Another way to reckon the success or failure of any specific campaign is to consider changes in public interest over the course of the traditional fall campaign period. This reckoning takes the level of public interest on Labor Day as given and asks how much the subsequent two months of campaign activity increased (or, conceivably, decreased) public interest. Changes in the average level of public interest in each campaign from Labor Day to Election Day are presented in figure 6.[6]

What seems most striking about the results in figure 6 is how few campaigns produced significant increases in public interest. There are as many negative estimates as positive ones, and while only one of these (in 1952) is large enough to be of much concern, the general pattern suggests that, by this reckoning, successful campaigns are rather uncommon. The campaigns of 1960 and 1992 stand out, as they did in figure 5; indeed, essentially all of the heightened interest in these two campaigns evident in figure 5 appears from figure 6 to have been generated between Labor Day and Election Day. The 1984 and (to a lesser extent) 1980 campaigns also generated significant interest, with increases of about ten and five points, respectively.

The positive results in figure 6 for three of the five campaigns since 1980 provide an important bit of perspective on the overall decline in campaign interest evident in figure 5. The relatively high levels of interest on Election Day shown in figure 5 for elections before 1980—with the notable exception of the 1960 campaign—result entirely from relatively high levels of interest on Labor Day rather than from public reactions to the fall campaigns themselves. Conversely, the overall decline in campaign interest in

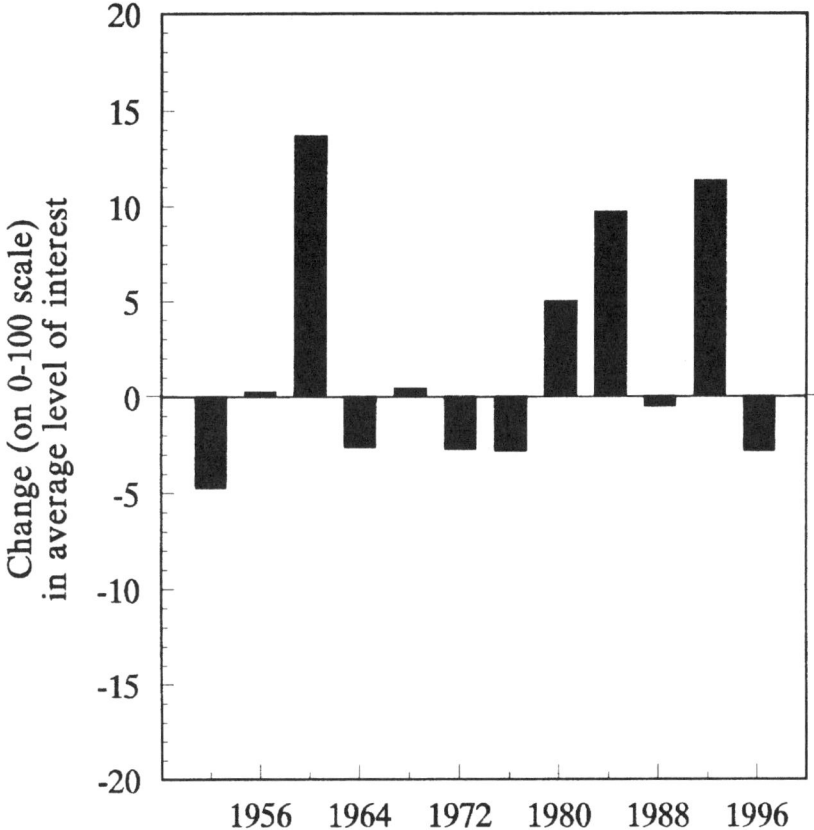

Fig. 6. Labor Day to Election Day changes in interest in the campaign

recent election cycles evident in figure 5 would have been even steeper had it not been for the increases in interest during the fall campaigns of 1992, 1984, and 1980. Thus, the relatively low levels of public interest in recent campaigns seem to be attributable to shortcomings of the long presidential nominating process—or of the political system more generally—rather than of the traditional general election campaign.

Evaluations of the Candidates

One of the most common complaints about contemporary political campaigns is that their triviality and meanness leave the public increasingly dissatisfied with the candidates, at least one of whom must then go on to function as a political leader lacking the reservoir of popularity he or she might otherwise command. The basis for this complaint—at least as it applies to recent presidential elections—is shown in figure 7, which displays average evaluations of the major-party candidates in each of the past twelve presidential elections. The evaluations are derived from responses to open-ended questions about the "good and bad points" of each candidate since 1952 and from ratings of each candidate on the "feeling thermometer" employed by NES since 1968. The individual-level correlation between these two measures is modest (.37), reflecting a good deal of measurement unreliability. However, as is clear from figure 7, the two measures track each other nicely at the aggregate level for the period where they overlap.

The general trend in figure 7 is clearly downward, but most of the decline in candidate evaluations is concentrated in the 1960s. The proportion of favorable open-ended responses declined from 69 percent in 1960 to 47 percent in 1972. Since 1972 there is no evidence of further decline. Open-ended candidate evaluations in each of the past seven elections have been about evenly divided between positive and negative responses, with a high of 54 percent positive in 1976 and a low of 46 percent positive in 1980. Thus it would not appear that presidential candidates have become increasingly unpopular over the past twenty-five years, as some indictments of the electoral process have suggested.

There is somewhat better evidence for a decline in the efficacy of the electoral process in figure 8, which shows the change in the favorability of candidate evaluations over the two months of each fall campaign. While there is clearly a good deal of election-specific variation—which presumably reflects the specific candidates and events of each campaign—there are more declines than increases in the favorability of candidate evaluations, especially in the past twenty-five years: the average decline in the favorability of open-ended responses over the course of fall campaigns from 1952 through 1972 amounted to half a percentage point, while the corresponding average decline from 1976 through 1996 was about three times that size.

However, neither of these average changes is especially large, and the difference between them is certainly not statistically significant. What may be more impressive is that there are so few instances of noticeable increases in the favorability of candidate evaluations over the entire period covered by the NES data. The 1960 and 1984 campaigns each produced an increase of five or six percentage points in the favorability of open-ended candidate evaluations, but none of the other ten campaigns came close to duplicating those successes. Thus, if we take changes in public evaluations of the can-

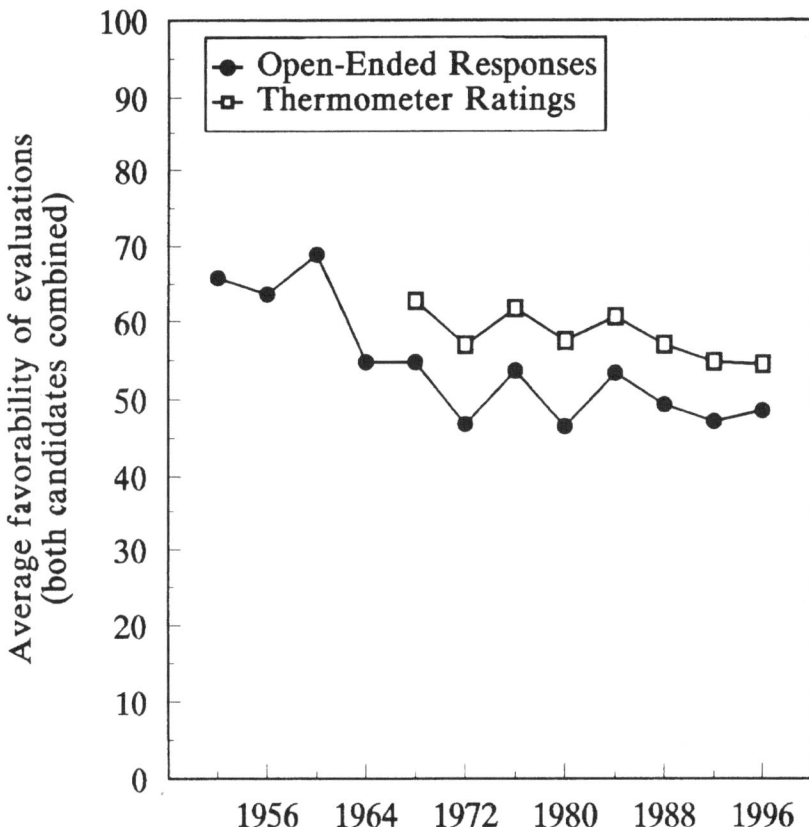

Fig. 7. Candidate evaluations.
Average evaluations of major party presidential candidates (using open-ended "likes" and "dislikes" and "feeling thermometers").

didates as a benchmark of campaign quality, we must conclude that the electoral process has been performing pretty dismally for more than forty years.

Faith in Elections

Perhaps the clearest and steadiest decline in public attitudes toward the electoral process evident in the NES survey data is displayed in figure 9, which presents average levels since 1964 of public faith in elections, as measured by a question about how much "having elections makes the government pay attention to what the people think." By this measure, faith in

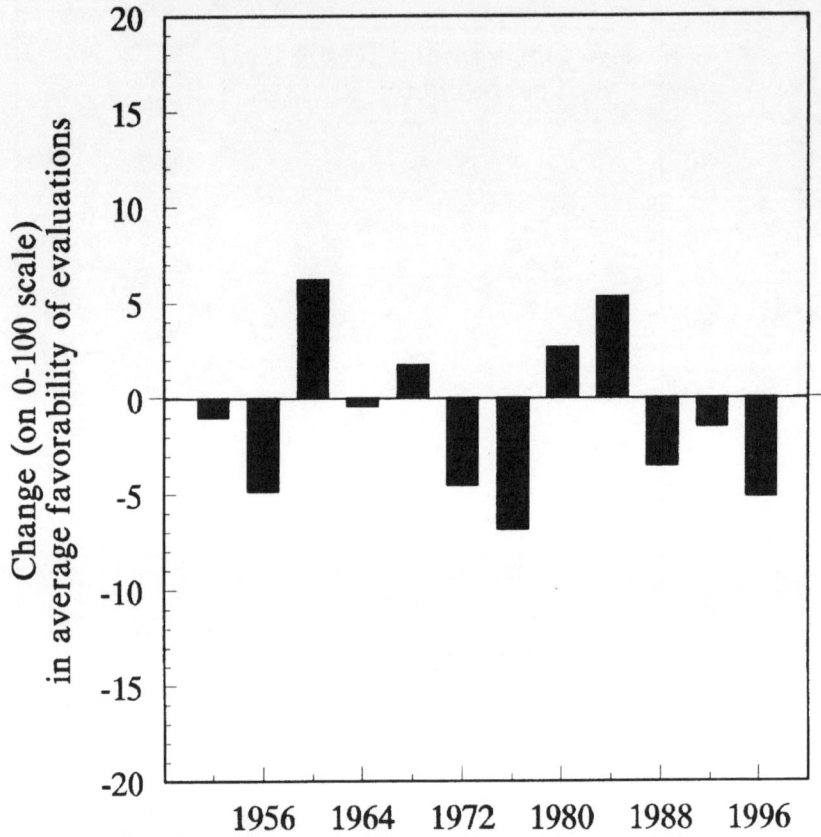

Fig. 8. Labor Day to Election Day changes in candidate evaluations

elections declined in all but one of the past eight election years, from a high of eighty-one points in 1964 to a low of fifty-six points in 1996. The only exception was in 1992, which saw a significant five-point rebound in faith in elections before the downward trend resumed in 1996.

Figure 9 also shows separate trend lines for faith in elections among NES respondents who said they followed government and public affairs "most of the time" and those who said they followed government and public affairs "only now and then" or "hardly at all." In every election year the former group attached considerably more importance than the latter group did to elections as a mechanism for ensuring political responsiveness. Although the trend lines for each of these two subgroups is somewhat

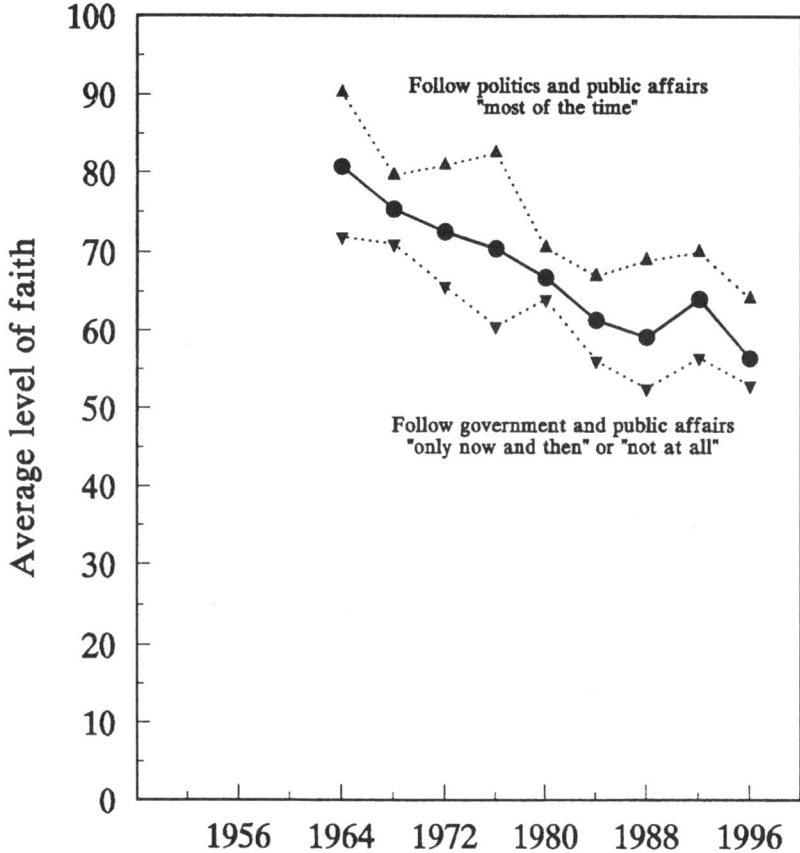

Fig. 9. Faith in elections.
"How much do you feel that having elections makes the government pay attention to what the people think—a good deal, some, or not much?"

more ragged than the overall trend line, both show the same marked decline in faith in elections over the past nine presidential election cycles.

Few time trends in the NES survey data match the steady downward slope evident in figure 9. However, those few are heavily concentrated in a battery of items concerning trust in government—a battery including the question on faith in elections from which figure 9 is derived. Other items in this battery include a general question on trust in government and more specific questions on how much tax money people in government waste, the extent to which government is run by a few big interests, and how many of the people running the government are crooked. Responses to all of these questions show more or less similar monotonic declines in trust over three decades, in most cases with a temporary rebound immediately following Ronald Reagan's landslide reelection in 1984.

These responses probably cohere, at least in part, because of a kind of verbal expressive momentum generated by survey respondents answering in quick succession a variety of similar questions on the general topic of trust in government. Thus, to capture public attitudes toward the electoral process more specifically, it may be desirable to purge the responses to the NES item on faith in elections of their correlation with responses to other items in the same battery. The trend line of faith in elections presented in figure 10 is derived from a regression analysis including as control variables individual responses to two other items in the battery on trust in government—one on whether the government is run "by a few big interests looking out for themselves" or "for the benefit of all the people," and the other on whether "people in the government waste a lot of money we pay in taxes." These items tap specific aspects of trust in government with no direct bearing on the electoral process. Thus, including them as control variables should capture the extent to which declining levels of faith in elections are simply one manifestation of a more general decline in trust in government.

The apparent decline in faith in elections is considerably less steep and less regular in figure 10 than in figure 9, as would be expected if the responses graphed in figure 9 reflect general attitudes about politics and government as well as more specific attitudes about the electoral process. Rather than declining almost steadily by three points per election cycle, faith in elections by this reckoning declined by only about two points per election cycle over the whole period and almost not at all since 1984. Conversely, the data presented in figure 10 clearly show that most of the declining faith in elections evident in figure 9 is not simply a manifestation of more general public dissatisfaction with the political system. Even holding constant respondents' attitudes toward government waste and corruption, the responses charted in figure 10 document a substantial decline throughout the 1960s and 1970s in public faith in the electoral process.

What Voters Learned

The data presented so far seem to confirm many observers' worst fears about the quality of presidential campaigns. Ads and news have become increasingly negative, candidates are generally less esteemed than they used to be, and the public's interest and faith in the electoral process have

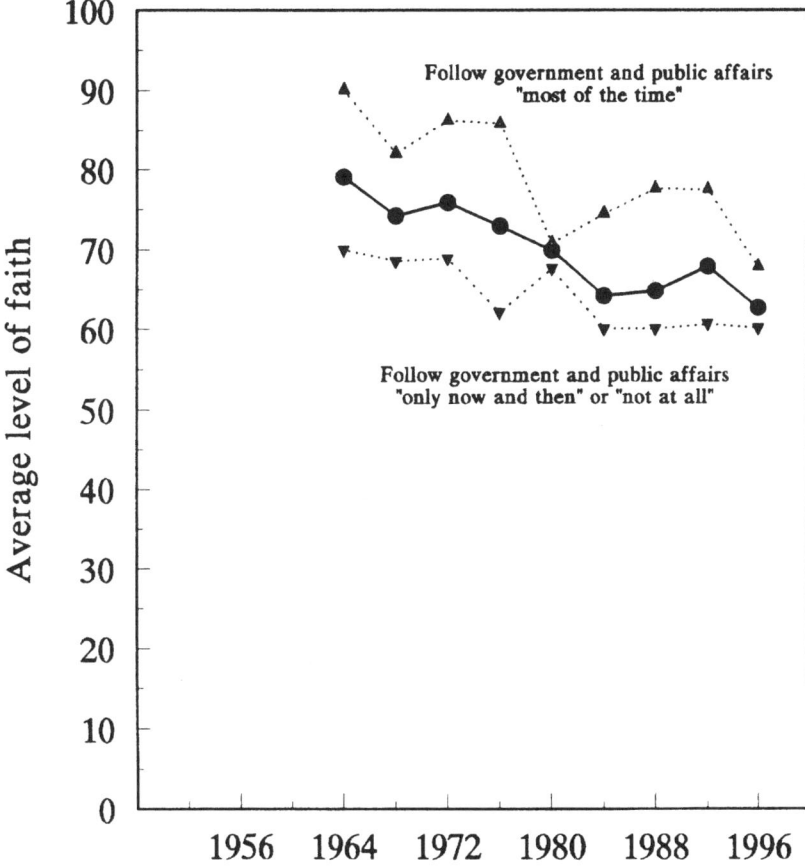

Fig. 10. Faith in elections, controlling for faith in government.
"How much do you feel that having elections makes the government pay attention to what the people think—a good deal, some, or not much?"

declined substantially. However, none of these data shed much direct light on the extent to which recent presidential campaigns may have fulfilled the "informing function" Kelley (1960, 8) proposed as a primary standard of evaluation. Despite all the negativity and public dissatisfaction, is there any evidence that recent presidential campaigns have "help[ed] voters make rational voting decisions?"

My approach to this question focuses on three different indicators of potential learning: prospective voters' knowledge of the candidates' relative positions on important political issues, the apparent richness of voters' general impressions of the candidates, and the extent to which voters mimic the voting behavior of more informed citizens with similar characteristics. Each of these indicators has significant limitations as a measure of campaign quality, but together they may shed significant light on the question of how well modern political campaigns succeed in educating prospective voters.

Knowledge of Candidates' Issue Positions

One of the first and most consistent findings of systematic survey research was that ordinary citizens know relatively little about political issues. As Berelson, Lazarsfeld, and McPhee pointed out,

> The democratic citizen is expected to be well informed about political affairs. He is supposed to know what the issues are, what their history is, what the relevant facts are, what alternatives are proposed, what the party stands for, what the likely consequences are. By such standards the voter falls short. (1954, 308)

Campbell et al. (1960, 170) similarly noted that "many people know the existence of few if any of the major issues of policy," and Converse (1964) provided a detailed demonstration of the apparent inconsistency and temporal instability of their issue preferences.

To use political issues as an effective basis for electoral choice, prospective voters must have a reasonably clear and accurate sense not only of what the issues are but also of whether and how the competing candidates' issue positions differ. It does prospective voters little good to know that they prefer increased defense spending or aid to the unemployed if they have no idea which candidate is more likely to satisfy those preferences. Thus, one of the things we might want campaigns to do is to give prospective voters a clearer sense of the candidates' positions on important issues of the day.

NES surveys for the past quarter century have asked respondents to place themselves, candidates, and political parties on a variety of seven-point issue scales. Some of these issue scales have been repeated consistently since 1972, while others have come and gone as the issues they represent have risen or receded on the political agenda. Here, I analyze placements of the presidential candidates on five issue scales, each of which has been included in NES surveys in at least four of the last seven presidential election years: general political ideology, guaranteed jobs, aid to blacks, defense spending, and the trade-off between government spending and services.

On each of these issues, Republican presidential candidates in this period have consistently taken more conservative positions than their Democratic opponents. Thus, my measure of issue knowledge requires prospective voters to place the Republican candidate to the right of the Democratic candidate on each issue scale. Those who did so are contrasted with those who declined to place either or both candidates, placed both candidates at the same point on the issue scale, or placed the Republican candidate to the left of the Democratic candidate.[7]

Table 1 shows the estimated probability of a typical survey respondent placing the Republican candidate to the right of the Democratic candidate on each issue in each presidential election year. The estimated probabilities range from less than 25 percent (on aid to blacks in 1976 and ideology in 1980) to more than 50 percent (on ideology in 1972 and government spending and services in 1996). A good deal of variability is evident both across issues and across elections; this variability presumably reflects both the relative salience of specific issues in specific election years and the relative distinctness of the competing candidates' actual issue stands. It is not surprising that Richard Nixon and George McGovern were clearly distinguished in 1972—especially with respect to ideology— or that Ronald Reagan and Walter Mondale were equally clearly distinguished with respect to defense spending and the trade-off between government spending and services (though not with respect to racial policy or ideology) in 1984. What may be more surprising is that Bob Dole and Bill Clinton were so clearly distinguished in 1996: for the three issues with comparable data going back to 1972, the average probability of placing the candidates in the correct relative positions was actually slightly higher in 1996 than in 1972.

Another way to evaluate the various campaigns is in terms of how much prospective voters learned about the candidates' relative issue positions between Labor Day and Election Day. The raw material for this sort of evaluation is presented in table 2, which shows how much a typical survey respondent's probability of correctly placing the Republican candidate to the right of the Democratic candidate changed for each issue in each fall campaign.

What may be most striking about the entries in table 2 is that they provide remarkably little indication of issue learning. There are almost as many negative entries in the table as positive ones, and the average gain in issue knowledge between Labor Day and Election Day (across both issues and election years) amounts to only one percentage point. By this standard, most recent presidential campaigns have been rather dismally unsuccessful. The only real exception is in 1972, when a typical prospective voters' probability of placing Nixon to the right of McGovern increased by an average of more than 5 percentage points between Labor Day and Election Day—a reminder of V. O. Key's (1966) metaphor of the electoral process as echo chamber. The corresponding average gains are between 2 and 3 percentage points in 1988 and 1996 and are even smaller in other recent election years.

Candidate Considerations

Analyses of what prospective voters did or did not learn about any specific issues in any given campaign are always subject to the criticism that those specific issues fail to reflect what that campaign was really about or what

TABLE 1. Issue Knowledge

Estimated probabilities of correct relative placements of major party presidential candidates on important issues, for a "typical" survey respondent, derived from year-by-year probit analyses including statistical controls for age, sex, race, education, family income, and panel status.

	Ideology	Guaranteed Jobs	Aid to Blacks	Defense Spending	Spending vs. Services
1996	.455	.430	.434	.281	.504
1992	.380	.338	—	.414	.316
1988	.318	.317	.282	.420	.344
1984	.343	.380	.337	.516	.459
1980	.238	.311	.378	.401	—
1976	.329	.305	.223	—	—
1972	.503	.384	.410	—	—

TABLE 2. Issue Learning

Changes in estimated probabilities of correct relative issue placements of major party presidential candidates during recent fall campaigns, for a "typical" survey respondent, derived from year-by-year probit analyses including statistical controls for age, sex, race, education, family income, and panel status.

	Ideology	Guaranteed Jobs	Aid to Blacks	Defense Spending	Spending vs. Services
1996	+.017	−.027	+.019	+.042	+.087
1992	+.011	−.004	—	+.054	−.059
1988	+.020	+.023	+.018	+.013	+.043
1984	−.032	+.021	−.038	+.061	+.004
1980	−.018	−.068	−.072	−.034	—
1976	−.029	+.032	+.039	—	—
1972	+.074	+.019	+.071	—	—

particular survey respondents really cared about. Kelley (1983) argued for a more flexible and heterogeneous approach to voting research, in which voting behavior is predicted and elections are interpreted on the basis of open-ended considerations volunteered by survey respondents rather than their responses to fixed questions selected and framed in advance by survey researchers. His work relied heavily on the same open-ended questions tapping "likes" and "dislikes" of the candidates that provided a measure of candidate evaluations in figures 7 and 8, but Kelley focused on the net balance of open-ended evaluations of the two candidates—both in the aggregate and in a variety of more or less specific subject areas such as "New Deal issues," "competence," and "governmental corruption"—rather than the extent to which both candidates were evaluated favorably or unfavorably.

A straightforward standard of campaign quality suggested by Kelley's work is that campaigns should enrich the stock of considerations on which prospective voters draw in formulating their vote choices. Citizens should have more to say—whether positive or negative—about the candidates in good campaigns than in bad campaigns, and the variety of considerations they report should increase more over the course of good campaigns than of bad campaigns. From this perspective, the specific content of prospective voters' perceptions of the candidates is less important than their ability to volunteer some more or less coherent reasons to vote for or against those candidates.

Figure 11 shows the average number of candidate considerations volunteered by a typical prospective voter in each presidential campaign since 1952, summing as many as five distinct responses to each of the four open-ended questions in the NES surveys: one each tapping reasons to vote for the Democratic candidate, against the Democratic candidate, for the Republican candidate, and against the Republican candidate. The figure shows a modest decline over the past thirty years in the number of candidate considerations volunteered by NES survey respondents, from an average of just over 5 mentions in the elections of the 1960s to between 4 and 4.5 in recent election years. However, so much of this decline occurs in a single year—1972—that it may be attributable to some change in the administration of the NES survey rather than to any real change in public perceptions of the candidates. In any case, aside from this one significant decline, there is surprisingly little variation from one election to another in the apparent richness of public perceptions of the candidates.

To the extent that some campaigns did elicit more candidate considerations than others, they tend to be the same campaigns that seemed in figure 5 to elicit more public interest as well. For example, the campaigns of 1960, 1968, and 1992 are relative high points both in figure 5 and in

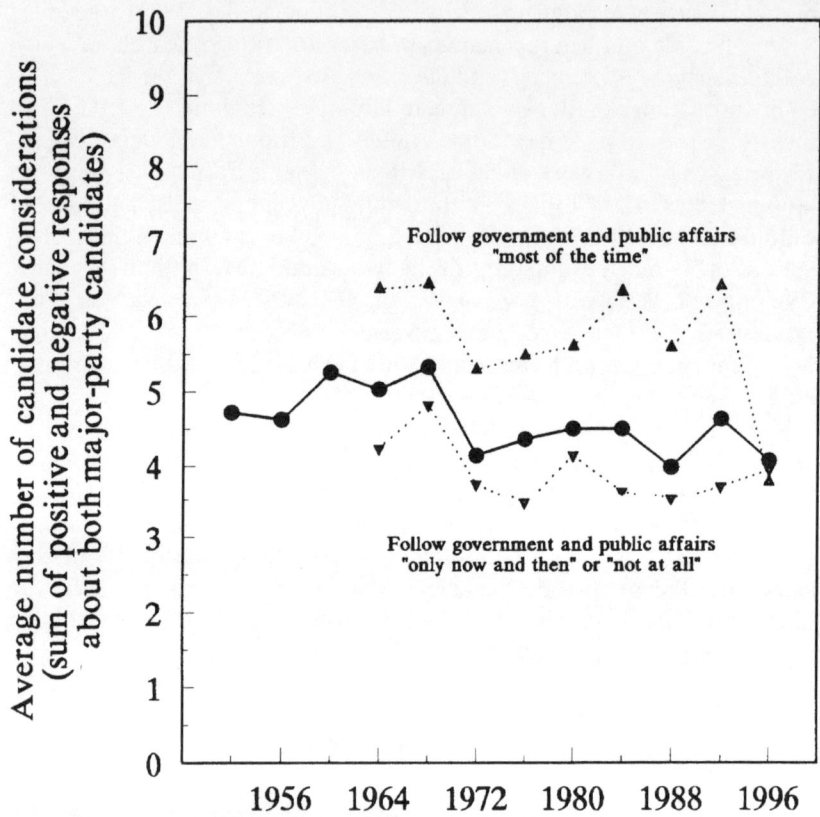

Fig. 11. Candidate considerations.
"Now I'd like to ask you about the good and bad points of the major candidates for president. Is there anything about [Republican/Democrat] that might make you want to vote [for/against] him?"

figure 11. Conversely, the campaigns of 1956, 1972, and 1988 were all marked by relatively low levels of interest, and all produced relatively few candidate considerations.

The apparent richness of candidate considerations declined once again in 1996, especially among those respondents who followed politics and public affairs most regularly. In fact, the average number of good and bad points about the candidates volunteered by this group declined by 40 percent from 1992 to 1996. The resulting average of 3.8 mentions was far lower than in any of the eight other elections for which breakdowns are available and—perhaps even more surprisingly—were no higher than for respondents who followed politics "hardly at all" or "only now and then." Moreover, much of this decline occurred during the course of the fall campaign. The average number of candidate considerations volunteered by respondents who followed politics "most of the time" declined from 5.0 on Labor Day to 3.8 on Election Day, a drop twice as large as the next largest for any group in any election year.

Figure 12 shows changes in the number of candidate considerations between Labor Day and Election Day for the entire electorate in each election year. There is clearly some tendency for the richness of candidate considerations to increase over the course of the fall campaign, but usually not by a great deal. The average increase in the total number of responses to the four open-ended questions tapping good and bad points of both candidates was about .5. In only three of the twelve election years—1960, 1976, and 1988—did the average citizen report as much as one additional reason to vote for or against either candidate by Election Day.

It appears from these results that the intensity of the fall campaign and the imminence of Election Day do relatively little to enrich or crystallize prospective voters' thinking about the presidential candidates. By this measure, at least, most of what voters know on Election Day is learned before the fall campaign is even under way.[8] If most citizens by Labor Day already had a richly detailed store of candidate considerations on which to draw, the modest further increases evident in figure 12 would probably not be surprising—or troubling. But when the average prospective voter enters the fall campaign with only four (often quite sketchy) reasons to vote for or against either candidate, the failure of most campaigns to provide most prospective voters with even one more consideration relevant to their choice is both surprising and troubling.

Campaigns, Information, and "Cue-Taking"

Another alternative to specific issue knowledge as a measure of campaign learning derives from the idea that busy citizens can make intelligent voting decisions on the basis of a variety of "cues," endorsements, and other informational shortcuts in the political environment. A significant "extenuationist" literature (the term is due to Luskin forthcoming) has emerged in recent years suggesting that campaigns may be quite successful at providing prospective voters with the cues they need to figure out which side they should be on, even when they lack the specific issue knowledge so dear to political scientists (McKelvey and Ordeshook 1986; Popkin 1991; Lupia 1992). As Page and Shapiro (1992, 387–88) put it, "People probably do not need large amounts of information to make rational voting choices.

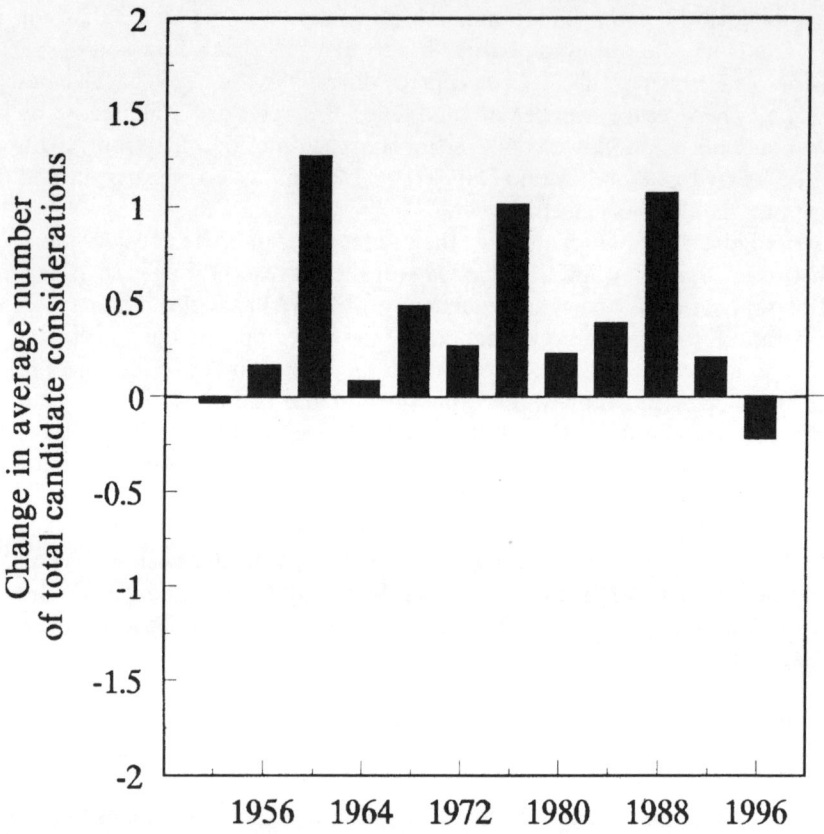

Fig. 12. Labor Day to Election Day changes in candidate considerations

Cues from like-minded citizens and groups (including cues related to demographic characteristics and party labels) may be sufficient, in an environment where accurate information is available, to permit voters to act as if they had all the available information."

The most direct empirical test of this extenuationist proposition is contained in my own recent work on "Uninformed Votes" (Bartels 1996). That work suggests that relatively uninformed voters only partially succeed in mimicking the behavior of those who are more informed. In presidential elections from 1972 through 1992, the average voter's probability of casting a Republican vote deviated by about ten percentage points from the corresponding probability for a "fully informed" voter with similar social characteristics. The year-by-year estimates of this average deviation, shown in the first column of table 3, range from 7.6 percentage points in 1976 up to 11.8 percentage points in 1984. All the deviations are clearly greater than zero, allowing the confident rejection of the hypothesis of fully efficient "cue-taking."

Many—but by no means all—of these deviations from "fully informed" individual voting behavior canceled out in the electorate as a whole. The estimates in the second column of table 3 suggest that aggregate deviations from hypothetical "fully informed" election outcomes ranged from less than one percentage point in 1976 to more than five percentage points in 1980 and averaged about three percentage points. The pattern of these deviations across the six elections included in the analysis suggests that incumbents did about five percentage points better and Democrats did about two percentage points better than they would have if all voters had been fully informed.

One standard of campaign quality suggested by this work is that good campaigns should help relatively uninformed voters mimic the choices made by more informed voters who are, in some relevant sense, similar. By this standard, the presidential campaigns of 1976, 1988, and 1972 appear from the results in table 3 to have been somewhat more successful than those of 1984, 1980, and 1992. Another standard of campaign quality suggested by this work is that discrepancies between actual and hypothetical

TABLE 3. Estimated Deviations from "Fully Informed" Voting

Individual-level deviations from hypothetical fully informed votes and aggregate-level deviations from hypothetical fully informed election outcomes (from Bartels 1996, 216). Standard errors of the estimates are shown in parentheses.

	Average Deviation (%) from "Fully Informed" Individual Vote	Aggregate Deviation (%) from "Fully Informed" Republican Vote Total
1992	10.62	+2.73
	(1.50)	(1.18)
1988	7.91	−3.01
	(1.54)	(2.13)
1984	11.80	+4.87
	(3.06)	(2.05)
1980	11.70	−5.62
	(2.38)	(3.35)
1976	7.58	+0.35
	(2.72)	(2.20)
1972	8.28	+1.71
	(2.06)	(2.20)

"fully informed" vote choices should diminish over the course of a campaign, as relatively uninformed voters absorb low-information cues allowing them to figure out which side they should be on. Evaluating a campaign by this standard requires estimation and comparison of discrepancies between actual and hypothetical "fully informed" vote choices at various points in the campaign.

Fournier's recent analysis (1997) took exactly this approach, using data from recent Canadian campaigns to study the evolution of information effects over time. "As campaigns proceed," Fournier concluded, "the discrepancies in decision rules between information groups diminish; the usefulness of political information to explain individual political behaviour declines; and the ability of uninformed voters to make decisions analogous to those of informed citizens with similar sociodemographic profiles increases" (18). The average individual-level deviation at the beginning of the five campaigns analyzed by Fournier (the 1992 constitutional referendum campaign in Quebec and in the rest of Canada and support for the Liberal, Conservative, and Reform parties in the 1993 election campaign outside of Quebec) was 16 percentage points; the corresponding average deviation at the end of these five campaigns was 9.4 percentage points.

Despite differences in setting and method, these deviations from hypothetical "fully informed" vote choices resemble in magnitude the average deviation of about ten percentage points in recent American presidential elections reported in table 3.[9] Thus, Fournier's analysis provides confirmation of the political significance of information effects in electoral settings. However, what is most original and interesting about his analysis is that it sheds light on the role of campaigns in producing approximate correspondence between actual and "fully informed" votes. The apparent reduction by a third or more in the average deviation from "fully informed" preferences during the weeks of active campaigning leading up to the vote suggests that relatively uninformed voters were a good deal more successful in mimicking the choices of better-informed voters with similar characteristics at the end of the Canadian campaigns Fournier studied than at the beginning of those campaigns. By this standard, these campaigns appear to have been surprisingly successful at providing relatively uninformed voters with useful political cues.

Evaluating Campaigns

Given the variety of reasonable standards that might be used to evaluate campaign quality—and the considerable disparity of results produced by applying these various standards to actual presidential campaigns in the preceding descriptive analysis—it is far from obvious that any meaningful global evaluations of campaign quality are possible. Nevertheless, it is not uncommon for observers to offer such evaluations, often with considerable confidence and a good deal of apparent agreement, and sometimes even with systematic evidence in support of their impressions. This seeming paradox seems to me to reflect an overly selective application of specific standards of evaluation in a setting that is normatively and empirically quite complex. Here, I illustrate this phenomenon by summarizing the implications of my analysis for assessments of campaign quality in the three most recent presidential campaigns.

A Tale of Two Campaigns, Reconsidered

There seems to be a broad consensus of opinion among political observers that the 1988 presidential campaign was one of the worst in recent memory. Germond and Witcover (1989) captured the widespread impression that the campaign was unusually nasty, brutish, and short on substance in the subtitle of their quadrennial election report: "The Trivial Pursuit of the Presidency." As Buchanan put it,

> George Bush, the victorious candidate, mounted an evasive, mean-spirited assault against the hapless governor of Massachusetts, Michael Dukakis. The media covered Bush's attacks, photo-ops at flag factories, Willie Horton, and horse-race polls. Reporters pressured neither candidate to discuss the issues or to clean up their ads. The campaign left voters ill-informed and dispirited. Only half bothered to vote. Dozens of editorials, op-ed pieces, news analyses, study commission reports, polls and books expressed everything from distaste to outrage in rejecting the tone, style, and content of the race. (1996, 1)

By contrast, there seems to be an equally broad consensus that the 1992 campaign was one of the best in recent memory. Robin Toner of the *New York Times* called it "a big, sweeping, utterly serious campaign" in which "the voters provided a merciless reality check on the candidates" (quoted in Buchanan 1996, 11). In a chapter entitled "A Tale of Two Campaigns," Buchanan (1996) contrasted the high levels of public interest and substantive focus in 1992 with the much lower levels in 1988; he attributed the difference to public concern about the economy and to the positive impact of independent candidate Ross Perot. Just et al. (1996, 243, 237) likewise considered the 1992 campaign "something of a surprising success" and asked "What enabled 1992 to be different from its lamented predecessor, the 1988 presidential election?"

The data presented here are in some respects quite consistent with the view that campaign quality was unusually low in 1988 and unusually high in 1992. The most supportive evidence comes from public attitudes toward the electoral process. Interest in the campaign jumped from a near-record low level in 1988 to a near-record high level in 1992 (figure 5), and much of this jump occurred during the two months of the fall campaign (figure 6). The monotonic decline in faith in the electoral process stretching back a quarter of a century or more continued in 1988 but was sharply reversed in 1992 (figure 9). Prospective voters had less to say about the candidates in 1988 than in any other campaign on record but more to say in 1992 than in any other campaign since the 1960s (figure 11). Citizens clearly were turned off by the 1988 presidential campaign but strongly engaged in 1992.

On the other hand, several of the measures of campaign quality proposed here put the comparison between 1988 and 1992 in a rather different light. Advertising tone declined slightly in 1988 but even more in 1992—to the lowest level on record (figure 1). Bad news in 1992 was down only slightly from the record level of 1988 (figure 2), while policy schema in news coverage became even scarcer—again, reaching the lowest level on record (figure 3). Thus, despite widespread consternation regarding Willie Horton and flag factories after the 1988 campaign, little seems to have changed in candidates' or the press's behavior. By these measures, 1992 represented a continuation rather than a reversal of long-standing trends.

The seemingly straightforward contrast between the "bad" campaign of 1988 and the "good" campaign of 1992 becomes even more muddled when we consider what prospective voters seem to have learned from each of these campaigns. While the number of candidate considerations volunteered by NES survey respondents was unusually low in 1988 and unusually high in 1992, these differences were already well in place before Labor Day. In fact, prospective voters "caught up" considerably during the 1988 fall campaign: the average number of open-ended evaluations increased from three on Labor Day to four on Election Day—the second-largest increase on record—while the corresponding increase in 1992 was only one-fifth as large (figure 12).

What is more, prospective voters seem to have learned a good deal more about the candidates' issue positions in the "trivial," "mean-spirited" 1988 campaign than in the "big, sweeping, utterly serious" 1992 campaign. The probability of correct issue placements increased at least slightly between Labor Day and Election Day on every issue in 1988 but declined on two of four issues in 1992 (table 2). On the (arguably) central issue of government spending and services, the proportion of the public that correctly placed Bush to the right of Dukakis in 1988 increased by more than four percentage points over the two months of the fall campaign, while the proportion that correctly placed Bush to the right of Clinton in 1992 decreased by almost six percentage points.

Finally, the apparent discrepancies between actual and hypothetical "fully informed" vote choices were somewhat smaller on average in 1988 than in 1992, although the net result of these discrepancies was of similar aggregate magnitude in both election years (table 3). Moreover, the comparison of actual and hypothetical "fully informed" election outcomes in table 3 suggests that a "fully informed" electorate in 1988 would have been a few percentage points more Republican, despite the "evasive" and "mean-spirited" nature of the Republican campaign, while a "fully informed" electorate in 1992 would have been a few percentage points more Democratic.

These comparisons make it clear that the various measures of campaign quality proposed here need not lead to similar evaluations of any given campaign. Citizens may be engaged but not informed or vice versa. They may develop unusually rich and detailed perceptions of the candidates but not like what they see. The same negative ads and bad news may seem to drive them to cynicism and despair in one campaign but coexist with rebounding interest and faith in the electoral process in another.

One implication of these facts is that serious global evaluations of campaign quality will require more careful weighing of disparate goods than has so far been common. There is, certainly, a meaningful sense in which the 1992 presidential campaign was markedly better than the 1988 campaign. But it certainly was not better in every meaningful sense, as some of the postmortems by pundits and political scientists seem to imply. Citizen engagement and satisfaction were clearly higher in 1992, the tone of ads and press coverage was not much different, and prospective voters learned less about the candidates' issue stands. To prefer the campaign of 1992 to the campaign of 1988 is, at least implicitly, to weigh the first of these criteria more heavily than the other two. That preference is not unreasonable, but neither is it beyond reasonable debate.

Another implication of the apparent disparity among different criteria for evaluating the same two campaigns is that the empirical connections among these various aspects of campaign quality may be weaker than scholars and pundits sometimes seem to suppose. If roughly similar behavior by candidates and the press can produce historically low levels of public interest in one campaign and historically high levels four years later, the variations in public interest are probably attributable less to the behavior of candidates and the press than to other aspects of the campaign context that may or may not be amenable to identification and alteration by would-be reformers. If the same two-month period can produce significant increases in public interest in the campaign but significant decreases in public knowledge of the candidates' issue stands, the assumption that "voters provided a merciless reality check on the candidates" may be mistaken.

The final section of this paper provides some exploratory analysis of the empirical relationships between campaign institutions and behavior on one hand and public evaluations, engagement, and education on the other. However, before pursuing those relationships, I turn to the question of how the 1996 presidential campaign stacked up against other recent campaigns when evaluated by the various standards proposed here.

1996 in Comparative Perspective

One advantage of the substantial time series provided by NES survey data is that it allows for the documentation of some long-term trends in public attitudes toward the electoral process. Another advantage is that the long time frame provides useful comparative perspective on the attitudes expressed in any given election year. Is it impressive or depressing that interest in the 1992 campaign averaged 57.7 on the 0 to 100 scale? Are the 4.07 candidate considerations volunteered by the average respondent in 1996 grounds for celebration or alarm? In the absence of meaningful absolute benchmarks, our evaluation of any one campaign is likely to be significantly affected by comparisons with other campaigns.

Given the long-term decline in several indicators of campaign quality documented earlier—and the surprising reversal of at least some of those trends in 1992—comparative benchmarks are especially relevant in any evaluation of the 1996 presidential campaign. For example, should we expect a resumption of the long decline in public interest and faith in the electoral process evident in figures 5 and 9 or a continuation of the significant rebounds in these indicators observed in 1992? Buchanan argued that the former expectation is more realistic:

> Occasionally, as in 1980 or 1992, a campaign will seem less offputting than usual. But regression to the norm is the long-term trend. Only the names, faces, and banner issues are likely to change much from one campaign to the next, giving some veneer of novelty to what are really quite fixed and recurring patterns. (1996, xvii)

The indicators of campaign quality considered here provide a good deal of support for Buchanan's argument. For the most part, the same benchmarks that made the 1992 campaign stand out as unusually successful saw the most dramatic reversions to long-term trend lines in 1996. Public interest actually declined during the course of the fall campaign (figure

6), reaching a new record low by Election Day (figure 5). Faith in the electoral process also declined markedly in 1996, more than canceling the upturn observed in 1992 to produce another record low (figures 9 and 10). By these standards, at least, things could and did continue to get worse.

The richness of prospective voters' perceptions of the candidates, as measured by their responses to open-ended "likes" and "dislikes" questions, also declined markedly, from 4.6 in 1992 to 4.1 in 1996 (figure 11). Moreover, most of this difference emerged during the fall campaigns, since the average number of open-ended responses increased by .2 between Labor Day and Election Day in 1992 but decreased by about the same amount in 1996 (figure 12).

The declines from 1992 to 1996 in campaign interest, faith in the electoral process, and candidate considerations were all concentrated disproportionately in the third or so of the public that claimed to follow government and public affairs "most of the time." This pattern is especially striking in figure 11, where a gap in candidate considerations that had been gradually widening for twenty years completely disappeared in 1996, leaving the most avid followers of public affairs with nothing more to say about the presidential candidates than the third or so of the public who claimed to follow public affairs "only now and then" or "not at all."

It is tempting to attribute this relative lack of engagement among politically aware citizens to another striking feature of the 1996 presidential campaign: the relative lack of engagement of the news media. Apparently believing that little was at stake and that the election outcome was foreordained, the media ignored the 1996 campaign in droves. Zaller coded just 7.2 minutes of campaign coverage on the average network news broadcast in October 1996—a third less coverage than the average for the other seven campaigns included in his content analysis and more than 40 percent less than in 1992 (figure 2).

Despite the relative paucity of campaign coverage in 1996, prospective voters saw and heard enough to evaluate the candidates significantly less favorably on Election Day than on Labor Day. The decline of 5.2 points over the course of the 1996 campaign in the percentage of open-ended evaluations that were favorable was exceeded only in 1976 and was roughly matched in 1956, 1972, and 1988 (figure 12).[10] Some of this decline may be attributable to the specific stimulus of Bill Clinton's well-publicized campaign finance irregularities; in any case, on this dimension, too, the 1996 campaign was notably unedifying.

The only indicators of campaign quality that registered any significant improvement in 1996 were measures of issue knowledge and issue learning. Prospective voters were much more likely to recognize the relative positions of the major party candidates on important issues in

1996 than in 1992—by more than seven percentage points on ideology, nine percentage points on guaranteed jobs, 15 percentage points on aid to blacks, and 18 percentage points on government spending and services. Indeed, on four of the five issues included in table 1 prospective voters were more likely to be able to place the candidates correctly in 1996 than in any election year since 1972. (The sole exception was the issue of defense spending, which played a very modest role in the 1996 campaign.) Moreover, at least part of this issue knowledge seems to have been acquired during the course of the fall campaign. Whereas in 1992 knowledge of the candidates' issue stands declined between Labor Day and Election Day on two issues out of four, in 1996 it increased by an average of 4 percent on four issues out of five. Overall, there appears to have been more issue learning in 1996 than in any campaign since 1972.

Thus, in a variety of respects—both positive and negative—the 1996 campaign resembled the campaign of 1988 more than that of 1992. While the complaints of pundits during and after the 1996 campaign focused less on negative ads and photo ops than in 1988 and more on a fundamental lack of political drama, both campaigns produced widespread public dissatisfaction and declines in prospective voters' evaluations of the candidates—but also a clearer sense of where the candidates stood on important political issues. Thus, by some standards, campaign quality in 1996 reached a low point unmatched in at least four decades, while by other standards it was higher than at any other time in recent memory.

Benchmarks for Reform: The Impact of Campaign Activities

To evaluate campaign quality is one thing, to improve it is another. My analysis so far has been essentially descriptive. But careful description may pave the way for improvement if it provides a basis for analyzing why some campaigns have been notably more successful than others in engaging and educating prospective voters. If careful measurement is the first step on the road to intelligent reform, then careful causal analysis is the second step.

I have already noted that much of the concern expressed by critics of negative advertising, "horse race" journalism, and other prominent features of modern campaigns stems from beliefs about the impact of those practices on citizens' attitudes and behavior. One aim of the descriptive exercise reported here is to provide the data necessary to test such beliefs. Where variations in campaign quality can be convincingly traced to specific political institutions and behavior, it may be possible, at least in principle, to engineer changes in those institutions and behavior that elevate the quality of political campaigns. In the absence of convincing causal links between specific political institutions and behavior on one hand and specific good or bad campaign outcomes on the other, would-be reformers must proceed on the basis of prejudice or guesswork.

Franklin's (1991) analysis relating the clarity of prospective voters' perceptions of incumbent senators' ideological positions to the campaign behavior of the senators and their opponents provides a good example of such a convincing causal link. If we take clarity of ideological perceptions to be valuable, Franklin's research provides good reason to expect that changes in campaign behavior could improve campaign quality. Of course, the practical problem remains of how to encourage campaigners to behave in ways that promote ideological clarity; but at least we can be reasonably confident that solving that practical problem will produce real, identifiable benefits.

Given the variety of alternative indicators of campaign behavior and public reactions canvassed here—and the variety and complexity of possible causal relationships among those indicators—I can only begin to explore the potential indirect effects of specific campaign activities on other aspects of campaign quality. My hope is that the examples offered in this section may encourage other analysts to examine a wide variety of plausible connections between campaign institutions and behavior on one hand and public engagement and education on the other. And while the manifest limitations of my data and analyses must make the specific conclusions offered here far from completely convincing, my tentative first steps may prod other analysts to do better.

The specific connections I explore here involve three prominent aspects of campaign behavior: debates, the volume and nature of media coverage of the campaign, and the tone of campaign ads. In the statistical analyses reported in tables 4, 5, and 6, these aspects of campaign behavior are related to various indicators of public engagement and education across a series of presidential campaigns. The dependent variable in table 4 is the favorability of public evaluations of the candidates; the analysis in table 5 is of interest in the campaign; table 6 focuses on knowledge of the candidates' issue positions. In each case, the explanatory variables include measures of individual survey respondents' age, sex, race, education, and income as well as contextual measures of campaign behavior, some treated as constant for all the survey respondents interviewed in a given year and others keyed to the point in the campaign at which each respondent was interviewed.[11]

The "Date" variable appearing in the tables is the number of days before Election Day that a given survey respondent was interviewed,

46   Campaign Reform

divided by –60. Thus, it runs from approximately –1 (for respondents interviewed at the beginning of the fall campaign, around Labor Day) to zero (for respondents interviewed on Election Day). One implication of this coding convention is that the coefficient for the "Date" variable represents the positive or negative change in the intercept level for each dependent variable over the entire fall campaign for a typical respondent in a typical election year.[12] Another is that the intercept itself represents the average value of the dependent variable for a typical respondent at the end of a typical campaign (when the "Date" variable reaches its maximum value of zero).

Contextual variables typically appear in the tables twice, once as main effects and again in interactions with the "Date" variable. In each

TABLE 4. Campaign Variables and Candidate Evaluations

Alternative regression analyses of open-ended evaluations ("like" and "dislikes") of major party candidates as a function of interview date, debates, advertising tone (Geer), bad news (Patterson), and volume of network news coverage of the campaign (Zaller). Controls for age, sex, race, education, family income, and panel status are included in the analyses but omitted from the table. Standard errors of the parameter estimates are shown in parentheses.

	(1)	(2)	(3)	(4)	(5)	(6)
Intercept	49.94	46.18	48.01	57.87	61.95	57.93
	(1.06)	(.85)	(.63)	(3.24)	(2.95)	(3.11)
Date	.18	–1.53	–4.27	13.51	14.28	13.00
	(1.90)	(1.33)	(.88)	(5.64)	(5.26)	(5.57)
Debates	1.78	1.01	1.72	1.88	1.92	1.83
	(.26)	(.25)	(.24)	(.33)	(.33)	(.32)
Advertising Tone	–.2144	.4258	0	.0521	.4180	0
	(.1045)	(.0624)	(—)	(.1493)	(.0863)	(—)
Advertising Tone × Date	–.4777	–.0166	0	.2244	.2728	0
	(.1828)	(.1003)	(—)	(.2482)	(.1554)	(—)
Bad News	–.4527	0	–.3473	–.2145	0	–.2383
	(.0603)	(—)	(.0357)	(.0826)	(—)	(.0482)
Bad News × Date	–.3176	0	–.0726	.0032	0	–.0997
	(.1100)	(—)	(.0594)	(.1448)	(—)	(.0908)
Network News	0	0	0	–.987	–1.661	–.946
	(—)	(—)	(—)	(.358)	(.275)	(.286)
Network News × Date	0	0	0	–1.771	–1.836	–1.526
	(—)	(—)	(—)	(.593)	(.469)	(.514)
adjusted R^2	.044	.038	.044	.022	.020	.020
standard error of regression	25.08	25.17	25.09	25.42	25.44	25.42
N	16,263	16,263	16,263	13,528	13,528	13,528
	(1960–92)	(1960–92)	(1960–92)	(1968–92)	(1968–92)	(1968–92)

case, the coefficient for the main effect represents the estimated impact of a one-unit change in the contextual variable on the average value of the dependent variable at the end of a typical campaign, and the coefficient for the interaction term shows how much of this estimated impact occurred during the two months of the fall campaign. For example, in the first column of table 4, the parameter estimate of −.4527 for "Bad News" indicates that an increase of one point in Patterson's "Bad News" variable (on the zero-to-one-hundred scale shown in figure 3) reduced the average favorability of candidate evaluations on Election Day by almost half a point (on the zero-to-one-hundred scale shown in figure 7). The parameter estimate of −.3176 for the "Bad News" × "Date" interaction in the same column of table 4 indicates that most of this effect occurred during the fall campaign.

TABLE 5. Campaign Variables and Interest in the Campaign

Alternative regression analyses of interest in the campaign as a function of interview date, debates, advertising tone (Geer), policy news (Patterson), and volume of network news coverage of the campaign (Zaller). Controls for age, sex, race, education, family income, and panel status are included in the analyses but omitted from the table. Standard errors of the parameter estimates are shown in parentheses.

	(1)	(2)	(3)	(4)	(5)	(6)
Intercept	43.40	50.91	43.43	24.33	56.83	32.91
	(1.71)	(1.19)	(1.71)	(7.00)	(3.99)	(6.49)
Date	1.48	7.26	1.48	5.32	17.75	15.44
	(2.70)	(1.86)	(2.65)	(11.55)	(7.11)	(10.90)
Debates	1.28	.03	.97	1.73	−.02	1.70
	(.38)	(.34)	(.35)	(.49)	(.44)	(.49)
Advertising Tone	−.1835	.1297	0	−.4386	−.1262	0
	(.1150)	(.0866)	(—)	(.1405)	(.1160)	(—)
Advertising Tone × Date	−.1337	−.0829	0	−.5760	−.7087	0
	(.2126)	(.1396)	(—)	(.2599)	(.2061)	(—)
Policy Schema	.2961	0	.2449	.5159	0	.3297
	(.0621)	(—)	(.0461)	(.1066)	(—)	(.0881)
Policy Schema × Date	.1210	0	.0965	.0813	0	−.1717
	(.1223)	(—)	(.0791)	(.1893)	(—)	(.1504)
Network News	0	0	0	1.288	−.483	.548
	(—)	(—)	(—)	(.490)	(.372)	(.435)
Network News × Date	0	0	0	−.117	−.561	−.946
	(—)	(—)	(—)	(.816)	(.632)	(.754)
adjusted R^2	.093	.090	.093	.099	.094	.098
standard error of regression	35.73	35.80	35.73	35.23	35.33	35.24
N	17,596 (1960–92)	17,596 (1960–92)	17,596 (1960–92)	14,861 (1968–92)	14,861 (1968–92)	14,861 (1968–92)

On Labor Day, one unit of "Bad News" depressed candidate evaluations by .4527 − .3176 = about .14 units, but this effect roughly tripled in magnitude between Labor Day and Election Day.

If the campaign variables included in these analyses affect the engagement and education of prospective voters, we would expect them to do so in exactly the way suggested by this example, with much (but perhaps not all) of the estimated effect appearing gradually over the two months of the fall campaign. A more puzzling pattern appears in the fourth column of table 4, which shows alternative parameter estimates for a different regression model with an additional contextual variable, "Network News," and a different time frame (omitting the elections of 1960 and 1964, for which Zaller's measure of network news coverage is unavailable). Here, the estimated effect of Patterson's "Bad News" at the end of the campaign is about half as large as in the first column of table 4 (−.2145 versus −.4527). But what seems odd is that this effect is essentially constant over the two months of the fall campaign, as indicated by the parameter estimate of .0032 for the "Bad News" × "Date" interaction. Since it seems implausible to suppose that bad news produces increasingly negative candidate evaluations up until Labor Day but has no effect thereafter, this pattern of

TABLE 6.   Campaign Variables and Issue Knowledge

Probit analyses of correct relative placements of major party presidential candidates on important issues as a function of date of interview, debates, and volume of network news coverage of the campaign (Zaller). Controls for age, sex, race, education, family income, and panel status are included in the analyses but omitted from the table. Standard errors of the parameter estimates are shown in parentheses.

	Ideology	Guaranteed Jobs	Aid to Blacks	Defense Spending	Spending vs. Services
Intercept	.1971	.2248	.5301	−.3381	.6728
	(.1178)	(.1185)	(.1216)	(.1559)	(.1546)
Date	.2004	.1654	.5234	.0136	.6222
	(.1995)	(.1992)	(.2102)	(.2373)	(.2451)
Debates	−.0201	−.0357	−.1362	.0505	−.0904
	(.0164)	(.0171)	(.0188)	(.0216)	(.0293)
Network News	−.0497	−.0512	−.0696	.0078	−.0712
	(.0105)	(.0105)	(.0111)	(.0129)	(.0149)
Network News × Date	−.0122	−.0074	−.0241	−.0071	−.0325
	(.0183)	(.0183)	(.0199)	(.0210)	(.0242)
log likelihood	−8,613	−8,392	−7,505	−5,980	−5,201
pseudo-R^2	.140	.088	.084	.121	.092
N	14,456	13,272	11,879	9,873	8,310
	(1972–96)	(1972–96)	(1972–88, 1996)	(1980–96)	(1984–96)

results probably reflects a misspecification of the regression model. For example, in this case the real causal relationship between bad news and candidate evaluations may actually be reversed: negative candidate evaluations earlier in the election year may produce bad news, but the bad news itself may have little or no additional effect over the course of the fall campaign.

As this example suggests, the opportunity to observe interactions between aggregate-level campaign variables and time provides crucial leverage for interpreting putative campaign effects. Thus, the apparent consistency or inconsistency of main effects and interaction effects for the campaign variables in tables 4, 5, and 6 will serve as a useful check on the plausibility or implausibility of the statistical results.

The Impact of Debates

In addition to the contextual campaign variables introduced in figures 1–4, the analysis presented in tables 4, 5, and 6 includes a variable measuring the potential exposure of each NES survey respondent to televised debates between the major presidential candidates. Debates have figured prominently in both empirical and normative analyses of political campaigns for almost forty years (Kelley 1960, 1962; Rahn, Aldrich, and Borgida 1994). On one hand, the Lincoln-Douglas debates provide a familiar (albeit quite unrepresentative) historical example of the substantive depth and sophistication of nineteenth-century campaigns. On the other hand, Kelley (1960) has pointed out how well at least some debate formats may satisfy general requirements for rational campaign communication by equalizing exposure to both candidates and allowing each to directly engage and, if possible, rebut the arguments of the other.

The data set for my analysis includes four presidential debates in 1960, none in 1964, 1968, or 1972, and from one to three in each election since 1976.[13] In each case, I use the date on which individual survey respondents were interviewed to construct a variable reflecting how many debates occurred before the point at which they were interviewed. Thus, the "Debate" variable takes the value zero for respondents interviewed at the beginning of each campaign and for respondents interviewed at any point in campaigns with no presidential debates. The variable takes the value one after the first debate in each fall campaign, two after the second debate, and so on up to a maximum value of four near the end of the 1960 campaign.

This measure of debate exposure appears in the various statistical analyses reported in tables 4, 5, and 6 as a potential influence on the favorability of major party candidate evaluations, interest in the campaign, and knowledge of the candidates' relative issue positions. The impact of debates on open-ended candidate evaluations is clearly positive in each of the alternative regression models reported in table 4. The average impact amounts to about 1.7 percentage points, which implies that prospective voters in a campaign with three presidential debates would end up about five percentage points more favorable toward the candidates than in a campaign with no debates. This difference in candidate evaluations represents about half of the total range of observed aggregate-level variation in open-ended evaluations over the past nine elections, from the low of 46.5 percent favorable in 1980 to the high of 54.8 percent favorable in 1964 and 1968. Making due allowance for the fact that debate audiences (though numbering in the tens of millions) are far from including the entire citizenry, the evidence in table 4 suggests that debates have a surprisingly potent positive effect on evaluations of the candidates.

The estimated impact of debates on interest in the campaign, shown in table 5, is also generally positive but is less consistent in magnitude than the estimated impact on candidate evaluations. In the two regression models including both Patterson's measure of policy coverage and Zaller's measure of network news coverage, the estimated effect of debates on interest is about 1.7 percentage points—comparable in magnitude to the estimated impact on candidate evaluations reported in table 4. In the two models including Patterson's measure but not Zaller's, the estimated effect is about 1.1 percentage points, while in the two models excluding Patterson's measure, the estimated effect is essentially zero. Since the models with the larger estimated debate effects are the ones that best fit the data, it seems likely that debates do generate significant additional interest in the campaign; however, given the range of estimates presented in table 5, the magnitude of this effect remains uncertain.

Finally, table 6 reports a variety of estimates of debates' impact on knowledge of the candidates' issue positions. Here the columns in the table do not represent alternative models using different explanatory variables to account for the same data but distinct analyses of a variety of issues using the same explanatory variables. The estimated effect of exposure to debates is more often negative than positive and is clearly negative for the two issues out of five where it is large enough to be potentially significant (aid to blacks and spending versus services). Thus, while debates clearly contribute to favorable evaluations of the candidates and may also spur public interest in the campaign, there is no reason to believe that debates contribute anything to prospective voters' knowledge of the candidates' issue positions.

Network News Coverage

Zaller's content analysis of television network news coverage, summarized in figure 2, revealed considerable variation across election years in the volume of news coverage of recent fall campaigns. The statistical analyses reported in tables 4, 5, and 6 provide estimates of the consequences of that variation. Unlike the measure of exposure to debates, which varies both across and within election years, Zaller's measure of network news coverage provides a single summary value for each campaign. However, to the extent that this summary value accurately reflects network news coverage of the corresponding campaign as a whole, the effects of that coverage should appear gradually over the two months of the fall campaign. Thus, the statistical analyses reported in tables 4, 5, and 6 include both main effects of network news coverage (reflecting the cumulative impact through Election Day of the year-to-year variations in coverage documented in figure 2) and interactions between news coverage and each respondents' date of interview (reflecting the portion of that cumulative effect specifically attributable to the two-month fall campaign).

The parameter estimates in table 4 suggest that every minute of additional daily network news coverage increased the proportion of negative candidate evaluations at the end of the campaign by about one percentage point. The estimates also suggest that this effect occurred during the two months between Labor Day and Election Day rather than reflecting decisions by the networks to provide relatively heavy coverage of campaigns in which the candidates were already relatively unpopular before Labor Day. Indeed, the relative magnitudes of the "Network News" and "Network News" × "Date" coefficients in table 4 suggest that the candidates were evaluated more positively at the beginning of fall campaigns that received relatively heavy network news coverage and became relatively unpopular only toward the end of these campaigns.

This apparent negative impact of network news coverage on candidate evaluations is comparable in magnitude to the apparent positive impact of debates: whereas each debate seems to have increased the favorability of candidate evaluations by a bit less than two percentage points, each additional minute per day of network news coverage seems to have decreased the favorability of candidate evaluations by roughly the same amount. Thus, a total of roughly sixty minutes of additional coverage over the two months of a fall campaign would counteract the positive effect on candidate evaluations of one debate.

What may be even more remarkable is that network news coverage also appears in table 6 to have depressed prospective voters' learning about the candidates' stands on campaign issues. These effects appear quite clearly for four of five issues included repeatedly in NES surveys, despite the different time periods (ranging from four to eight campaigns) covered by the different issues. The dependent variables in table 6 are dichotomous measures of correct relative candidate placements, and the parameter estimates reported in the table are from probit analyses. Translating the probit coefficients into probability effects, each additional minute of daily network news coverage seems to have decreased prospective voters' probability of correctly placing the candidates on these four issues by an average of about two percentage points, with about one-third of this effect occurring during the two months of the fall campaign.

How are we to interpret these rather surprising results? Given their relative precision and consistency across a variety of issues and time periods, it seems difficult to suppose that they are merely coincidental. One possibility is that they represent an artifact of the Downsian relationship between issue clarity and electoral competitiveness: the same campaigns in which issue differences between the candidates were relatively clear (1972, 1984, 1996) also received relatively little attention from the press, presumably at least in part because their outcomes seemed predictable well in advance of Election Day. The fact that the coefficients in table 6 for the interaction terms representing the gradual effects of network news coverage over the course of each fall campaign are considerably smaller in magnitude than the estimated main effects seems to support this artifactual interpretation. Nevertheless, the apparent negative effects of network news coverage are sufficiently consistent, despite their statistical imprecision, to suggest that here, as in the case of candidate evaluations, network news coverage of recent presidential campaigns may have produced reductions in, rather than positive contributions to, campaign quality.

Conversely, there is no real evidence of an effect of network news coverage on campaign interest in table 5. The parameter estimate for the "Network News" × "Date" interaction is negative in each of the three models where it appears, but the estimates vary greatly in magnitude and are in any case quite imprecise. The estimated main effect of network news coverage also varies greatly across the various model specifications, and the one fairly large positive estimate (in the fourth column of table 5) seems more likely to reflect the impact of campaign interest on the volume of news coverage than the reverse.

Negative News, Negative Ads

While the apparent negative effects of network news coverage on candidate evaluations (in table 4) and issue learning (in table 6) are certainly intriguing, it seems natural to wonder what it is about network news coverage that produces these effects. In the case of candidate evaluations, at least, the most plausible potential culprit is the increasing negativity of campaign news documented by Patterson (1993) and displayed in figure 3. Indeed, the single most plausible potential connection between campaigners' behavior and citizens' attitudes is probably the one between the negativity of campaign communications and public evaluations of the candidates. It stands to reason that if citizens are bombarded for months with negative news coverage and negative ads, people will end up thinking less of the candidates than if they are subjected to an uninterrupted stream of positive news coverage and self-promotional ads. These plausible connections are put to the test in table 4.

Across the range of alternative regression analyses reported in table 4, negative news always has the expected negative impact on candidate evaluations, and the magnitude of this impact is fairly substantial. For example, the implied effect of a forty-point increase in the negativity of news coverage—roughly the increase observed by Patterson between 1960 and 1988—ranges from about 9 to 18 percentage points. Since the observed decline in the favorability of candidate evaluations over this period is about 20 percentage points, it is tempting to conclude that negative news is a major cause of that decline. However, the portion of this effect that appears from the parameter estimates for the "Bad News" × "Date" interaction to be directly attributable to press coverage of the fall campaigns varies considerably across the various regression models, from zero up to about 13 percentage points. Thus, the causal underpinnings of the strong correlation between bad news and negative candidate evaluations remain rather uncertain.

The situation with respect to advertising tone is even less clear. More positive ads seem to produce more positive candidate evaluations in the two regression models in table 4 where bad news does not also appear as an explanatory variable, but even in these models one of the corresponding interaction terms is strongly positive and the other is close to zero. In the models where bad news appears as an additional variable, the strong negative correlation between bad news and advertising tone produces either implausible negative estimates (in the first column of table 4) or null results (in the fourth column) for the effect of advertising tone on candidate evaluations. Thus, there appears to be no real support in these data for the presumed relationship between negative campaign ads and negative candidate evaluations.

Nor in table 5 does advertising tone appear to be systematically related to interest in the campaign. As in table 4, the apparent effect of advertising tone in table 5 varies a good deal across the alternative regression specifications and is never very precisely estimated. However, most of the main effects of advertising tone and all of the interaction effects suggest that, if anything, campaigns with more negative advertising generate more public interest, while those with more elevated ads are less interesting to prospective voters. Despite the plausibility of a systematic relationship between the three-decade trend in negative advertising tone documented in figure 1 and the general decline in campaign interest over the same period documented in figure 5, there is no evidence here of a causal connection.

By comparison, there is some evidence in table 5 suggesting that public interest in presidential campaigns is higher when press coverage is framed in terms of "policy schema" and lower when coverage is framed in terms of "game schema." The estimated main effect of Patterson's "Policy Schema" measure is strongly positive in each of the four columns of table 5 where it appears as an explanatory variable. These parameter estimates imply that the difference in campaign coverage between 1960 (with 54 percent of front-page *New York Times* stories framed in policy terms) and 1992 (with only 15 percent framed in policy terms) reduced public interest by from ten to twenty points, an effect that would account for most of the difference between the highest levels of public interest recorded in figure 5 (around sixty points in 1960 and, despite the "game schema," 1992) and the lowest levels (about forty points in 1988 and 1996). However, the interaction terms reflecting the gradual impact of policy coverage over the course of each campaign are a good deal smaller, much less precisely estimated, and in one case negative rather than positive. Thus, there is little reason to interpret the observed relationship between policy coverage and campaign interest as reflecting a causal impact of press behavior on public interest, at least over the course of the fall campaign.

Conclusions

My analysis suggests that assessments of campaign quality depend crucially on our choice of normative standards for evaluation.

By some standards—especially those focusing on voter knowledge and learning—campaign quality has not declined and may even have increased over the period covered by my analysis. Voters knew more about the candidates' issue stands in 1996—and probably learned more about those stands during the two months of the fall campaign—than in any presidential election since 1972 (tables 1 and 2). The richness of their impressions of the candidates has remained essentially unchanged over the same period (figure 11) and in any case has only occasionally increased markedly over the course of a general election campaign (figure 12). A comparison of actual voting behavior with hypothetical "fully informed" votes shows no apparent increase either in individual-level deviations or in aggregate deviations between actual and hypothetical "fully informed" election outcomes (table 3). And there is some evidence from Fournier's (1997) analysis of Canadian data that campaign processes do a good deal to reduce these deviations by providing relatively uninformed voters with useful cues and informational shortcuts.

By other standards—especially those focusing on public attitudes toward the candidates and the electoral process—campaign quality has declined substantially over the period covered by my analysis. Interest in presidential campaigns has declined unevenly since 1960, reaching a new low in 1996 (figure 5). Evaluations of the candidates have become significantly less favorable over the same period (figure 7), and all of the last three presidential campaigns have seen declines in the favorability of candidate evaluations between Labor Day and Election Day (figure 8). Public faith in the ability of elections to ensure political responsiveness reached a new low in 1996, continuing a substantial and almost continuous decline going back more than three decades (figure 9), even after making allowances for declining trust in government more generally (figure 10).

Even here, however, systematic comparisons over a long period of time suggest some caveats to the familiar complaints about the dismal state of contemporary political campaigns. Public attitudes are clearly subject to short-term improvements, as the experience of 1992 nicely demonstrates. Moreover, most of the long-term erosion of public satisfaction with campaigns and candidates evident in my analysis is concentrated in the 1960s and early 1970s rather than in more recent election cycles. There is no clear trend in campaign interest since 1972, although 1992 represents a (temporary) high point and 1996 a (perhaps equally temporary) low point. Indeed, recent campaigns seem from the data presented in figure 6 to have been more successful than those before 1980 (with the notable exception of the 1960 campaign) in generating additional public interest between Labor Day and Election Day. Presidential candidates have not become any less popular since 1972, either. Faith in elections has continued to decline, but most of the decline in recent years seems to reflect a lack of faith in the political system generally rather than in elections specifically. While the crisis of public dissatisfaction with campaigns is by no means over, it does not appear to have worsened significantly in the past twenty years.

This stabilization of public attitudes provides a striking counterpoint to the continuing decline of campaign tone as measured by the negativity of television ads (figure 1) and news coverage (figure 3). Judging from Geer's data, the tone of ads became more positive between 1964 and 1976, but public attitudes toward the candidates and the campaign process became more negative; the tone of ads became more negative between 1976 and 1992, but public attitudes toward the candidates and the campaign process did not. Conversely, Patterson's data on the negativity of news coverage show an increase through the 1960s, when public attitudes were becoming more negative, but also through the 1970s, when for the most part they were not.

Discrepancies of this sort between the observed behavior of campaigners and the apparent reactions of prospective voters seem to call out for empirical analysis. While my own attempts in this direction have been quite tentative and only begin to address the formidable problems of data collection and analysis that bedevil any effort to make convincing causal inferences about a process as complex and multifaceted as a modern presidential campaign, they suggest that some familiar assumptions about the relationships among various aspects of campaign quality may require significant revision.

For example, there is little or no evidence in my analyses that negative advertising makes prospective voters less favorable toward the candidates (table 4) or less interested in the campaign (table 5). If anything, the results in table 5 suggest that negative ads are more likely to stimulate public interest in the campaign than to reduce it. Televised candidate debates seem to reduce rather than increase prospective voters' knowledge of the candidates' issue stands (table 6). In each case, these counterintuitive results may turn out on further analysis to be simply wrong, but in the meantime, they should raise significant cautions regarding the potential dangers of proceeding too hastily from description and evaluation to prescription.

The practical problem of what might be done to improve the quality of political campaigns is further complicated by the fact that the same campaign activities may have both positive and negative effects. For example, while campaign debates seem to reduce prospective voters' knowledge of the candidates' issue stands (table 6), they also make the candidates more popular (table 4) and may stimulate public interest in the campaign (table 5). Assuming for the sake of argument that all of these effects are real, which is most important? This potential practical dilemma is another manifestation of the normative complexity of political campaigns.

In a variety of ways, then, my analysis brings us back to where Kelley (1960, 8) started almost forty years ago: "A set of standards for evaluating campaign discussion is logically prior to useful criticism of it or suggestions for reforming it." I would add that we need not only a set of standards but also some way of adjudicating among potentially conflicting standards for evaluating campaign quality. We also need a clearer sense of the causal connections relating the behavior of campaigners to the reactions of prospective voters, if we are to have any confidence in our grasp of the likely consequences of proposed campaign reforms.

Genuine improvements in campaign quality will require more than righteous indignation about the state of contemporary campaign discourse. Intelligent reforms must be based on systematic description, hardnosed evaluation, careful causal analysis, and sensitivity to the various political obstacles that must be overcome if we hope to turn our ideals into practice. For political scientists who are also concerned citizens, much remains to be done.

NOTES

The Pew Charitable Trusts, the John Simon Guggenheim Memorial Foundation, and Princeton University contributed generous support for the research reported here. Lynn Vavreck provided helpful advice and assistance at various points. John Geer, Thomas Patterson, and John Zaller shared data from their content analyses of campaign advertisements and news coverage. The American National Election Studies project collected, archived, and distributed a wealth of relevant survey data. E. J. Dionne Jr., Shanto Iyengar, Stanley Kelley Jr., and Thomas Mann offered stimulating comments on a previous version of the analysis in a roundtable session conducted at the 1997 annual meeting of the American Political Science Association in Washington, DC. To all of these individuals and institutions I offer my thanks, along with the usual caveat that none of them is responsible for the views expressed here, which are solely my own.

1. Data for 1952–92 are from the Cumulative Data File on the *American National Election Studies 1948–1994* CD-ROM released by NES and the Inter-University Consortium for Political and Social Research (May 1995). Data for 1996 are from the April 1997 release of the 1996 American National Election Study. I have merged them with the Cumulative Data File.

2. This portion of Geer's more extensive content analysis parallels an earlier effort by Kaid and Johnston (1991) using the same campaign ad archive. The correlation between Geer's aggregate-level measure of negativity by election year and Kaid and Johnston's measure is .91 (Finkel and Geer 1998), which suggests a reassuring degree of intercoder reliability.

3. Since Geer's data set includes no information on how often or how widely specific ads were aired, each appeal is weighted equally. Goldstein's (1997) analysis of ad buys in the 1996 presidential campaign suggests that more realistic weighting might produce somewhat different results. For example, "while only 47 percent of the Dole commercials were 'negative,' 55 percent of the buys were 'negative' and 70 percent of the spots shown were 'negative'" (Goldstein 1997, 19).

4. The unit of analysis for Geer's coding was the specific appeal rather than the entire spot. Thus, any one ad could and often did include a mixture of positive and negative appeals.

5. An independent content analysis cited by Cappella and Jamieson (1997, 246) documented comparable declines in media coverage of the 1996 campaign.

6. The change in campaign interest from Labor Day to Election Day in each campaign is calculated from a statistical analysis with campaign interest regressed on the respondents' dates of interview, age, sex, race, education, family income, and panel status. This approach captures any linear trend in campaign interest between Labor Day and Election Day while smoothing out temporary fluctuations in interest over the course of each campaign. Elsewhere (Bartels 1997), I have adopted a similar approach to examine priming and persuasion in recent presidential campaigns.

7. Until recently, NES respondents were not asked to place the presidential candidates if they had already declined to place themselves on the same issue scale. Thus, to preserve comparability across election years, I classify all respondents who did not place themselves along with those who did not place the candidates or placed them incorrectly, even if they could and did provide correct relative candidate placements. This restriction reduces the apparent levels of issue knowledge reported in table 1, especially for the ideology scale, where a substantial proportion of respondents declined to place themselves in every election year.

8. These results are consistent with Just et al.'s (1996, 206) finding, derived from more general open-ended questions included in in-depth interviews, of "a substantial increase" in the number of considerations offered by citizens about the candidates early in the 1992 campaign but a much smaller increase between September and October. More generally, these results are also consistent with Bartels's (1993) finding that prospective voters' perceptions and evaluations of the candidates in the 1980 presidential campaign were largely fixed by the spring of the election year.

9. The similarity is even more marked for the results from the 1993 election campaign, where Fournier (1997, 34) found average deviations of 13.1 percentage points at the beginning of the campaign and 8.6 percentage points at the end of the campaign. The deviations in the 1992 referendum campaign were much larger outside of Quebec though similar in magnitude within Quebec.

10. The change in average candidate evaluations as measured by ratings on the "feeling thermometer" was smaller—about 1.6 points—but in the same direction.

11. Only the estimated effects of contextual variables are shown in tables 3, 4, and 5. The control variables are included in the analyses to capture individual-level variation, but their estimated effects are omitted from the tables.

12. All of the survey data are reweighted to give equal weight to each election year regardless of how many respondents were interviewed in each year's NES survey.

13. I exclude vice presidential debates as well as Ronald Reagan's debate with independent candidate John Anderson in 1980.

REFERENCES

Adasiewicz, Christopher, Douglas Rivlin, and Jeffrey Stanger. 1997. *Free Television for Presidential Candidates: The 1996 Experiment.* Philadelphia: Annenberg Public Policy Center, University of Pennsylvania.

Ansolabehere, Stephen, and Shanto Iyengar. 1995. *Going Negative: How Political Advertisements Shrink and Polarize the Electorate.* New York: Free Press.

Ansolabehere, Stephen, Shanto Iyengar, Adam Simon, and Nicholas Valentino. 1994. "Does Attack Advertising Demobilize the Electorate?" *American Political Science Review* 88:829–38.

Bartels, Larry M. 1992. "The Impact of Electioneering in the United States." In *Electioneering: A Comparative Study of Continuity and Change,* ed. David Butler and Austin Ranney. Oxford: Clarendon Press.

Bartels, Larry M. 1993. "Messages Received: The Political Impact of Media Exposure." *American Political Science Review* 87:267–85.

Bartels, Larry M. 1996. "Uninformed Votes: Information Effects in Presidential Elections." *American Journal of Political Science* 40:194–230.

Bartels, Larry M. 1997. "How Campaigns Matter." Unpublished manuscript, Princeton University.

Berelson, Bernard R., Paul F. Lazarsfeld, and William N. McPhee. 1954. *Voting: A Study of Opinion Formation in a Presidential Campaign.* Chicago: University of Chicago Press.

Broder, David. 1990. "Putting Sanity Back in Elections." *Washington Post,* January 14, D1.

Buchanan, Bruce. 1996. *Renewing Presidential Politics: Campaigns, Media, and the Public Interest.* Lanham, MD: Rowman and Littlefield.

Campaign Discourse Mapping Project. 1996. *Assessing the Quality of Campaign Discourse: 1960, 1980, 1988, 1992.* Philadelphia: Annenberg Public Policy Center, University of Pennsylvania.

Campbell, Angus, Philip E. Converse, Warren E. Miller, and Donald E. Stokes. 1960. *The American Voter.* New York: Wiley.

Cappella, Joseph N., and Kathleen Hall Jamieson. 1997. *Spiral of Cynicism: The Press and the Public Good.* New York: Oxford University Press.

Converse, Philip E. 1964. "The Nature of Belief Systems in Mass Publics." In *Ideology and Discontent,* ed. David E. Apter. New York: Free Press.

Finkel. Steven E. 1993. "Reexamining the 'Minimal Effects' Model in Recent Presidential Campaigns." *Journal of Politics* 55:1–21.

Finkel, Steven E., and John Geer. 1998. "A Spot Check: Casting Doubt on the Demobilizing Effect of Attack Advertising." *American Journal of Political Science* 42:573–95.

Fishkin, James S. 1995. *The Voice of the People: Public Opinion and Democracy.* New Haven: Yale University Press.

Fournier, Patrick. 1997. "The Impact of Political Campaigns on the Effects of Political Sophistication." Paper presented at a conference on capturing campaign effects, Vancouver, British Columbia.

Franklin, Charles H. 1991. "Eschewing Obfuscation? Campaigns and the Perceptions of U.S. Senate Incumbents." *American Political Science Review* 85:1193–213.

Geer, John G. 1998. "Campaigns, Competition, and Political Advertising." In *Politicians and Party Politics,* ed. John G. Geer. Baltimore: Johns Hopkins University Press.

Germond, Jack W., and Jules Witcover. 1989. *Whose Broad Stripes and Bright Stars? The Trivial Pursuit of the Presidency, 1988.* New York: Warner Books.

Goldstein, Kenneth M. 1997. "What Did They See and When Did They See It? Measuring the Volume, Tone, and Targeting of Television Advertising in the 1996 Presidential Election." Department of Political Science, Arizona State University. Revised version of a paper presented at the annual meeting of the Midwest Political Science Association, Chicago.

Greenfield, Jeff. 1982. *The Real Campaign: How the Media Missed the Story of the 1980 Campaign.* New York: Summit Books.

Holbrook, Thomas M. 1996. *Do Campaigns Matter?* Beverly Hills, CA: Sage.

Jamieson, Kathleen Hall. 1992. *Dirty Politics: Deception, Distraction, and Democracy.* New York: Oxford University Press.

Just, Marion R., Ann N. Crigler, Dean E. Alger, Timothy E. Cook, Montague Kern, and Darrell M. West. 1996. *Crosstalk: Citizens, Candidates, and the Media in a Presidential Campaign.* Chicago: University of Chicago Press.

Kaid, Lynda Lee, and Anne Johnston. 1991. "Negative versus Positive Television Advertising in U.S. Presidential Campaigns, 1960–1988." *Journal of Communication* 41:53–64.

Kelley, Stanley, Jr. 1960. *Political Campaigning: Problems in Creating an Informed Electorate.* Washington, DC: Brookings Institution.

Kelley, Stanley, Jr. 1962. "Campaign Debates: Some Facts and Issues." *Public Opinion Quarterly* 26:351–66.

Kelley, Stanley, Jr. 1983. *Interpreting Elections.* Princeton: Princeton University Press.

Key, V. O., Jr., with the assistance of Milton C. Cummings Jr. 1966. *The Responsible Electorate: Rationality in Presidential Voting, 1936–1960.* Cambridge: Harvard University Press.

Kinder, Donald, Tali Mendelberg, Michael Dawson, Lynn Sanders, Steven Rosenstone, Jocelyn Sargent, and Cathy Cohen. 1989. "Benign Neglect and Racial Codewords in the 1988 Presidential Campaign." Paper presented at the annual meeting of the American Political Science Association, Atlanta.

Lau, Richard, Gerald Pomper, and Erlinda Mazeika. 1995. "The Effects of Negative Campaigning." Paper presented at the annual meeting of the American Political Science Association, Chicago.

Lupia, Arthur. 1992. "Busy Voters, Agenda Control, and the Power of Information." *American Political Science Review* 86:390–403.

Luskin, Robert C. Forthcoming. "From Denial to Extenuation (and Finally Beyond): Political Sophistication and Citizen Performance." In *Thinking about Political Psychology,* ed. James H. Kuklinski. New York: Cambridge University Press.

Mayer, William G. 1996. "In Defense of Negative Campaigning." *Political Science Quarterly* 11:437–55.

McKelvey, Richard D., and Peter C. Ordeshook. 1986. "Information, Electoral Equilibria, and the Democratic Ideal." *Journal of Politics* 48:909–37.

Mendelberg, Tali. 1997. "Executing Hortons: Racial Crime in the 1988 Presidential Campaign." *Public Opinion Quarterly* 61:134–57.

Page, Benjamin I. 1978. *Choices and Echoes in Presidential Elections: Rational Man and Electoral Democracy.* Chicago: University of Chicago Press.

Page, Benjamin I., and Robert Y. Shapiro. 1992. *The Rational Public: Fifty Years of Trends in Americans' Policy Preferences.* Chicago: University of Chicago Press.

Patterson, Thomas E. 1993. *Out of Order.* New York: Knopf.

Pew Research Center for the People and the Press. 1996. *Campaign '96 Gets Lower Grades from Voters.* Washington, DC: Pew Research Center for the People and the Press.

Popkin, Samuel L. 1991. *The Reasoning Voter: Communication and Persuasion in Presidential Campaigns.* Chicago: University of Chicago Press.

Rahn, Wendy M., John H. Aldrich, and Eugene Borgida. 1994. "Individual and Contextual Variations in Political Candidate Appraisal." *American Political Science Review* 88:193–99.

Taylor, Paul. 1996. "Politics in Prime Time: Free TV Airtime for Candidates Is a Partial But Worthwhile Fix." *New Democrat* (September–October): 40–41.

Tufte, Edward R. 1978. *Political Control of the Economy.* Princeton: Princeton University Press.

Zaller, John R. 1992. *The Nature and Origins of Mass Opinion.* New York: Cambridge University Press.

Zaller, John R. Forthcoming. *A Theory of Media Politics.* Chicago: University of Chicago Press.

Chapter 2

Assessing Attack Advertising: A Silver Lining

John G. Geer

When Americans are asked about the health of our electoral process, the response is quite discouraging. Citizens lack faith in how campaigns work and in the men and women who run in them. For example, more than three-quarters of the electorate in January 1996 thought that candidates for major political office do not mean what they say during the campaign ("Thinking about the Political Process" 1998, 44). This dissatisfaction with electoral campaigns has led many reformers to offer recommendations to improve the conduct of elections. However, all too often the "solutions" presented by scholars and pundits have only made matters worse. Reformers need systematic data to guide and to shape their proposals. But reformers cannot live by data alone. They must also have clear and defensible standards of judgment to assess and to interpret empirical findings.

I argue here that sound recommendations require close attention to the intersection of standards and evidence. I make this broader point by focusing on "negative" campaigning. As Bruce Buchanan notes in his contribution to this volume, one of the public's biggest concerns about campaigns is their negativity. In fact, there is a widespread belief among informed observers of the political process that negative campaigns have many detrimental effects (e.g., Ansolabehere and Iyengar 1995). This perception is not, however, consistent with much of the recent evidence (e.g., Finkel and Geer 1998; Freedman and Goldstein 1999; Jamieson, Waldman, and Sherr 1998). I seek to raise further doubts about the accuracy of this perception by demonstrating that short, negative ads have a number of advantages over longer, positive ads. These advantages may not be enough to say that negativity is good for the electoral process. But the evidence I present should caution against any blanket call for decreasing the negativity of campaigns, while it forges a better understanding of attack advertising in American elections. Given widespread concerns about the ill effects of negative campaigning, it is critical that we learn more about the costs and benefits of attack politics.

Why Negative Appeals May Be More Substantive

If we were to canvass political observers, there would be a consensus that campaigns should be more positive and more substantive. Buchanan (1996, 68) represents this perspective when he argues that "positive and substantive campaigns are central to 'protective' democracy." While this view has normative appeal, I shall contend that these goals actually work at cross-purposes. That is, negative campaigns tend to produce more "substance" than do positive campaigns. So, attempts to lessen the frequency of attacks during elections will have the unintended consequence of also lessening the frequency of substantive exchanges between candidates.

The underlying reason for this connection between negativity and substance can be found in the requirements of attack politics. An effective attack places different demands on the candidate than do self-promotional appeals. For example, Clinton could (and did) claim in 1992 that he wanted to grow the economy—that he wanted to create jobs by investing in people and training them for the twenty-first century. This kind of rhetoric played well against the sounding board of a recession. He did not go into great detail about his plans—he just focused on his general goals. But when Clinton went on the attack, it was not enough just to say that Bush opposed economic growth, favored higher unemployment, or opposed job training. Such claims were not true. Bush's policies may have been misguided, but they were not designed intentionally to derail the economy or give people their pink slips. Rather Clinton had to take his attacks against Bush one step further. He had to say what about Bush's policies caused the economic problems and setbacks. Attacks, in sum, usually demand more specifics than does a simple positive claim about economic growth.

Jamieson (1992, 103) lends support to this point, arguing that the "stronger the attack, the greater the amount of specific factual content." There is, of course, not a one-to-one correspondence between factual content and substance, but some commonalities exist. Credible attacks require evidence to back up the claims, which come, for example, from "nonpartisan authorities such as a newspaper" (103). Using such sources makes arguments more effective and more substantive. Assertions usually have a hollow ring. It is simply not very substantive to assert that Dukakis favors a tax increase and leave it at that. However, if the claim is supported by an accurate count of the number of bills he signed that increased taxes or a clip from a Boston newspaper accusing him of raising taxes, the attack not only becomes believable but also adds to the campaign discourse.

A possible counter to this argument is that attacks tend to focus on unfair personal statements against the opposition rather than policy-oriented criticisms. So the reason for lessening attacks in campaigns may really stem from a concern about the mudslinging aimed at candidates' personal lives. However, the data do not support the idea that traits are a more common target for attack than are issues. Of all the appeals made in presidential ads aired on TV from 1960 to 1996 (discussed subsequently), only 8 percent were trait-based criticisms. By contrast, one-fifth of all appeals involved attacks on the opposition's policy stances.

Among the reasons why candidates attack on issues more frequently than on traits may be the need for evidence to make them work. As with issues, a candidate cannot just claim the opposition is morally flawed. The public will not react favorably to unsubstantiated personal attacks. It is harder to document that someone is personally flawed than that someone is misguided on policy matters. Consider the increased difficulty in documenting that a candidate is a "weak leader" compared to supporting a claim that the contender has a tendency to raise taxes. In the case of the latter, it is easier to produce the necessary evidence. There is a paper trail. A key exception to this claim involves a candidate's honesty. Has the individual told the truth? Have they misled the public? Have they said one thing and done another? Most candidates have a written and spoken record that provides a way to answer such questions. And nearly 75 percent of all personal attacks focus on a candidate's integrity and honesty—data consistent with this argument (see Geer 1998).[1]

So even though many pundits may think that negativity is mostly composed of personal attacks, there is both evidence and reason to suggest otherwise.

Toward a Definition of Substance

Devising an all-encompassing definition of *substance* is beyond the scope of this essay, but I can employ a few useful indicators to permit an assessment of how negative appeals stack up to their positive counterparts. For starters, informed observers tend to view the discussion of issues during a campaign as an important sign of substance. Just consider the amount of attention scholars have paid to studying the subject of issue voting. That interest is fueled in part by the belief that such voting is superior to casting ballots on the basis of personality. Carmines and Stimson (1980, 79) observe that "the common—indeed universal—view has been that voting choices based on policy concerns are superior to decisions based on party loyalty or candidate image." While discussion of issues is an important indicator of substance, I do not want to cheapen the value of personal traits to voters' decisions. Some scholars (e.g., Kelley 1960) have noted the relevance of this dimension for electoral choice. My point is simply that on average, the more substantive a campaign, the more it focuses on policy debates.

Looking only at the frequency of issues is a crude indicator of substance. To develop a more refined measure of this concept, I also need to assess the quality of issues discussed in the campaign. Such an assessment can take a number of different directions. For example, the accuracy of appeals is one criteria that springs to mind. In fact, there has been a presumption that attack advertising is more misleading than is positive advertising. Interestingly, Jamieson, Waldman, and Sherr (1998, 1) report that "in most presidential general elections deception is as likely in ads and speeches that are self-promotional as those that are oppositional." That finding is potentially important in the unfolding debate over negative advertising.

I, however, pursue an alternative strategy to assess the quality of issues by estimating whether campaigns "expose the grounds on which candidates disagree and the differences between candidates" (Kelley 1960, 14). Kelley has argued that such discussion during campaigns helps promote a more informed electorate and, hence, more rational voters. The reasoning here is that by more clearly spelling out the differences between candidates, campaign appeals will help voters make decisions that are consistent with their own preferences on policy. When a candidate favors economic growth, that appeal will hardly help voters understand what the contender plans to do once in office or help sort out the differences between nominees. Conversely, specific information about the candidate's tax policy or willingness to increase the minimum wage would be useful.

To move toward such an analysis, I rely on Donald Stokes's famous essay questioning the merits of the Downsian approach to politics. In that article, Stokes (1966, 170) drew a distinction between "valence" issues and "position" issues.[2] A position issue involves advocating governmental action "from a set of alternatives over which a distribution of voters' preferences is defined" (170). By contrast, a valence issue links the candidates or parties "with some condition that is positively or negatively valued by the electorate" (170–71). While Stokes's argument was aimed at raising doubts about the underlying assumptions of Downs's theory, one can use this distinction to evaluate the content of campaign appeals. A call for economic growth, as mentioned earlier, would count as a valence appeal, while a call for a higher level of military spending would be treated as a position issue.

The judgment that position issues are superior to valence issues is open to some debate. Candidates who call for an end to corruption or mismanagement of government can be sending an important and serious signal to the public about government's potential direction. Valence issues, therefore, can be important to the electorate. But my point is that on average, campaigns become more substantive if they contain a higher share of position issues.

The Data

Political advertising on television has become a staple in national and most state-level campaigns (e.g., Jamieson 1996; Luntz 1988). At the presidential level, major party nominees are spending two-thirds of their federally sponsored campaign budget on producing and airing televised spots (West 1997). Not only do candidates put a lot of stock in advertising, but pundits and journalists pay a great deal of attention to the spots aired by candidates. Given the importance of political advertising, scholars have spent a good deal of time examining the ads' content. Patterson and McClure (1976) were among the first to recognize the importance of this medium, but many others have followed suit (Buchanan 1996; Diamond and Bates 1984; Jamieson 1996; Joslyn 1980; Just et al, 1996; Kahn and Kenney 1998; Kern 1989; West 1997; and others).

I too have undertaken an analysis of televised political advertising in presidential elections. My content analysis draws from the many strengths of this past work but differs in a number of important ways that allow me to offer new insights about presidential campaigns. First, I seek to understand the messages politicians send to voters during the campaign, not to examine ads per se. This goal required a different approach to collecting the data. Most previous work has sought to capture the message of the full spot, treating it, for example, as an issue or trait ad. That tactic makes good sense when the questions motivating the analysis are about ads themselves. But to understand the politicians' appeals to the public requires an examination of the specific content of each ad. Hence, the unit of analysis is the appeal within the political spot (the data can be aggregated in a variety of ways, as we shall see).

Politicians send multiple messages to voters through advertising, and my content analysis sought to capture those appeals. The result is a coding scheme that is unusually detailed. I have more than 1,700 different codes for issues alone. And I know whether the specific issue was offered as a reason to vote for the candidate or to vote against the opposition (i.e., positive and negative appeals). I also have detailed information on candidates' personal appeals during the course of the campaign, with nearly two hundred unique categories. In addition, I have coded references to values, such as freedom or democracy, that generated one hundred different codes.

This coding scheme permits me to secure a much more detailed reading of the presidential candidates' appeals than does previous work.

My approach also avoids one of the pitfalls identified by Jamieson, Waldman, and Sherr (1998)—the tendency to pigeonhole ads as either negative or positive. This distinction, as they argue, oversimplifies matters. These scholars advocate the use of a third category: contrast ads. My scheme goes even further by using the appeal as the key unit of analysis. I can measure the content of ads by estimating the share of appeals that are negative or positive. Few ads are completely negative or positive. For example, among ads I coded as negative, 3 percent of appeals were positive. For positive spots, the share of negative appeals was 12 percent. And for contrast ads, about 41 percent of all appeals were negative. These data underscore the need to develop as refined a set of measures as possible for assessing the content of political advertising.

Another advantage of my data set is the number of years under study. Using the Julian P. Kanter Political Commercial Archive at the University of Oklahoma, I have examined sixty-second and shorter ads from 1960 to 1996. Having ten elections to evaluate increases the generalizability of the results. All in all, my data set includes 757 ads from general elections (see Geer 1998 for details on the sample used).[3]

While my data have a number of assets, they also have flaws. Most troubling is that I do not know how often or where the ads under study were aired, forcing me to weight each ad equally. Goldstein (1997) has recently discussed a new technology that may get around this problem for 1996 and future elections (see also Freedman and Goldstein 1999). But Goldstein's solution does not solve the problem for past elections. Jamieson, Waldman, and Sherr (1998) have offered a partial solution for past elections, trying to weight ads by campaign spending on ads. The spending data are not only spotty but also potentially misleading (see Goldstein 1997). Geer and Lau (1998) have devised another way to get around this problem, developing hypothetical strategies that permit scholars to adjust ad content across different campaign settings. This approach opens up new avenues to examine the effects of campaigns, but one has to subscribe to their assumption that it is possible to deduce a reasonable set of strategies that rational candidates might pursue.

Here, I simply assign equal weight to all ads. A key reason for this decision is that it is not clear that weighting would greatly alter my results. Both the work by Freedman and Goldstein (1999) and that by Geer and Lau (1998) suggest that the equal-weighting assumption may not pose serious problems for the accuracy of many statistical analyses. Freedman and Goldstein, for example, gathered detailed readings on the public's exposure to ads aired during the recent Virginia gubernatorial election to assess whether negativity demobilizes the electorate. These data represent an improvement over Finkel and Geer's (1998) approach, which assumed that all voters had the same exposure to ads. But even though Freedman and Goldstein's data are superior in regard to when and where ads were aired and who was watching them, the results did not tell a different tale than from what Finkel and Geer report: attack advertising does not demobilize citizens. Without a well-developed way to weight ads over the entire time frame under study or clear evidence that such schemes will greatly alter the results, I will treat all appeals within each ad the same for this analysis.

Assessing Campaigns' Substance

In the remaining pages of this chapter, I present two measures of substance in presidential campaigns arising from the preceding discussion and determine whether and how they correlate with the length and negativity of ads. First, I examine the frequency of issue appeals within different types of political ads. Second, I assess the quality of issue appeals within ads, operationalizing Stokes's (1966) notion of valence versus position issues.

The Proportion of Issues

Table 1 breaks down the ratio of issues to traits for positive, contrast, and negative ads.[4] I include contrast ads, as noted earlier, because Jamieson, Waldman, and Sherr (1998) have argued convincingly that these spots represent an important analytical category. The data show that positive ads pay less attention to issues (47 percent) than do both negative and contrast ads (61 and 62 percent, respectively).[5] Table 2 provides an additional breakdown by comparing the share of issues in thirty-second and sixty-second ads.[6] The shorter spots tend to pay more attention to issues than longer spots. Since sixty-second ads dominated the 1960s and thirty-second spots were the most common in the 1980s, table 2 also reports the breakdown for issues and traits for sixty-second ads aired between 1980 and 1996 to control for period effects. The attention paid to issues declined even further for the sixty-second spots run since 1980.

Table 3 takes the next logical step, examining the length and tone of the ad together. As one can see, thirty-second, negative ads contained the largest amount of issue discussion, with nearly two-thirds of their appeals dealing with issues. And this focus on issues seems to come mostly at the expense of values, which decline to just 7 percent of appeals. This finding makes sense. Values tend to be references to such things as peace, liberty, community. It would be difficult to document Clinton's opposition to liberty. The data also show that sixty-second negative ads are fairly rare—only 5 percent of the total sample falls in this category. It may be that political consultants fear a backlash from the electorate when attacks go on for longer than thirty seconds. Perhaps the public's tolerance of negativity has a time limit. Among those sixty-second negative spots, there is a greater focus on traits than in previous results. Contrast ads, like thirty-second negative ads, score well on the "maximizing issues" criterion, with more than 60 percent of appeals about issues.

The fact that negative thirty-second ads devote a good deal of time to issues is hardly sufficient evidence to support the call for more such ads. But for those who want to see issues play a bigger role in campaigns—a reasonable goal—shorter, negative spots have something to recommend them. The next section will extend this analysis further by examining the quality of issue information contained in spots.

The Quality of Issue Information

Because my coding scheme is very detailed, I am able to distinguish between issue appeals that are very general and ones than are more specific. I start by expanding Stokes's core distinction between valence and

TABLE 1. Proportion of Values, Issues, Traits by Type of Presidential Ad, 1960–96

	Positive Ads	Contrast Ads	Negative Ads
Values	27%	13%	8%
Issues	47%	62%	62%
Traits	25%	25%	30%
N	4,842	2,071	2,016

Source: Data compiled by author.

TABLE 2. Proportion of Values, Issues, Traits by Length of Presidential Ad, 1960–96

	30-Second Ads	60-Second Ads	60-Second Ads, 1980–96
Values	15%	25%	30%
Issues	58%	49%	43%
Traits	28%	25%	26%
N	4,645	3,841	1,484

Source: Data compiled by author.

position issues. This effort seeks not only to shed more light on the substantive content of attack advertising but also to build confidence in my data and coding scheme. Table 4 has five separate categories for different types of appeals. One refinement involves Rabinowitz and Macdonald's (1989) idea of "directional" issues. While these types of issues qualify as position issues, the appeals are not framed spatially. Instead, citizens can learn the general direction of policy. Does a candidate support a tax cut? Does the nominee favor decreasing defense spending? The second refinement comes from experiences when conducting the content analysis. Contenders often just say that they "care" about an issue. Even though such appeals fall under the valence umbrella, I have (for the moment) provided a separate category for them. Next, the "general" category also has valence overtones. Here the candidate just mentions the topic without any further comment. One can implicitly assume that the candidate cares about the issue and wants to solve the problem, but no explicit reference to such opinions are made. The final label—"specific"—concerns those appeals either that are spatially framed or where the candidate advocates a detailed policy proposal (i.e., the line-item veto).[7]

As one can see, Stokes's original insights hold up very well. Nearly 50 percent of all appeals are explicitly valence. Another 29 percent (general and caring) also can be thought of as valence issues. Only 6 percent are specific appeals, with an additional 18 percent falling under Rabinowitz and Macdonald's directional issues. These results have face validity as well, which bolsters one's faith in the data. For example, issues raised by

TABLE 3. Proportion of Values, Issues, Traits by Length and Type of Presidential Ad, 1960–96

	30-Second Positive Ads	30-Second Contrast Ads	30-Second Negative Ads
Values	25%	12%	7%
Issues	47%	61%	65%
Traits	28%	27%	28%
N	1,617	1,466	1,530
	60-Second Positive Ads	60-Second Contrast Ads	60-Second Negative Ads
Values	28%	16%	12%
Issues	47%	62%	51%
Traits	25%	22%	37%
N	2,832	469	440

Source: Data compiled by author.

Democrats tend to stress "caring" more than do those raised by Republican candidates (8 to 3 percent). That finding makes sense, since the Democrats' bread-and-butter issues concern social welfare. It is easier to care about helping the elderly than about building an MX missile. At the same time, nominees from the "in" party use more directional appeals and fewer valence appeals than do contenders from the "out" party. That finding too is reasonable, since the incumbent party has been in office and has had to take positions on various policy matters.

The remaining analyses will collapse the five categories into two—position versus valence. By so doing, I capture the key analytical difference for assessing whether negative or positive appeals better inform voters about candidates' policy differences. As stated earlier, valence issues will tell voters what the candidates care about and their goals for the country. But position issues are more likely to allow voters to cast informed ballots, since they will help voters better understand candidates' policy disputes.

Table 5 returns us to the discussion about the length of ads and their negativity. If we value more position issues over fewer, then longer, positive ads appear to have some drawbacks. The lowest share of position appeals can be found among sixty-second positive spots (12 percent). The thirty-second positive spots do better, with 18 percent of appeals qualifying as positional. Both types of negative ads perform much better, netting about 30 percent position appeals. Thirty-second contrast ads score the highest on this dimension, with 37 percent position appeals.

Negative appeals generally are more specific than positive appeals. Among all negative appeals raised since 1960, 32 percent qualified as position issues. The comparable percentage for positive appeals drops to 18. These findings support the earlier argument that negative appeals have a different dynamic than their counterparts. That is, when making a positive appeal, candidates have a greater tendency to be vague, for example, calling for a "sound Social Security system." But when attacking the opposi-

TABLE 4. Varying Types of Substantive Appeals in Presidential Ads, 1960–96

Valence	48%
Caring	6%
General	23%
Specific	6%
Directional	18%
N	4,891

Source: Data compiled by author.

tion, there is a greater need for evidence and reasoning. It is just not a very viable strategy for a candidate to say only that the opposition wants a "weak Social Security system." Rather, an attack encourages the attacker to say why electing the opponent will lead to a stagnant economy or poses a threat to Social Security. The data here are consistent with this position.

It is worth noting, however, that positive appeals do not always fall prey to vagueness. If one takes a closer look at contrast ads, positive appeals are quite specific. I broke the share of position issues within these ads into negative and positive appeals. Among negative issues, 41 percent were position appeals. For positive issues, the share stood at 33 percent. That proportion is higher than for either kind of negative ad. Whether contrast ads in general have this characteristic is not clear. Clinton used thirty-second contrast ads extensively in 1996, with these ads making heavy use of position appeals (more than 50 percent). If Clinton is dropped from the analysis of thirty-second contrast ads, the number of position issues in such spots declines to 26 percent. Clinton's campaign may be misleading or may signal a change in content of contrast ads. We cannot be sure. Regardless of interpretation, spots that explicitly compare candidates seem to offer a promising format.

Explaining the Share of Position Issues in Campaigns

My final task is to develop a more complete account of the share of position issues in campaigns. As we have seen, the type of ad appears to affect how issues are framed. But to forge a more systematic reading of the issue content of ads, I develop a multivariate account that controls for potentially confounding factors. In this analysis, I move from the appeal to each nominee's campaign as the unit of analysis. That is, what explains why

TABLE 5. Proportion of Position Appeals, by Length and Tone of Ad, 1960–96

	30-Second Positive Ads	30-Second Contrast Ads	30-Second Negative Ads
Position Appeals	18%	37%	30%
Number of Ads	143	115	145
	60-Second Positive Ads	60-Second Contrast Ads	60-Second Negative Ads
Position Appeals	12%	21%	29%
Number of Ads	193	38	39

Source: Data compiled by author.

some presidential candidates offer fewer valence issues than do others? One causal variable that will be examined is simply the share of negative issue appeals in that candidate's bid for the White House. A second variable will be the proportion of contrast ads in that campaign. We saw earlier that these ads are worth thinking about as a separate category. I also include a variable measuring the share of thirty-second spots in a campaign. Thirty-second ads contain more position appeals than do sixty-second spots (28 percent to 17 percent). That fact results in part at least from the greater negativity of thirty-second spots. But with a multivariate setting, I can explicitly assess the impact of thirty-second spots on the shape of appeals.

Two other variables worth exploring involve the context of the particular election. The first is the competitiveness of the contest. As competitiveness increases, the tendency to be vague may also increase. The reason for this hypothesis is twofold. A close campaign may encourage candidates to avoid staking out clearly defined positions. In addition, close contests may not be as negative as lopsided elections, where the trailing candidates are forced to attack as a way to get back into the race. The next contextual variable is incumbency. Here the idea is that incumbents will be more specific since they have a record to run on and to defend. As a candidate, it may be possible to say, "I favor making Social Security solvent." But as president, specific policies will be adopted that affect Social Security's workings. Stokes (1992) himself noted that campaigns are often made of valence issues, whereas governing forces politicians to adopt position issues to meet the demands of the office.

The dependent variable in my analysis is the share of position issues in each of the twenty presidential campaigns of major party candidates from 1960 to 1996. I have calculated the share of negative issues, the share of contrast ads, and the proportion of thirty-second spots for each campaign. I measured competitiveness by the amount the candidate was ahead or behind in the first Gallup Poll trial heat taken in September.[8] To measure incumbency, I created a three-part ordinal scale. The first category was simply challengers, the second was sitting vice presidents, and the third was presidents seeking reelection. The normal distinction is between incumbents and challengers, but between 1960 and 1996, three sitting vice presidents ran as their parties' presidential nominees. These contenders were partially tied to their administrations and had to defend some of those policies. Bush could not completely separate himself from Reagan in 1988. Such candidates constitute an "in between" category, yielding the three-part measure.

Table 6 presents the results of this regression. As one can see, the model works fairly well. The share of negative issues and contrast ads have a sizable impact on the amount of position appeals in a campaign. For every 10 percentage points more negativity, there is a 7 percentage point jump in position appeals. Contrast ads have an impact as well, although it is far less substantial than the impact of negative appeals. Incumbency too appears to have a substantive and statistically significant effect. The coefficient indicates that incumbents, on average, have 11 percentage points more position appeals than do pure challengers. Interestingly, an increase in the share of thirty-second spots, when controlling for other variables, decreases the amount of position appeals in a campaign. This finding is potentially important, since it suggests that shorter ads per se do not encourage more specific appeals. It appears that the thirty-second format is more conducive to negativity than the sixty-second format, leading to the appearance of more specific appeals. Shorter spots are an artifact of that phenomenon rather than actually contributing to the type of issue appeal.

Competitiveness does not appear to have much impact. With so few cases, I dropped competitiveness to see if it changed the estimates of the other variables. Incumbency gains a bit in strength, both substantively and statistically, while negativity and share of contrast ads hold about the same level of influence.[9]

The lessons from this analysis are potentially important. For starters, it suggests an independent role for both negativity and contrast ads. We need, however, to be cautious about overstating the impact of contrast ads. If one drops Clinton's campaign from the analysis, negativity and incumbency remain powerful, but the coefficient for contrast ads shrinks, no longer reaching statistical significance. Contrast ads may have an effect, but we should avoid making any strong claims about them.

These results also point to an upper limit on the share of position appeals. Using the highest values for each of the variables under study

TABLE 6. Explaining the Share of Position Issues in Presidential Campaigns, 1960–96

Variable	Parameter Estimate	Standard Error	Beta	t-statistic	Significance
Constant	−11.91	7.19	—	−1.66	.120
Incumbency	5.75	2.71	.39	2.12	.052
% of Negative Issues	.71	.23	.78	3.09	.008
% of Contrast Ads	.44	.21	.36	2.05	.059
% of 30-Second Ads	−.15	.08	−.43	−1.79	.095
Competitiveness	.12	.14	.15	.87	.399

$N = 20$ R-squared = .68   Adjusted R-squared = .57

(i.e., an incumbent who went on the attack and used numerous contrast spots), the predicted share of position appeals is slightly more than 50 percent. By comparison, a challenger's campaign that was very positive and relied on very few contrast ads could in fact yield a share of position issues close to zero. Consequently, the quality of campaign appeals can vary dramatically. But even under the most favorable conditions, candidates will use valence issues extensively—a finding quite consistent with Stokes's insight offered thirty-five years ago.

Conclusion

At least two general lessons may be drawn from these results. First, calls for less negativity in campaigns may have more drawbacks than well-intentioned reformers anticipate. Reforms usually have unexpected effects, and the data here provide a few clues to what some of them may be. Given that campaigns should be, as this volume's concluding chapter argues, "more informative, more engaging, and more edifying," we need to be cautious in our recommendations about the tone of campaigns. Jamieson, Waldman, and Sherr (1998, 18) make a similar pitch, questioning whether "scholars and pundits should continue [to advocate] an increase in 'positive advertising.'" Perhaps our real responsibility is to find better ways to communicate some of our results to the larger public. By showing that the typical assumptions about the drawbacks of negative advertising are overstated, we may be able to lessen the widespread public dissatisfaction with political advertisements. The perception rather than the reality poses the real threat.

Second, we need to be very clear about the standards we use when judging and trying to reform the quality of campaigns. Even though this chapter contends that attack advertising has some underappreciated benefits, I do not endorse the increased use of attack spots. Rather, my point is that under some reasonable criteria, such as increasing the number of position issues, more negative ads may be a good thing. Hence, we need to not only be clear about the criteria we use to evaluate campaigns but also justify the particular ones employed. I am fully aware that other very defensible standards have not been considered here. Nonetheless, campaigns that pay more attention to issues and discuss issues in ways that inform voters better about the candidates' positions have something to recommend them. For these reasons, attack advertising in American presidential elections does indeed have a silver lining.

NOTES

I thank Lynn Vavreck and an anonymous reviewer for University of Michigan Press for helpful comments on this essay.

1. It is also worth noting that attacks concerning misleading the public or dishonesty do not concern merely personal traits. When criticizing Clinton for breaking his word on a middle-class tax cut, Dole was attacking the president on two counts: the president did not keep his word, and he failed to cut taxes. In short, attacks about honesty blur the distinction between issue- and trait-based appeals.

2. Scholars have offered other distinctions between different types of issues (see, e.g., Berelson, Lazarsfeld, and McPhee 1954; Carmines and Stimson 1980). The advantage of Stokes's approach is that it focuses on how candidates frame issues rather than how voters think about them.

3. The Kanter Archive holds the largest number of presidential ads available for analysis. Jamieson (Campaign Discourse Mapping Project 1996) has raised questions about the Kanter Archive, noting that the Annenberg Archive at the University of Pennsylvania contains many more ads from the 1960 Kennedy campaign. That is true. However, for Reagan's 1980 bid for the White House and Dukakis's run, the Kanter Archive has many more ads (136 to 17 in 1980 and 126 to 46 in 1988) than does the Annenberg Archive. Over the four elections reported, the Annenberg Archive has about 41 ads per candidate's campaign (Campaign Discourse Mapping Project 1996, 24). For the same four elections, the Kanter Archive has nearly 63 ads per campaign. My point here is not to cast doubt on the value of the archive at the University of Pennsylvania: it is a rich resource that can provide scholars important insights into elections. Instead, my goal is to ease any concerns about the holdings available at the Kanter Archive.

4. I did a simple breakdown of appeals made in all political spots aired in presidential campaigns from 1960 to 1996. The proportion of issues stands at 54 percent, with traits 26 percent and values 20 percent. The amount of attention devoted to issues squares with previous content analyses (e.g., Joslyn 1980), providing faith in the data's accuracy.

5. Others too have found that negative spots contain more issue information than do positive ads (see Jamieson, Waldman, and Sherr 1998; Kaid and Johnston 1991; West 1997).

6. One concern about comparing thirty-second ads to sixty-second ads may be the timing of the spot. That is, sixty-second spots could be used for bios and hence run earlier in the campaign and contain fewer policy appeals. In each analysis, I examined the date of the ad (which I know for ads from 1972 to 1996) to test this rival hypothesis. There is no relationship between length of ad and date of creation. In each month from August to October, about 30 percent of the spots in my data set were sixty seconds long.

7. On request, I can supply the codes that underlie these categories. When developing the original coding scheme, I had the benefit of talking directly to Donald Stokes about it. He suggested a number of improvements in the coding scheme that allowed it to better reflect his notion of valence versus position issues.

8. Specifically, I calculated the difference in vote intention between the two major party nominees. So if Clinton was ahead of Dole 52–37, Clinton scored a –15 and Dole a –15. I measured competitiveness in other ways, and in no instance did the basic results change.

9. These results are available on request. I also ran a number of different specifications, and the estimates associated with the share of negative issues and incumbency were very stable. I also checked the Durbin-Watson statistic to make sure autocorrelation was not a problem.

REFERENCES

Ansolabehere, Stephen, and Shanto Iyengar. 1995. *Going Negative: How Political Advertisements Shrink and Polarize the Electorate.* New York: Free Press.

Berelson, Bernard R., Paul F. Lazarsfeld, and William N. McPhee. 1954. *Voting.* Chicago: University of Chicago Press.

Buchanan, Bruce. 1996. *Renewing Presidential Politics.* New York: Rowman and Littlefield.

Campaign Discourse Mapping Project. 1996. *Assessing the Quality of Campaign Discourse: 1960, 1980, 1988, 1992.* Philadelphia: Annenberg Public Policy Center, University of Pennsylvania.

Carmines, Edward, and James Stimson. 1980. "Two Faces of Issue Voting." *American Political Science Review* 74:78–91.

Diamond, Edwin, and Stephen Bates. 1984. *The Spot.* Cambridge: MIT Press.

Finkel, Steven E., and John G. Geer. 1998. "Spot Check: Casting Doubt on the Demobilization Hypothesis." *American Journal of Political Science* 42: 573–95.

Freedman, Paul, and Kenneth Goldstein. 1999. "Measuring Media Exposure and the Effects of Negative Campaign Ads." *American Journal of Political Science* 43:1189–1208.

Geer, John G. 1998. "Campaigns, Party Competition, and Political Advertising." In *Party Politics and Politicians,* ed. John G. Geer. Baltimore: Johns Hopkins University Press.

Geer, John G., and Richard Lau. 1998. "A New Way to Model Campaign Effects." Paper presented at the annual meeting of the American Political Science Association, Boston.

Goldstein, Kenneth. M. 1997. "What Did They See and When Did They See It? Measuring the Volume, Tone, and Targeting of Television Advertising in the 1996 Presidential Election." Department of Political Science, Arizona State University. Revised version of a paper presented at the annual meeting of the Midwest Political Science Association, Chicago.

Jamieson, Kathleen Hall. 1992. *Dirty Politics.* New York: Oxford University Press.

Jamieson, Kathleen Hall. 1996. *Packaging the Presidency.* 3d ed. New York: Oxford University Press.

Jamieson, Kathleen Hall, Paul Waldman, and Susan Sherr. 1998. "Eliminate the

Negative?" Paper presented at the conference on "Political Advertising in Election Campaigns," Washington, DC.
Joslyn, Richard. 1980. "The Content of Political Spot Ads." *Journalism Quarterly* 57:92–98.
Just, Marion R., Ann N. Crigler, Dean E. Alger, Timothy E. Cook, Montague Kern, and Darrell M. West. 1996. *Crosstalk.* Chicago: University of Chicago Press.
Kahn, Kim Fridkin, and Patrick Kenney. 1998. "Do Negative Campaigns Mobilize or Suppress Turnout." Unpublished manuscript, Arizona State University.
Kaid, Lynda Lee, and Anne Johnston. 1991. "Negative versus Positive Television Advertising in U.S. Presidential Campaigns, 1960–1988." *Journal of Communication* 41:53–64.
Kelley, Stanley, Jr. 1960. *Political Campaigning.* Washington, DC: Brookings Institution.
Kern, Montague. 1989. *30-Second Politics.* New York: Praeger.
Luntz, Frank. 1988. *Candidates, Consultants, and Campaigns.* New York: Blackwell.
Mayer, William G. 1996. "In Defense of Negative Campaigning." *Political Science Quarterly* 111:437–56.
Page, Benjamin. 1978. *Choices and Echoes in Presidential Elections.* Chicago: University of Chicago Press.
Patterson, Thomas, and Robert McClure. 1976. *The Unseeing Eye.* New York: Putnam.
Rabinowitz, George, and Stuart Elaine Macdonald. 1989. "A Directional Theory of Issue Voting." *American Political Science Review* 83:93–122.
Stokes, Donald E. 1966. "Spatial Models of Party Competition." In *Elections and the Political Order,* ed. Angus Campbell, Phillip Converse, Warren Miller, and Donald Stokes. New York: Wiley.
Stokes, Donald E. 1992. "Valence Politics." In *Electoral Politics,* ed. Dennis Kavanagh. Oxford: Clarendon Press.
"Thinking about the Political Process." 1998. *Public Perspective* 9:44.
West, Darrell. 1997. *Air Wars.* 2d ed. Washington, DC: CQ Press.

Chapter 3

How Does It All "Turnout"? Exposure to Attack Advertising, Campaign Interest, and Participation in American Presidential Elections

Lynn Vavreck

Introduction

The keystone of American democracy is the political campaign—a critical link through which potential governors communicate with citizens about problems, solutions, and basic ideologies. Candidates sell their ideas, their histories, and even themselves while voters listen, evaluate, and eventually cast ballots. It is a system in symbiotic balance. Voters need information, but not too much (Popkin 1990), and candidates want to provide information, but only specific kinds. The balance, however, may be shifting. It appears that citizens have lost faith in government, and their participation in elections continues to decline. Voters seem to want something more from candidates—but what? In this chapter I explore whether and why Americans are tuning out presidential campaigns and, more importantly, if the campaigns themselves have anything to do with the phenomenon.

Throughout our political history, citizens have lauded the clever wit of candidates. Who can resist smiling at Blaine's slogan highlighting Cleveland's illegitimate child during the 1884 campaign, "Ma, Ma, where's my Pa?" To which Cleveland replied, once elected, "Gone to the White House, ha ha ha!" Invective and vituperative strategy routinely amuse voters and may even draw them into the process. The intemperance and revelry of campaigns were so burdensome that in 1860, perhaps the most important election in American history, Abraham Lincoln said very little about his ideas and policies for fear his words would be severely distorted by his opponents. Instead, he and the Republican Party organized "Wide Awakes"—torchlight parades in which young men 6' 4" and taller marched alongside rail-splitters' battalions in support of Lincoln (Boller 1996). Today, many people speculate that these types of campaigns (low on information and high on drama) can be blamed for repelling voters from the process (Alliance for Better Campaigns 1998; Center for Global Ethics 1998; League of Women Voters 1998; Taylor 1996). But the important 1860 election, with all of its attack and exceptional antics, still managed to attract 81.2 percent of eligible voters to the polls. Negativity has not always meant low participation levels.

It is true that as campaigns have become more attack oriented from 1952 to 1996, campaign interest and electoral participation have also declined. Because of this correlation, many reformers and political observers suggest a causal relationship. They cry out that today's elections lack substance and that contemporary campaigns are nasty, mean-spirited, and shallow (Cain 1998; Johnson 1998; McAllister 1998). In a June 18, 1998, *Washington Post* article about campaign consultants, Frank Luntz, a well-known Republican political consultant, quipped, "I think the biggest problem in politics today is the lack of substance" (McAllister 1998). It appears that no one disputes that the delicate equilibrium between candidates and citizens appears to be disrupted—the debate is over the cause and the cure.

There are those who explore the idea that the lack of "color"—the lack of torchlight parades and barbecues—has changed political campaigns from entertainment to pure instruction (Zaller 1998). These adherents argue that if campaigns were more entertaining, if voters could get something out of them other than information (such as social time with family and friends), more people would participate. Others contend that candidates have become more interested in attacking their opponents than in promoting themselves and that this negativity, for lack of a better word, has demobilized and disengaged the electorate (Ansolabehere and Iyengar 1995; Campaign Discourse Mapping Project 1996; Lau, Pomper, and Mazeika 1995; but see Finkel and Geer 1998 and Geer's chapter in this volume). Finally, some scholars view the declining trends among voters as part of a larger societal shift, a general weakening of trust in a variety of political and social institutions (Putnam 1995). The explanation for the disruption of the balance between candidates and voters, wherever its roots, is likely to be made up of elements from all three of these possibilities and still others.

In addressing the downward participatory trends among voters, campaign reform has emerged as a potential panacea. Reformers argue that if voters are unhappy with American politics, then current campaign practices must be largely to blame (Alliance for Better Campaigns 1998; Project on Campaign Conduct 1998; Taylor 1996). These reformers suggest that if candidates would stop attacking one another, if we could remove money from the system, if reporters would be less cynical—if just one of these reforms could be implemented, citizens might once again become politically attentive.

This chapter explores the implications of one of these potential reforms—the effects of suppressing campaign attacks on campaign interest and political participation.[1] I begin the analysis by examining why political observers believe campaign attacks might be warding off citizens, and from there I explore whether there is evidence to suggest that attack advertising is systematically leading to a decline in campaign interest and participation. These questions are important, for if attack advertising does not adversely affect campaign interest and participation, then eliminating or decreasing it would be ineffective—meaning that it would not change whatever trends reformers want changed—and might even produce negative consequences not yet contemplated.

Preserving the Public Good

Policy reforms are aimed at preserving or creating a public good. In the case of campaign reform, the public good that is being preserved can be thought of as an informed and engaged electorate. This electorate is by no means "perfect"—the public good as it exists, or existed in the early parts of this century, is simply an electorate in which many but not all of the eligible voters take the time to learn about candidates and vote in elections. Specifically, those who do participate care about whether their preferred policies are enacted into legislation. Those who do not participate do so for any number of reasons. Perhaps they have four kids and no spare time to learn about politics, or they recently moved to a new home and did not register to vote. Whatever their reasons for being disinterested in campaigns and not participating in elections, their absence from the system is either an irregularity (they usually vote but did not this time because of some circumstance independent of the campaign itself) or it is habitual (they never vote). The informed and engaged electorate survives despite these types of nonparticipants.

What should worry scholars of campaigns and political reformers is when citizens who are usually interested in politics and vote in elections stop doing so because the system itself has spurned them. This changes the modestly sized informed and engaged electorate into a disgruntled and pessimistic electorate in which few citizens enjoy civic duties and only a small percentage participate. When citizens who care about seeing their policy preferences passed into law do not participate because the system discourages them from doing so, a "public bad" is created.

Some scholars believe the preponderance of attack-based campaigning in contemporary campaigns is the catalyst that has started the shift toward a public bad (Ansolabehere and Iyengar 1995; Campaign Discourse Mapping Project 1996; Lau, Pomper, and Mazeika 1995; Patterson 1993). The story, however, may not be that simple. Bartels's chapter in this volume suggests that public satisfaction with campaigns and elections has been declining steadily over four decades—but also that people know more now about candidates' issue positions than they have at any time in the past three decades. Some scholars claim that attack or negative campaign ads have actually increased the amount of issue information available to the electorate, have disseminated that information clearly to voters, and have generated concern about election outcomes (Geer in this volume; Finkel and Geer 1998; Mayer 1996). Do campaign attacks destroy interest and participation or provide clear and easy information to voters about candidates? Do attack antics detract from the public good, leave it unaffected, or enrich it?

To get a handle on answering this question one must decide on what criteria the public good is evaluated. In his introductory chapter, Bartels argues that we can evaluate campaigns on two fronts—how they affect public attitudes toward the electoral process and how they affect voter learning about candidates during campaigns. Attack advertising may negatively affect people's attitudes about the electoral process (making it bad for voters since it gets in the way of their instrumental policy goals) but may increase the level of voter learning about candidates' issue positions (making it good for candidates who want to efficiently and effectively distinguish themselves from their opponents). I turn now to sorting out which, if any, of these scenarios is at work.

Does Attack Disengage and Demobilize?

In what is perhaps the most elaborate experimental investigation of this relationship, Ansolabehere and Iyengar (1995) find that attack advertising demobilizes the electorate, particularly disarming those who have weak partisan affiliations. As in any experimental setting, these scholars have the ability to control what the subjects see and how much attention the subjects pay to what is being shown (in essence, they force the subjects to pay attention). This experimental setup has strong internal validity, giving many insights into the kinds of psychological effects attack advertisements may have, given the controlled level of attention to the advertisement. But this design cannot shed any light on how attack advertising might affect the levels of attention people pay to campaigns (attack ads may make people pay less or more attention). Nor can this setup assess the dynamic and endogenous relationship between attack advertising and participation. If we care about reforming attack-based electioneering, we must discover whether it creates interest in campaigns or destroys it and whether it encourages people to pay attention to campaigns or makes them tune out. To ascertain answers to these questions, both variables must be allowed to change: attention to attack advertisements and interest (or participation) must vary simultaneously since the two are related to one another in a system, not unlike supply and demand.

In a subsequent survey-based study, Finkel and Geer (1998) came to a contrary conclusion about the relationship of campaign negativity to participation. Their results indicate no relationship between declining turnout and campaign tone. Additionally, they find that although campaign tone is associated with lower levels of efficacy, negative campaign tone is also associated with greater concern about the election outcome. Again, however, Finkel and Geer have investigated the same problem that Ansolabehere and his colleagues examined—the effects of campaign negativity given a certain, or controlled, level of interest, exposure, or attention. To carefully ascertain the effects of attack-based campaigning on people's interest, attention, and participation, all of these variables must be allowed to influence one another.

A New Approach: A System of Effects

To investigate how attack advertising influences campaign interest and participation, I make one simple assumption—that is, that attack advertising can affect only people who pay attention to the campaign in the media and see, hear, or read about the campaign. Therefore, paying attention to the campaign in the media becomes a proxy for having been exposed to some percentage of attack campaigning.[2]

One possible relationship between paying attention to the campaign in the media and campaign interest is as follows: the more attention you pay to the campaign in the media, the more interested you become in the campaign, and the more interested you become in the campaign, the more attention you pay to the campaign in the media. This is a positively related system. Of course, the opposite could also be true: the more attention you pay, the less interested you become, and the less interested you become, the less attention you pay. This is a negatively related system. Finally, these variables might have no relation to one another. Paying attention to the campaign might not make you any more or less interested in the campaign, and your level of interest might not encourage or discourage your attention level. This is a neutral relationship.[3]

Reformers believe we are currently in a negatively related system. People watch campaigns on television or read about them in the papers, and the attack-based strategy of candidates and coverage makes people less interested in the campaign, which then makes them pay even less attention. The same story is true for participation—you pay attention to the campaign and you become less likely to vote, but the less likely you are to vote, the less attention you pay to the campaign. Both of these systems are fueled by what people see when they pay attention to campaigns. Reformers argue that if we can change the content, style, and tone of campaigns, we can shift these systems out of negative relationships and into positive ones. But no one has investigated these systems to see if they are in a negative, positive, or neutral state. Instead, scholars have explored one component of the system (how exposure to campaign negativity affects interest or participation) without looking at the other half of the relationship (how interest or participation affects exposure to campaign negativity). To study the complete system, I test the following two hypotheses and corollaries:

System 1

H1: Paying attention to the campaign in the media is positively associated with campaign interest.

C1: Campaign interest is positively associated with paying attention to the campaign in the media.

System 2

H2: Paying attention to the campaign in the media is positively associated with electoral participation.

C2: Electoral participation is positively associated with paying attention to the campaign in the media.

First Element: Has the Tone of Campaigns Changed?

The level of attention a person pays to the campaign in the media is a critical variable in the relationships among campaign attacks, interest, and participation. Exposure to the campaign is a necessary condition for being affected by the campaign. Therefore, since the percentage of negative ads and attack-based news coverage is known for each election year, a voter's attention to the campaign in any given year indicates exposure to these attack strategies. But just how much attack-based campaigning occurs in American presidential elections?

In figure 1, I present the percentages of negative campaign advertisements over six presidential election years (Geer 1998) and the percentage of negative news coverage over the same period (Patterson 1993). As is easily observed, American presidential campaigns have become more negative over the course of this period, culminating in the 1996 election, in which almost half of all campaign appeals were negative in tone.[4] In addition, the tone of news coverage of presidential campaigns has also declined steadily over this period.[5] The first link in the reformers' chain has been substantiated—campaigns today are more attack oriented than they were twenty years ago.

Second Element: Have Levels of Interest and Participation Changed?

In figure 2, I present data that bear on the questions of campaign interest and voter participation. The turnout data are the aggregate voting rates recorded for each election. The survey data were collected by the National Election Study.

The trend in campaign interest presented in figure 2 is replicated from figure 5 in Bartels's introductory chapter. These data are the average levels of campaign interest for a typical survey respondent (a forty-five-year-old white female with a high school diploma and median family income). It appears from these data that interest in campaigns has declined gradually over time, with the exception of the 1960 and 1992 campaigns.[6] In 1996, campaign interest sank to its all-time low, just under 40 percent. Simultaneously, participation dropped to an all-time low. As interest deteriorates, so does participation. The correlation of these two time trends is .86.

The second element of the reformers' story is confirmed. Campaign interest and electoral participation are declining over time, and campaign negativity is increasing. It is easy to understand why scholars and reformers are anxious to blame candidates' behavior in campaigns for the electorate's disengagement and demobilization. But a more rigorous test of this claim is possible.

Specifying a Systems Model

A unique feature of the relationship between campaign interest and exposure to attack-based campaigning is that both variables affect one another. Essentially, both are dependent variables, even though I want to use each of

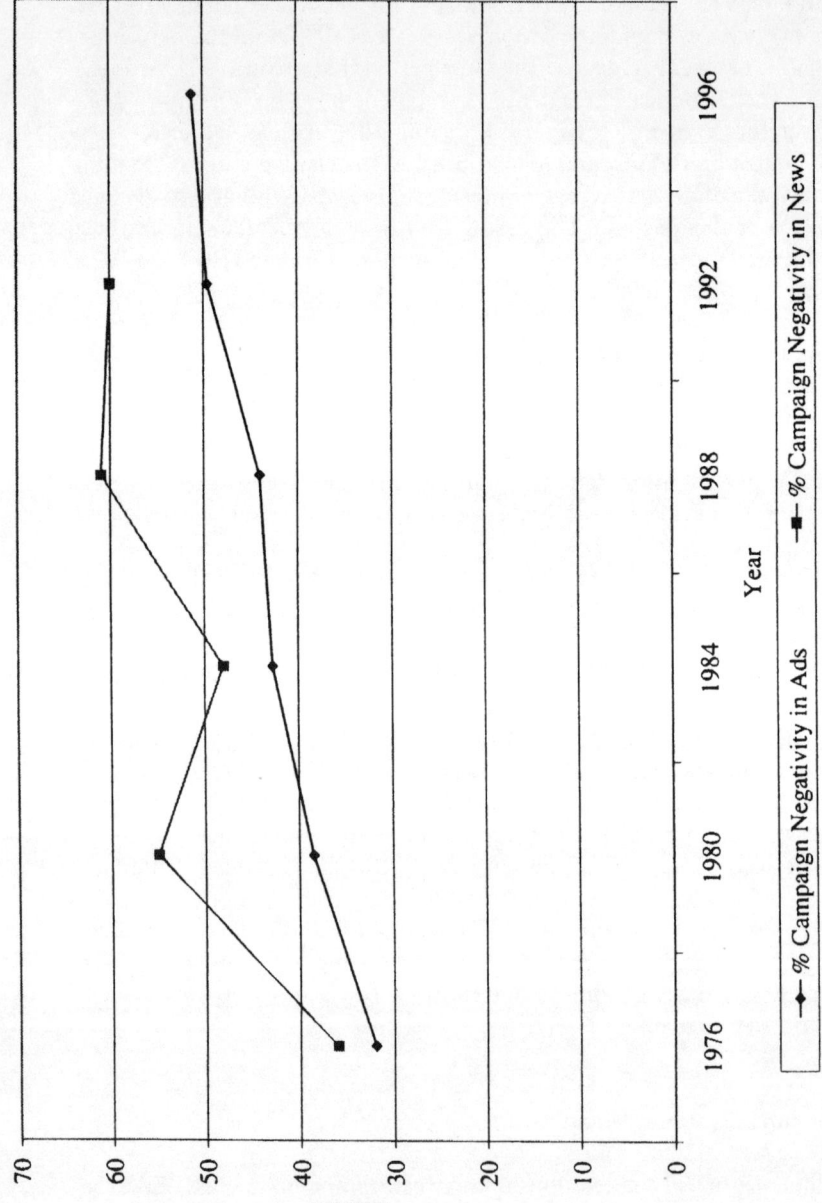

Fig. 1. Increases in campaign negativity over time, 1976-96

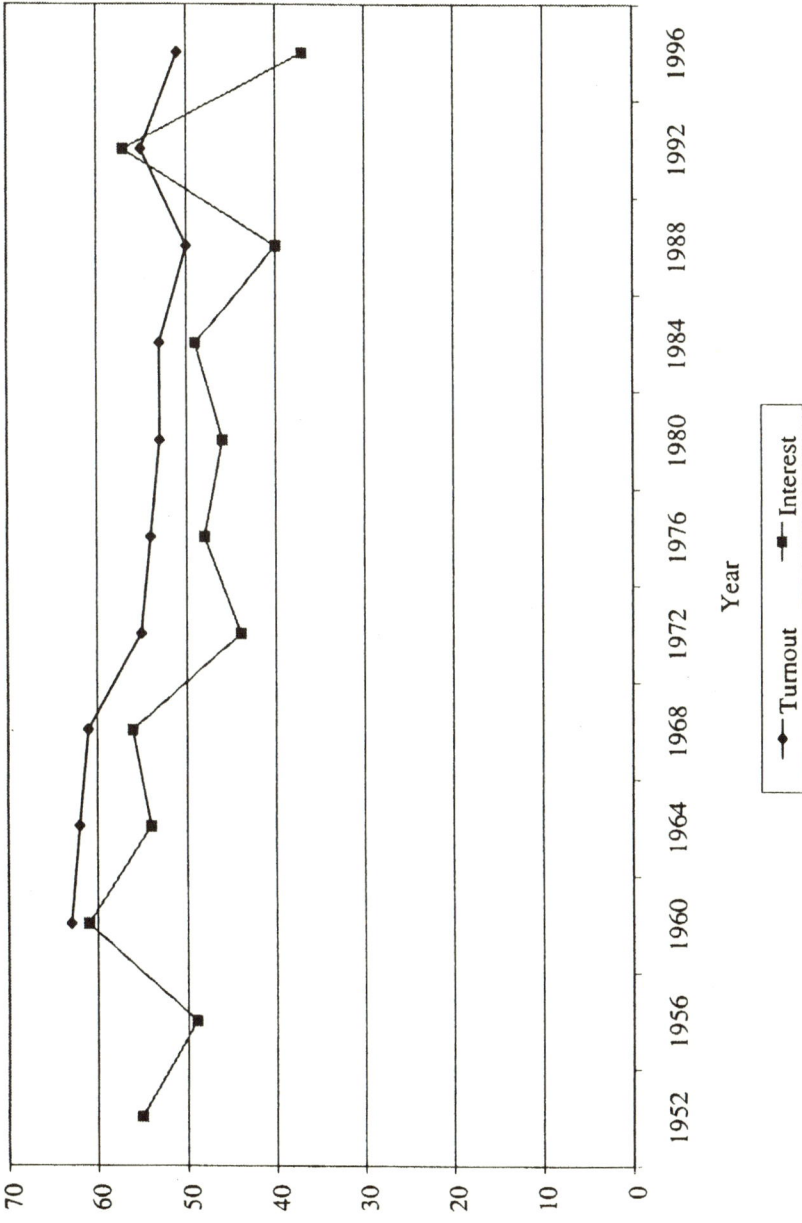

Fig. 2. Campaign interest and electoral participation over time, 1976-96

them as an independent variable to explain the other. Estimating endogenous relationships such as the one between exposure to attacks and campaign interest (or exposure and participation) requires special methodological attention. In simultaneous equation modeling there is more than one equation to estimate in each system; there is one equation for each endogenous variable. In system 1, I estimate one equation for campaign interest and another equation for campaign attention (which is serving as a measure of exposure to campaign attacks). Then, for system 2, I estimate one equation for campaign attention and one equation for participation. In this type of work, one cannot estimate the parameters of a single model without taking into account the information provided by the other equations in the system. To ignore the simultaneity by simply using ordinary least squares would result in biased and inconsistent estimates—that is, as the sample size increased indefinitely, the estimates would not converge to their true population values. Therefore, some other method should be used.

As a solution to this problem I use a full information maximum likelihood (FIML) model.[7] This approach allows me to estimate all of the equations in the system at the same time, taking full account of the endogeneity.[8] Although in this case FIML is the best possible choice among estimators, these models are not without drawbacks.[9]

Data, Variables, Models

The survey data for these analyses are provided by the American National Election Study (NES). The NES surveys a random sample of the American population before and after every presidential election. I draw here on the surveys from 1976 to 1996.[10]

I begin with system 1—the simultaneous relationship between campaign attention (exposure to campaign attacks) and campaign interest.

System 1

$$\text{Interest} = \alpha_0 + \alpha_1 \text{ Traits} + \alpha_2 \text{ Turnout}_{t-1} + \alpha_3 \text{ Reside} + \alpha_4 \text{ Attention} + \varepsilon_1$$

$$\text{Attention} = \beta_0 + \beta_1 \text{ Traits} + \beta_2 \text{ Newspaper} + \beta_3 \text{ Television} + \beta_4 \text{ Urban} + \beta_5 \text{ Interest} + \upsilon_1$$

"Traits" include categorical variables for gender, race, education, and partisan strength along with an ordinal variable constructed from the log of income. These variables are believed to influence campaign interest and attention in typical sociological and psychological ways (Campbell et al. 1960; Lazarsfeld, Berelson, and Gaudet 1948; Wolfinger and Rosenstone 1980). The variables that identify the attention equation are "Turnout$_{t-1}$," which is a measure of whether the respondent voted in the last presidential election, and "Reside," which is the number of years a respondent has lived at his or her current address. These variables should be positively related to campaign interest.

"Newspaper," "Television," and "Urban" are variables that identify the interest equation. The first two variables measure the number of days in a given week the respondent reads a daily newspaper or watches television news. These variables track the respondent's use of nonpolitical media (thereby assessing to how much political media he or she might be exposed). "Urban" is a measure of the level of development of the respondent's community. This variable traces how many news organizations a respondent can possibly be exposed to; for example, a large urban area has many more sources of news than does a small rural area. These instruments for news exposure should be positively associated with campaign attention.[11] Campaign interest is an ordinal measure of a respondent's interest level (the options are "very much," "somewhat," or "not at all" interested). Campaign attention is measured similarly but with four possible categories of response ("a lot," "some," "a little," or "no" attention).

The second system, which details the relationship between campaign attention and participation, is exactly the same as the first except the dependent variable in the first equation is "Turnout$_t$," which represents vote in the current presidential election.

System 2

$$\text{Turnout}_t = \gamma_0 + \gamma_1 \text{ Traits} + \gamma_2 \text{ Turnout}_{t-1} + \gamma_3 \text{ Reside} + \gamma_4 \text{ Attention} + \varepsilon_2$$

$$\text{Attention} = \lambda_0 + \lambda_1 \text{ Traits} + \lambda_2 \text{ Newspaper} + \lambda_3 \text{ Television} + \lambda_4 \text{ Urban} + \lambda_5 \text{ Turnout}_t + \upsilon_2$$

Results: System 1

Does Exposure to Campaign Attacks Lead to a Decline in Interest?

The short answer to this question is no—exposure to campaign attacks does not appear to lead to a decline in campaign interest among voters. Consider the results of the analysis on the first system of equations.

In the first half of table 1 I present results from the first equation in system 1, the equation explaining campaign interest. The control variables behave as anticipated. In many cases, being older, male, Caucasian, educated, and a high wage earner increases interest in the campaign. The instrumental variables also meet their expectations. Having voted in the previous presidential election systematically increases interest in the cur-

TABLE 1. The Endogenous Relationship between Exposure to Attack Advertising and Campaign Interest, 1976–96

Variable	1976	1980	1984	1988	1992	1996
System 1: Dependent Variable **Campaign Interest**						
Age	−0.004	**0.007**	**0.008**	0.002	0.0004	−0.00002
Female	0.13	−0.11	**−0.14**	−0.1	0.012	−0.05
White	0.11	−0.15	−0.14	−0.06	**0.2**	−0.02
High school	0.17	**−0.4**	**−0.3**	0.04	0.05	0.12
College	0.03	−0.09	−0.11	**0.4**	**0.3**	0.3
Graduate work	−0.003	0.14	0.02	0.5	**0.6**	0.22
Income (log)	−0.005	**0.02**	**0.01**	−0.0007	−0.003	−0.006
Turnout$_{t-1}$	**−0.47**	**0.59**	**0.5**	**0.6**	**0.62**	**0.15**
Reside	**0.09**	−0.008	**−0.06**	−0.01	−0.03	−0.03
Partisan	−0.134	**−0.13**	0.02	0.09	0.02	**−0.12**
Constant	3.08	0.05	0.08	−0.08	−0.33	**0.7**
Campaign Attention	−0.32	0.15	**0.34**	**0.31**	**0.41**	0.008
N	1,529	1,390	1,928	1,919	1,670	1,455
Log-likelihood	−1404.44	−2623.06	−3262.22	−3219.16	−2535.03	−2675.01
System 1: Dependent Variable **Campaign Attention**						
Age	**0.01**	**0.007**	**−0.005**	0.001	0.003	−0.002
Gender	0.1	0.02	0.03	**−0.17**	**−0.16**	−0.11
Race	−0.1	**0.24**	0.11	0.07	−0.11	0.03
High school	−0.06	**−0.41**	**−0.21**	**0.22**	0.07	−0.144
College	−0.22	**−0.33**	**−0.17**	**0.36**	**0.26**	0.12
Graduate work	0.03	**−0.17**	−0.06	**0.56**	0.25	0.2
Income	**0.03**	**0.02**	−0.006	−0.0004	−0.002	−0.005
Newspaper	**0.53**	**0.11**	**0.03**	−0.004	0.007	**0.03**
Television	**0.54**	**−0.2**	**0.4**	**0.31**	**0.18**	**0.4**
Urban	−0.03	−0.04	−0.04	−0.06	0.11	**0.2**
Partisanship	0.13	−0.1	0.05	−0.02	0.02	0.06
Constant	5.64	0.25	0.11	**−0.55**	**0.1**	−0.08
Campaign Interest	−0.04	**0.21**	**0.15**	**0.23**	**0.23**	−0.04
N	1,529	1,390	1,928	1,919	1,670	1,455
Log-likelihood	−1404.44	−2633.06	−3262.22	−3219.16	−2535.03	−2675.01

Note: Cell entries are FIML Endogenous Ordered Probit Coefficients (z-scores). Bold indicates coefficient is significant at the .01 level (two-tailed)

rent campaign, although how long a person lives at his or her current address has little effect on campaign interest.

For half of the years under investigation the variable of importance, attention to the campaign in the media, confirms the hypothesis that the more attention one pays to the campaign, the more interested one becomes in the campaign. In the other three years, this variable has no effect on interest. In no case, even when campaigns were at their dirtiest, does paying attention to the campaign in the media result in a decrease in campaign interest. A graphical presentation of these findings may help to illustrate the relationship between exposure to campaign negativity and campaign interest.

One thing that is notable about figure 3 is that progression along the X axis is representative not only of increases in campaign negativity but also of the passage of time. Based on these data, I infer that in the elections of 1980, 1984, and 1988, paying attention to the campaign in the media resulted in an increase in campaign interest among citizens. Particularly interesting is 1988, in which the number of negative appeals in advertisements rose to almost 50 percent. In this highly negative campaign year, paying attention to the campaign in the media increases a voter's likelihood of being interested in the campaign by the largest amount on record.

There does not appear to be a negative relationship between exposure to campaign attacks and campaign interest. In fact, when there is any relationship at all between these variables, it is a positive relationship. Campaign attacks seem to be increasing the level of voter interest in campaigns or leaving it unchanged. One thing can be said with considerable certainty: there is no evidence that attacks are causing voters to lose interest in presidential campaigns.

Does Being Interested in Campaigns Cause People to Pay More Attention?

Now I present data on the second half of system 1—the effect of being interested in the campaign on the level of attention one pays to the campaign in the media. In the previous section I showed that paying attention leads to either no change in interest or to an increase in interest. In those years when interest is increased, what happens to the level of attention? The second half of table 1 presents these data.

Once again, controls and instrumental variables behave mostly as anticipated. Being older, male, educated, white, and a high wage earner increases the probability of paying attention to campaigns in the media. The number of days a respondent watches television news is highly and positively related to the amount of attention he or she pays to the cam-

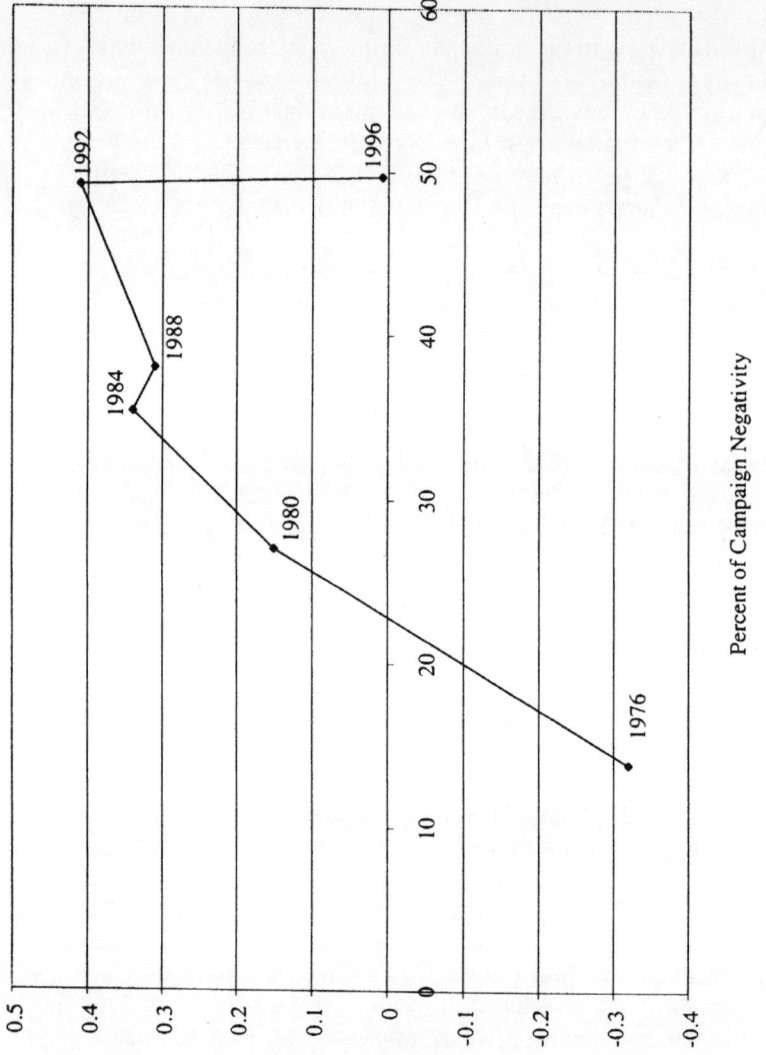

Fig. 3. Endogenous effects of exposure to campaign attacks on campaign interest

paign in the media. The number of days a respondent reads a daily newspaper also shows a positive, albeit more modest, relationship to campaign attention. In only one year (1996) did the size of the respondent's community affect his or her level of attention.

Once again, campaign interest and attention are positively related. In four of the six cases in the analysis, as people became more interested in the campaign, they paid more attention to the campaign in the media. In the two remaining years, no significant relationship was found in either direction. In figure 4, I graphically present these results.

From 1980 through 1992 interested citizens paid more attention to campaigns. These years show significant increases in negativity, and as I mentioned earlier, 1988 and 1992 exhibit particularly large increases in attack. Despite this growth in distasteful campaigning, people who were interested in campaigns increased their attention levels. This is another significant finding: attack-based campaigning does not seem to have a negative relationship with campaign attention. That is, campaign attacks are not causing citizens to ignore campaigns.

In fact, it appears that the opposite is true. Here is where evaluating the relationship, as a system, becomes important. This analysis, which allows for endogeneity between campaign interest and attention, suggests that as people pay attention to the campaign, even and especially in highly attack-oriented campaign years, they become more interested in the campaign. As people become more interested in the campaign, they pay more attention to it in the media. This phenomenon is represented by the positive and significant coefficients on campaign interest and campaign attention in the equations from system 1. These variables are related to one another positively—not negatively, as many reformers believe.

Results: System 2

Does Attack Campaigning Lead to Lower Participation on Election Day?

It is possible that even as negative campaigns attract people's interest, such campaigns discourage citizens from participating in elections. A person might be curious about the campaign, attracted to the colorful antics, and still be left with a feeling of lowered political efficacy—a feeling that his or her vote cannot affect the system or the outcome in any way. Negative campaigns may interest but not inspire voters—in short, such campaigns may, despite their interest, cause voters to stay away from the polls. In the first half of table 2, I present data on this possibility.

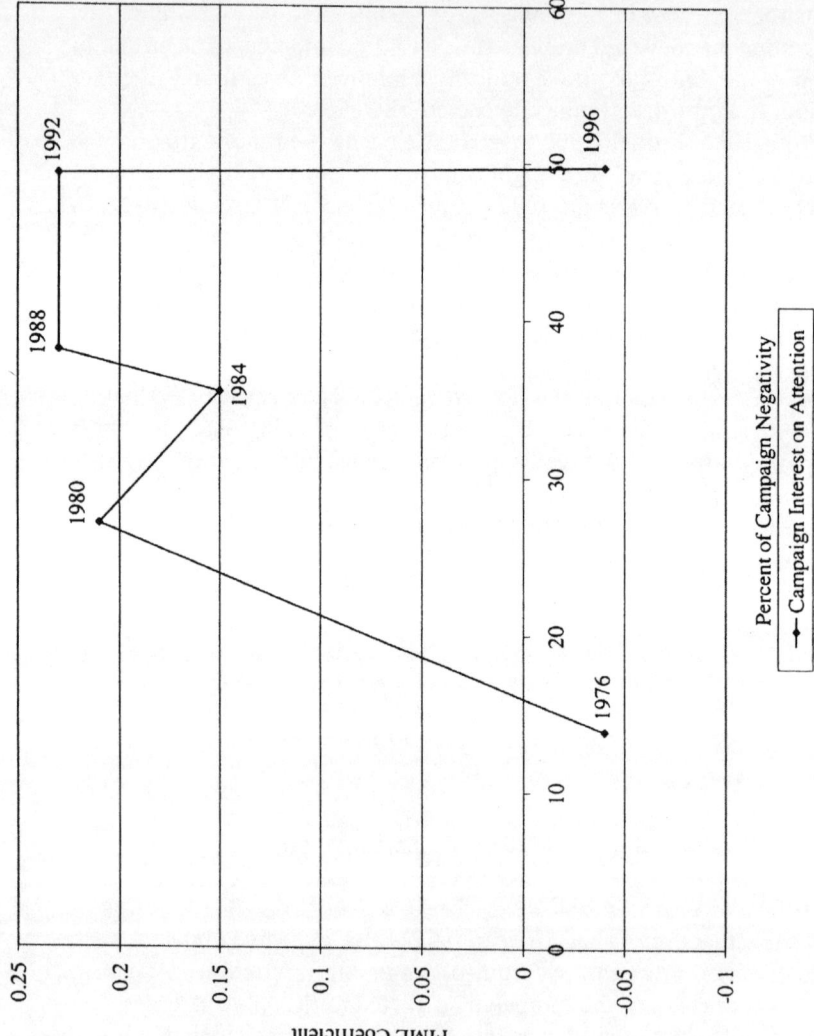

Fig. 4. Endogenous effects of campaign interest on campaign attention

The results in table 2 once again confirm that being older, white, male, educated, and a high wage earner positively affect the probability of voting in a presidential election. Furthermore, having voted in the previous presidential election makes it more likely that a person will vote in the current election, as does having lived at an address for a long time. Even being a strong partisan makes turnout more likely.

TABLE 2. The Endogenous Relationship between Exposure to Attack Advertising and Electoral Participation, 1976–96

Variable	1976	1980	1984	1988	1992	1996
System 2: Dependent Variable **Turnout**						
Age	−.003	−.005	−.006	−.01	−.01	.007
Gender	−.12	−.10	−.17	−.082	**.14**	−.084
Race	−.13	−.13	−.16	.1	−.20	.16
High school	−.21	−.6	−0.9	.12	**.28**	**.30**
College	−.07	.1	.21	**.46**	**.56**	**.69**
Graduate work	.17	.10	.07	**.82**	**.70**	**.79**
Income	**.03**	**.03**	**.04**	−.003	.002	−.001
Previous Voter	**1.4**	**1.5**	**1.9**	**2.11**	**1.31**	**1.32**
Years in Residence	**.12**	**.18**	**.16**	**.17**	**.13**	**.10**
Partisanship	**.16**	**.12**	.03	.03	**.16**	**.18**
Constant	−1.36	−.07	−.09	−1.3	−.78	−1.63
Campaign Attention	.11	**.47**	**.13**	.05	**.15**	**.09**
N	1,535	1,390	1,928	1,919	1,651	1,599
Log-likelihood	−937.81	−2519.06	−2567.22	−2230.36	−1878.46	−1978.17
System 2: Dependent Variable **Campaign Attention**						
Age	**.01**	**0.007**	−0.003	.00	.004	−.002
Gender	.1	0.02	0.05	−.14	−.12	−.11
Race	−.1	**0.24**	0.17	.08	−.09	.01
High school	−.03	**−0.41**	**−0.34**	.14	.04	−.12
College	−.2	**−0.33**	**−0.23**	**.42**	**.24**	.06
Graduate work	.007	**−0.17**	−0.08	**.63**	**.28**	.11
Income	**.03**	**0.02**	−0.008	−.007	.00	**−.006**
Newspaper	**.51**	**0.11**	**0.06**	−.006	.00	.008
Television	**0.52**	**−0.2**	**0.5**	**.37**	**.18**	**.38**
Urban	−0.02	−0.04	−0.07	−.02	**.11**	**.14**
Partisanship	0.1	−0.1	0.02	.00	−.01	.07
Constant	5.66	0.25	0.37	−.49	1.1	−.004
Turnout	**.12**	**0.21**	**0.10**	**.13**	**.13**	**.14**
N	1,535	1,390	1,928	1,919	1,651	1,599
Log-likelihood	−937.81	−2519.06	−2567.22	−2230.36	−1878.46	−1978.17

Note: Cell entries are FIML Endogenous Ordered Probit Coefficients (z-scores). Bold indicates coefficient is significant at the .01 level (two-tailed).

Paying attention to the campaign increases the likelihood of voting in four of the six years under analysis. Even in 1996, when almost half of all campaign appeals were negative, people who paid attention to these appeals were more likely to vote than those who did not. In figure 5 I present this relationship graphically.

As with the relationship between campaign attention and interest, the relationship between campaign attention and turnout is positive. Particularly interesting is 1992—a year when negative campaign appeals rose by almost 10 percent. In that year, paying attention to the campaign made people more likely to vote in the November election—even more than in 1988 or 1984, two elections that were much more positive than the 1992 election. There seems to be no indication that paying attention to campaigns, even negative ones, decreases voter turnout.

Does Planning to Vote Cause People to Pay More Attention to the Campaign?

As one might hope, the answer to this question is yes. Turning out (or planning to turn out) and campaign attention are positively related to one another. I present these data in the second half of table 2 and graphically in figure 6.

Again, the control and instrumental variables behave as anticipated. Planning to vote in November significantly increases the probability that a person will pay attention to the campaign in the media in every year since 1976. Furthermore, when people use the media, they become more likely to vote, as the first part of system 2 explained. These two variables, turnout and attention, are related to one another in a positive system, just like interest and attention. The more attention people pay to the campaign in the media, the more likely they are to vote in the election, and the more likely they are to vote in the election, the more attention they pay to the campaign in the media. Once again, reformers' hunches have not been substantiated.

In short, these results do not comport with reformers' notions that attack-based campaigning is causing citizens to lose interest in campaigns and disengage from the electoral process. When campaign interest, participation, and attention are allowed to endogenously affect one another, the results indicate that these variables positively influence one another.

Conclusion: New Standards

Campaign attacks neither cause voters to stay away from the polls nor constitute the roots of declining interest in campaigns. In fact, in some

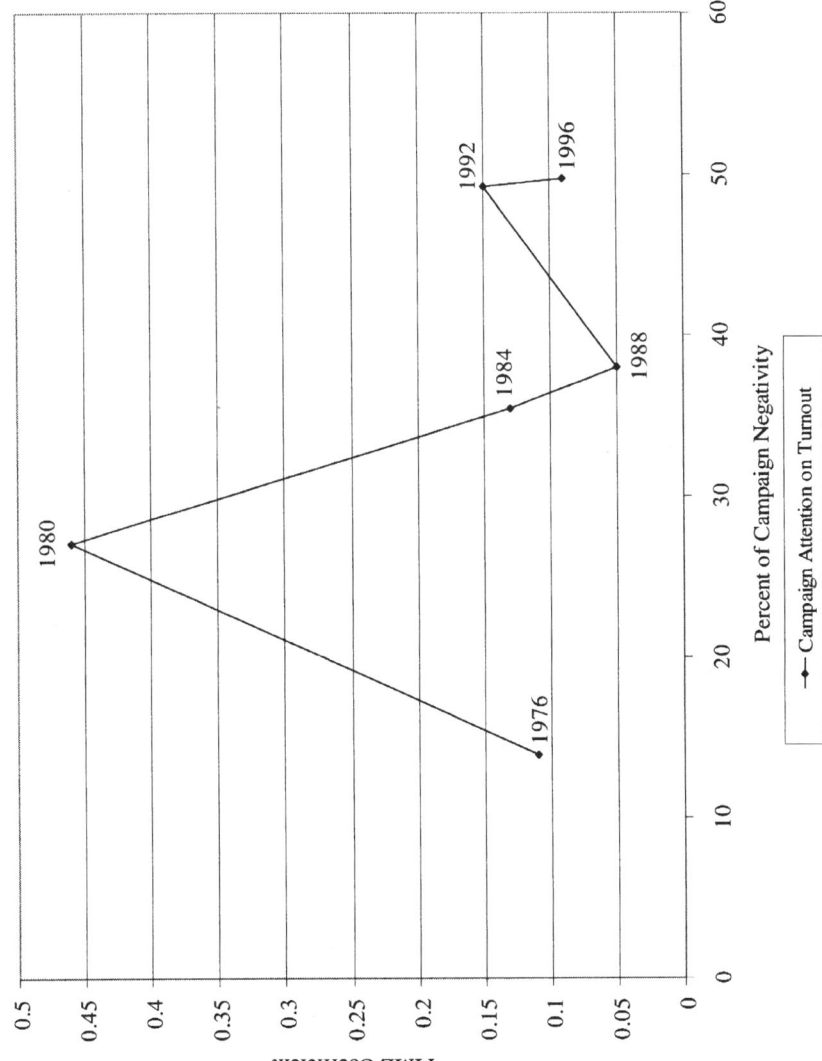

Fig. 5. Endogenous effects of exposure to campaign attacks on turnout

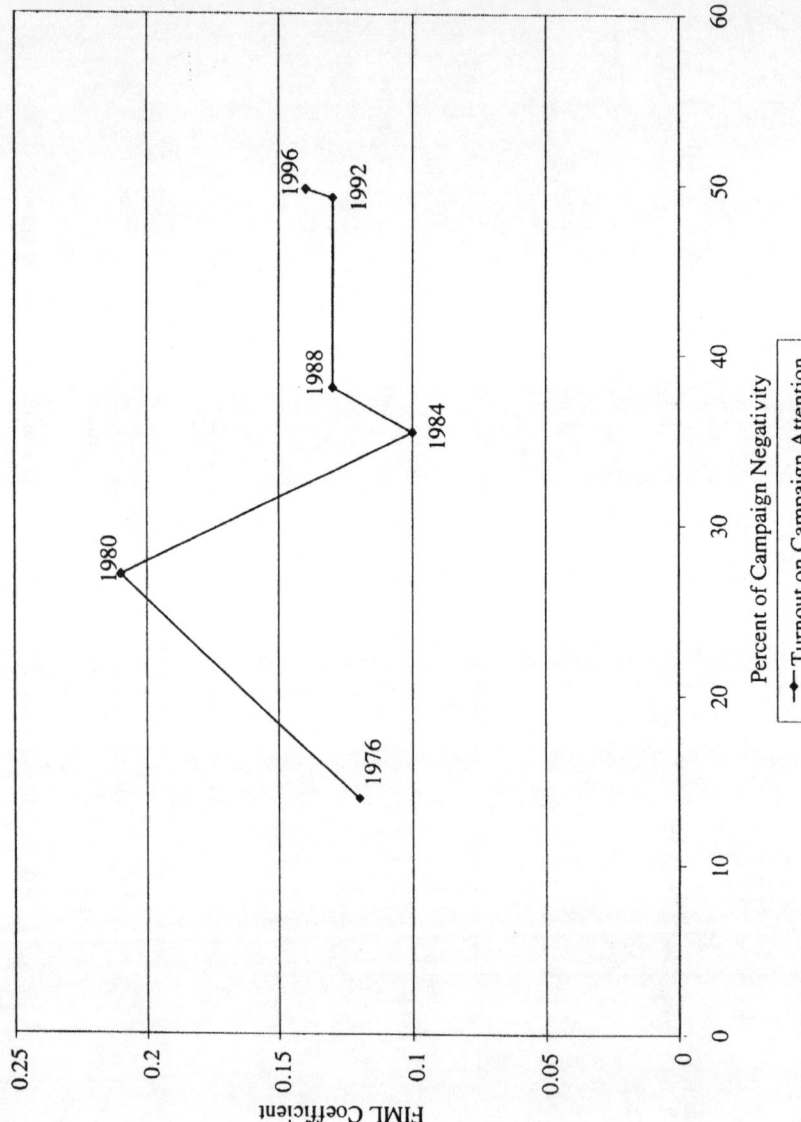

Fig. 6. Endogenous effects of turnout on campaign attention

years campaigns that contain negative appeals increase voter interest and participation. But, of course, in some years they do not. These results indicate that increased negative appeals do not lead to demobilization or disengagement of the electorate.

The results appear to put me in the somewhat awkward position of defending negative campaigning, but that is not what I intend to do. These data do not suggest that attack advertising is good for the electorate or, for that matter, good for candidates. There is no evidence to substantiate the belief that the more negative appeals a candidate makes, the more people become interested or the more turn out to vote. Yes, in some years increased negativity leads to increased interest and turnout, but those years may also have other campaign features that lead to both negative campaigning and increases in interest and turnout.

For example, a close race might lead both candidates to make more negative or attack appeals while creating heightened voter interest and turnout. A third-party candidate might also increase the amount of overall negativity in an election while increasing interest and turnout. Finally, an election that is centered or focused on one issue, about which all the candidates constantly debate, might attract more negative appeals and more voter participation. These spurious possibilities might be the actual cause of heightened voter participation and increases in negative campaigning.

Moreover, there may be other standards by which we want to judge political campaigns and the public good. Earlier, I described two possible ways in which we could evaluate campaigns: learning about the candidates' policy positions and attitudes about the electoral process. There may, however, be other possible criteria for evaluating campaigns that would better showcase the poor effects of negativity and attack.

One possible criterion for the evaluation of campaigns is how they affect system legitimacy or support (Buchanan in this volume). Broader than just attitudes toward the campaigns and the current election, this guideline illuminates people's confidence in their entire system of governance. As political scholars and reformers, we may care about these types of beliefs even though they do not appear to have any behavioral manifestations at the current time. We should care because one day the level of support for the system might sink to such a profound low that people begin abstaining from elections on these grounds. If campaign negativity were driving feelings of loss of legitimacy, it would also be to blame for this eventual demobilization.

A second possible standard for judging campaigns might be their effect on politicians' credibility once elected. In a recent survey conducted by the Project on Campaign Conduct (1998) at the Institute for Global

Ethics, 84 percent of respondents reported that they believe at least some candidates use outright lies during a campaign; 46 percent believe most candidates do. Furthermore, in a separate survey released by the Pew Research Center (Thurber, Nelson, and Dulio 1998), 84 percent of political consultants said they thought it was perfectly ethical to use factually true statements out of context to get a candidate elected. People are losing respect for politicians, and this attitude is likely a direct result of candidates' (and consultants') campaign behavior.

In the Campaign Conduct survey (1998), 78 percent of respondents suggested that negative, attack-oriented campaigning produces leaders who are less ethical and less trustworthy. Even more of the sample said that they lose faith in an elected official when he or she lies. Citizens may not be voicing this disrespect with their feet (abstaining from elections or punishing candidates who behave poorly), but the fact remains that politicians are not held in high regard.

The larger problem associated with this lack of respect for politicians is one of candidate recruitment. As respect for elected officials goes down the number of quality challengers for political positions also declines. In the survey of campaign consultants funded by the Pew Charitable Trusts (Thurber, Nelson, and Dulio 1998), 42 percent of consultants claim that the quality of candidates for congressional races is falling, and another 48 percent rate the overall quality of congressional candidates as only fair or poor. This is certainly a public bad about which scholars and reformers should care.

What can be done to curb some campaigners' distasteful and misleading practices and at the same time restore respect to political leaders? Some of the reforms proposed to combat negative campaigning because it was believed to disengage and demobilize may be appropriate reforms toward this end. The adwatch is a reform that was used extensively in 1992 and less in 1996 to discourage candidates from using misleading images and statements in their ads. Essentially, an independent organization (usually a media outlet such as CNN or the *Washington Post*) checks each frame of a political advertisement for its "truth." When done appropriately (Jamieson 1992), these adwatches can discourage candidates from running questionable ads because they do not want to bear the cost of being found to be misleading voters. The adwatch works because it affects candidates' incentives. Candidates behave better because of the adwatch.

Another reform that may go a long way toward restoring respect for elected leaders is free television advertising time with format restrictions. If the government pays for a certain amount of television time for candidates, the government could legally apply restrictions on what candidates who accept the free time do during their spots. One idea is that the candidates must appear in the ads themselves, with no voice-overs or music—just the candidate talking to the camera. This talking-head format was used in 1996 on several networks that provided free TV time to candidates. Although few voters recall seeing such ads, there is no evidence from network ratings that people changed the channel or turned off the television when these spots came on (Taylor 1996; *Free Air Time and Campaign Reform* 1997). Further, there is evidence that indicates that when candidates have to speak about their campaigns themselves, they do not do so in negative or attack-oriented ways but instead use positive promotional styles and substantiate claims with evidence (Adasiewicz, Rivlin, and Stanger 1997).

Finally, the most promising of potential reforms being put forth in this election cycle is the Campaign Code of Conduct effort promoted by the Institute for Global Ethics and funded by The Pew Charitable Trusts. During the fall 1998 elections in two states, Ohio and Washington, candidates in each race were asked to come together to draft and sign a set of pledges that structured the acceptable behavior in their particular election. The institute provided a framework for the activity of drafting the Campaign Code of Conduct, but candidates in the races wrote the actual document. The code includes things like an agreement to participate in at least one public debate, a promise to refrain from demeaning references and demeaning visual images of each other, a pledge to disclose campaign finances on the Internet, and an agreement not to use or allow to be used personal attacks, innuendo, or stereotyping against each other. Citizens are the ultimate judges of what behavior may cross these lines.

Voters in Ohio and Washington clearly believe that these codes of conduct are appealing (Project on Campaign Conduct 1998). Seventy-nine percent of voters claimed that they have more respect for a candidate who signs a pledge of good conduct. Further, 74 percent of voters indicated that they would be more likely to vote for a candidate if he or she signed such a pledge. These projects can raise the level of respect for political candidates and elected officials and can make it more appealing for high-quality challengers to participate in politics.

Paying attention to campaigns in the media, even with the large portion of discourse that is offensive to voters, does not make people lose interest in campaigns or abstain from voting. Reformers who use these two ideas to motivate change in the campaign system would do well to find other values that are adversely affected by negative campaigning and begin to justify suppressing attack campaigning in terms of these new concepts. Perhaps the best way to subjugate the amount of low-level campaigning that occurs in American elections is to recruit candidates who would not use such tactics, even if doing so would increase their chances of winning. As reformers, we have our work cut out for us.

NOTES

I thank Doug Rivers for helping me to conceptualize this problem and Jeffrey B. Lewis for writing the program that generated the endogenous ordered probit FIML estimates. I am grateful to Larry Bartels, whose grant supported this work and who provided a productive and provocative place for me to think about campaign reform. I am thankful to The Pew Charitable Trusts for their support of this project and many others like it that aim to restore honor to politics.

1. The term *campaign attack* refers to a number of different things in this chapter. *Campaign attack* refers primarily to two items: the advertising aired by candidates and the news coverage presented by journalists. Other scholars have provided data for my analysis, so I defer to their definitions of *attack*. Attack advertisements as measured by Geer 1998 are ads that are "negative" in tone. Attack ads as defined by Jamieson in the Campaign Discourse Mapping Project (1996) are unsubstantiated attacks, whether negative or positive in tone. Attack news as measured by Patterson 1993 is essentially coverage based on nonpolicy schema, with very little directly quoted from candidates and a heavy reliance on reporters' own opinions or assessments. Throughout this chapter the use of the terms *campaign attack, negative campaigning,* and *attack strategies* will imply this behavior by candidates and the press.

2. I have this percentage on record for every year since 1976 courtesy of John G. Geer, Vanderbilt University.

3. It is of course also possible that paying attention causes interest to increase, but this increased interest level does not lead to paying more attention, and vice versa. One might call this a partially related system.

4. Geer codes the individual appeals made in campaign advertisements rather than the entire ad itself. For example, one advertisement might have a positive appeal on the economy and a negative appeal on character.

5. For a precise explanation of what constitutes "negative" news coverage, see Patterson 1993.

6. These data on campaign interest suggest that other institutional factors, such as the number of candidates, the amount of campaign news coverage, the types of issues debated, the candidates' experience levels, or the quality of the campaigners, might affect people's interest levels in campaigns. For example, the 1960 and 1992 elections are years in which the "challenging" or "insurgent" party candidates ran highly effective campaigns (Vavreck 1997). It is not surprising that John F. Kennedy's and Bill Clinton's clever campaigns generated interest among voters (compared to, for example, Michael Dukakis's and George McGovern's less-effective insurgent-party campaigns).

7. Since the systems I wish to estimate involve ordered categorical dependent variables, FIML was the only solution that could itself generate consistent and efficient results. Limited-information techniques, such as a two-stage ordered probit model, would not have corrected for errors in the variance-covariance matrix, leaving the resulting estimates inefficient. Full details regarding the assumptions and restrictions used to generate the FIML estimates and Monte Carlo results are available from the author. The endogenous ordered probit FIML estimation pro-

gram is available on request and was written by Jeffrey B. Lewis, Department of Politics, Princeton University.

8. For a detailed technical discussion of FIML models, see Greene 1993, 612. For a simple discussion of the method, see Christ 1966, 395.

9. The disadvantages are primarily computational and presentational. The burden of estimating a FIML model is slightly greater than that of a limited-information model because the investigator must typically program the estimation routine. Also, because these models generate solutions that are highly nonlinear in the parameters, the coefficients are not easily interpreted. To best display the substance of the results, I rely on graphical presentations of the effects, although I present the complete results in tabular form as well. The nonlinearity in the parameters also makes it difficult to interpret compound variables such as interactions. So, while I agree with one reviewer that it would be interesting to pool these data and do the analysis on all years combined, doing so would be computationally complex.

10. Prior to 1976 the NES did not ask respondents about levels of attention paid to the campaign in the media.

11. For a detailed yet intuitive explanation of the trade-offs and difficulties in selecting instrumental variables, see Bartels 1991.

REFERENCES

Adasiewicz, Christopher, Douglas Rivlin, and Jeffrey Stanger. 1997. *Free Television for Presidential Candidates: The 1996 Experiment.* Philadelphia: Annenberg Public Policy Center, University of Pennsylvania.

Alliance for Better Campaigns. 1998. Web page available at http://www.better-campaigns.org (accessed September 1).

Ansolabehere, Stephen, and Shanto Iyengar. 1995. *Going Negative: How Political Advertisements Shrink and Polarize the Electorate.* New York: Free Press.

Bartels, Larry M. 1991. "Instrumental and 'Quasi-Instrumental' Variables." *American Journal of Political Science* 35:777–800.

Boller, Paul F., Jr. 1996. *Presidential Campaigns.* New York: Oxford University Press.

Cain, Bruce. 1998. Remarks at the University of Virginia's Sorenson Institute for Political Leadership Conference on Campaign Ethics, January 18–21, Charlottesville.

Campaign Discourse Mapping Project. 1996. *Assessing the Quality of Campaign Discourse: 1960, 1980, 1988, 1992.* Philadelphia: Annenberg Public Policy Center, University of Pennsylvania.

Campbell, Angus, Philip E. Converse, Warren E. Miller, and Donald E. Stokes. 1960. *The American Voter.* New York: Wiley.

Center for Global Ethics. 1998. Web page available at http://www.globalethics.org (accessed September 1).

Christ, C. F. 1966. *Econometric Models and Methods.* New York: Wiley.

Finkel, Steven E., and John G. Geer. 1998. "A Spot Check: Casting Doubt on the Demobilizing Effect of Attack Advertising." *American Journal of Political Science* 42:573–595.

Free Air Time and Campaign Reform. 1997. Report of the Conference held by the Annenberg Public Policy Center of the University of Pennsylvania and the Free TV for Straight Talk Coalition. Report 15. Philadelphia: Annenberg Public Policy Center, University of Pennsylvania.

Geer, John G. 1998. "Campaigns, Competition, and Political Advertising." In *Party Politics and Politicians,* ed. John G. Geer. Baltimore: Johns Hopkins University Press.

Greene, William H. 1993. *Econometric Analysis.* 2d ed. New York: Macmillan.

Jamieson, Kathleen Hall. 1992. *Dirty Politics: Deception, Distraction, Democracy.* New York: Oxford University Press.

Johnson, R. G. 1998. "Negative Campaigners Can Learn from Alabama." *Atlanta Journal and Constitution,* July 24, D2.

Lazarsfeld, Paul F., Bernard R. Berelson, and Hazel Gaudet. 1948. *The People's Choice: How the Voter Makes Up His Mind in a Presidential Campaign.* 2d ed. New York: Columbia University Press.

Lau, Richard R., Gerald Pomper, and Erlinda Mazeika. 1995. "The Effects of Negative Campaigning." Paper presented at the annual meeting of American Political Science Association, Chicago.

League of Women Voters. 1998. Web page available at http://www.lwv.org (accessed September 1).

Mayer, William G. 1996. "In Defense of Negative Campaigning." *Political Science Quarterly* 11:437–55.

McCallister, B. 1998. "Consultants' Ethics: Politics Survey Finds Attitude of 'Don't Blame Us.'" *Washington Post,* June 18, C2.

Patterson, Thomas E. 1993. *Out of Order.* New York: Knopf.

Popkin, Samuel. 1990. *The Reasoning Voter.* Chicago: University of Chicago Press.

Project on Campaign Conduct. 1998. Web page available at http://www.campaignconduct.org (accessed September 1).

Putnam, Robert D. 1995. "Bowling Alone: America's Declining Social Capital." *Journal of Democracy* 6:65–78.

Rosenstone, Steven J., and John Mark Hansen. 1993. *Mobilization, Participation, and Democracy in America.* New York: Macmillan.

Taylor, Paul. 1996. "Politics in Prime Time: Free TV Airtime for Candidates Is a Partial But Worthwhile Fix." *New Democrat* (September–October): 40–41.

Thurber, James A., Candice J. Nelson, and David A. Dulio. 1998. "Political Consultants: A Portrait of the Industry." Paper presented at the annual meeting of the American Political Science Assocation, Boston.

Vavreck, Lynn. 1997. "More than Minimal Effects: Explaining the Behavior of Clarifying and Insurgent Presidential Campaigns in Strategy and Effect." Ph.D. diss., University of Rochester.

Wolfinger, Raymond E., and Steven J. Rosenstone. 1980. *Who Votes?* New Haven: Yale University Press.

Zaller, John R. 1998. "Let's Make Campaigns Fun Again." Paper presented at Princeton University conference on campaign reform, June 18.

Chapter 4

Watching the Adwatches

Kathleen Hall Jamieson and Paul A. Waldman

Adwatches have the potential to enhance the quality of campaigns by creating disincentives for candidates to make dubious claims and by inviting a backlash from the knowledgeable citizenry if the ads overstep the line. Adwatches can have undesirable consequences in both areas as well. When adwatches carefully examine the accuracy and fairness of ads, they provide a powerful disincentive for campaigns to lie or launch unfair attacks. When adwatches are performed regularly, they help citizens evaluate not only specific candidate claims but the persuasive process in general.

Adwatching emerged in large part as a response on the part of the journalistic community to the 1988 presidential election. Among the reasons that that general election campaign was noteworthy is the fact that for the first time in the television age, ads for one major party presidential candidate lied blatantly. Specifically, Bush's "tank" ad charged falsely that Dukakis had opposed "virtually every defense system we have developed." Among others, the Democrat favored the Trident II submarine and the D5 missile and SSN21 Seawolf attack submarine. "He opposed the Stealth bomber" said the ad, when, in fact, Dukakis supported that project. Another of the Bush ads invited the false inference that Dukakis freed 268 first-degree murderers to rape and kidnap. In fact, four were furloughed and then only after their sentences had been downgraded from "first-degree murder not eligible for parole." And of these convicts, only one, William Horton, kidnapped and raped (Jamieson 1992).

Nor were the Democrats above reproach in 1988. An ad for Dukakis claimed that Bush had cast the "tie-breaking Senate vote to cut Social Security benefits" when instead, the Republican had voted to eliminate a cost-of-living adjustment in benefits, thus eroding purchasing power but not diminishing the actual level of benefits. Many reporters and editors felt that the Bush campaign successfully focused coverage on distracting issues. By repeating Bush's ads' claims without an accompanying assessment of their accuracy and relevance to governance, the press allowed the campaign to center on the Horton case, the Pledge of Allegiance, and Boston Harbor rather than the emerging savings and loan crisis or the demise of the Soviet Union. Consequently, the door was opened for a news format that would critique candidate advertising with two goals in mind: keeping candidates and consultants honest and creating a more informed electorate.

In an effort to address this issue, CNN worked with Kathleen Hall Jamieson and a research team at the University of Pennsylvania's Annenberg School for Communication to devise a broadcast format for critiquing ads. The primary challenge was to focus viewers' attention on the recontextualization offered by the reporter as opposed to the dynamic visual, verbal, and musical elements of the ad itself. Tests indicated that the most effective format had four basic elements. First, when a portion of the ad was shown, it would be placed in a mock television screen moved to the background and set at an angle to the viewer. Second, a news logo and a notice that this was a political ad for a candidate would be present on screen when the ad was being shown. Third, relevant portions of the ad would be shown with the screen frozen when the reporter commented on a portion of the ad. Finally, print correctors such as the words *correct, false,* or *misleading* would be placed across the screen when the reporter evaluated an ad's claim. These elements were designed to increase the likelihood that viewers would focus on the reporter's reframing.

Adwatching in 1992

As adwatches became common in 1992, consultants surmised that clearly false ads would run the risk of exposure by the press and of subsequent negative effects at the ballot box. Although the level of attack in the 1992 presidential ads was high, so too was the level of accuracy. When distortions occurred, they fell into the category of failing to tell the whole story. So, for example, while as a Clinton ad claimed, Bush did "sign the second biggest tax increase in American history," that act required the complicity of the Democratic Congress. And yes, as another Clinton ad averred, 17,000 Arkansans had moved "from welfare to work" since July 1989. But during that time, noted reporters, the number on the welfare rolls actually increased as new recipients of Aid to Families with Dependent Children and food stamps replaced the beneficiaries of the Clinton jobs program.

The distortions in a 1992 radio ad forecast one that would dominate the 1996 Democratic television ads. In it, Republican plans to cap entitlements at the rate of inflation became "slashing benefits for nearly 30 million older Americans." And a Bush television ad populated with working folk about to be taxed into the poorhouse foreshadowed the central false claim of the 1996 Republican ads; instead of raising taxes on upper-income earners, the ad forecast that the Democrat planned to raise taxes on the middle class.

While the number of people who see a single broadcast or print adwatch may be small, candidates can use adwatches against their opponents in subsequent ads to counter misleading claims. "George Bush is running attack ads," noted the unseen announcer in a 1992 Clinton ad. "He says all these people [the ad shows those pictured in the Bush ad] would have their taxes raised by Bill Clinton. 'Misleading,' says the *Washington Post*. And the *Wall Street Journal* says, 'Clinton has proposed to cut taxes for the sort of people featured in Bush's ad.'" This spot was seen by many more voters than had read either adwatch in the two newspapers.

As important, the adwatches had a prophylactic effect. One television newsperson told Times Mirror that the debunking of the ads "is the primary reason why no Willie Horton ads or their cousins have appeared in this [1992] campaign. Our coverage is keeping the bastards honest." Seventy-seven percent of the reporters surveyed after the election approved of these policing efforts. "We'll need a Teddy White to come along later to see if those who planned commercials really sat around worrying about whether we'd criticize them or not," another editor told the surveyors (Times Mirror Center 1992).

After the 1992 election, we asked the consultants that question. "It was a terrible feeling when I used to open the [*New York*] *Times* and they used to take my commercial apart, or [when I would] watch CNN and watch them take it apart. . . . I think these reality checks made our commercials less effective," observed Bush-Quayle adman Harold Kaplan at an Annenberg School conference. "I spent more time talking about economics and the latest statistics from the Bureau of Labor statistics and the Bureau of Census than I thought a creative person ever would in her lifetime," recalled Clinton-Gore ad director Mandy Grunwald. "Gene Sperling, who was the economic director of the Clinton campaign, and I talked far more than almost any two people in the campaign [determining whether it was] appropriate to use this statistic or not."[1]

Judging from these comments, it appears that in 1992, adwatches were satisfying one of the two criteria for success: they made media consultants more careful about accuracy, reducing the likelihood of misleading claims appearing in advertising. The change, however, was short-lived.

Adwatching in the Health Care Reform Debate

Between September 8, 1993, and July 15, 1994, under a Robert Wood Johnson Foundation grant, an Annenberg School research team analyzed more than $50 million worth of advertising directed at legislators through voters as well as press coverage of the policy debate. At issue was pending legislation on health care reform. If 1992 illustrated the success of adwatches, the health care reform debate showed where press scrutiny of ads can go wrong. Less than 10 percent of the reporting on ads examined their fairness or accuracy. Instead, press commentary focused on strategy: the tactics behind the ads, the groups being appealed to, and the advertising's effect on the Clinton plan's prospects. This is a particularly glaring lapse, given the complexity of the health care issue and the lack of public understanding of the different proposed plans.[2] The 10 percent of the reporting that focused on accuracy was clustered in the first three weeks of February 1994, when a problematic ad by the Democratic National Committee (DNC) elicited broadcast adwatches by Lisa Myers of NBC and Brooks Jackson of CNN as well as editorial condemnation by the *Washington Post*.

"The Republicans," says the announcer of the DNC ad. "First they said there was no recession. Now they say there is no health care crisis. They just don't get it." To the consternation of the Democrats, the idea that there was no health care "crisis" entered the national debate on the decidedly Democratic lips of New York's Senator Daniel Patrick Moynihan. Minority Leader Bob Dole then took up the claim. Moynihan specified that the crisis was not in health care but in health care coverage and cost. A number of Republicans took essentially the same position, including Republican Governors Christine Todd Whitman and Carroll Campbell. "There's a crisis for people who don't have health care. And there is a crisis in financing. But there is not a crisis in the whole medical system," said Campbell on a Sunday interview show. The DNC ad reduced that statement to Campbell saying "There's not a crisis." Rather than correcting the ad's misstatement of Campbell's view and explaining the importance of identifying the precise areas of need, most news accounts reduced the exchange to the level of partisan bickering, what some call "he said/she said" journalism.

So, for example, the *Wall Street Journal* (February 16, 1994, B5) headed its coverage "Democrats' Ad for Health Care Reform Distorts Governor's Position, GOP Says." After initially treating the exchange as charge and countercharge without offering arbitration, the *Washington Post* broke from "he said/she said" to print Campbell's actual words and to editorialize against the DNC's distortion of them. The ad's producer, Mandy Grunwald, was given space to respond on the *Post*'s op-ed page. The ad also contained other distortions, which were pointed out in the broadcast adwatches which, for balance, also examined misleading statements in a number of ads opposing the Clinton plan.

There was, in other words, a three-week period in February 1994 that contained a flurry of adwatching. With what, if any, effect? Ads about the health care reform debate had begun airing in the fall of 1993 and continued through the summer of 1994. On average, one out of two of the ads aired in each week up to the second week in February had contained at least one misleading statement. For the three weeks following the burst of adwatching, that average dropped to one in five before returning to an average of one in three. That jump in misleading claims did not elicit adwatching. The proportion then inched back to just over one of two—a level that continued until April when, for a week, three out of four of the ads contained some form of deception. Then as the debate began to subside, so too did the level of inaccuracy, which dropped to just below one out of two with minor variation through the rest of the debate. The number of ads aired per week did not drop after the adwatching; the proportion of pro-Clinton (1/3) and anti-Clinton plan (2/3) ads did not change; the only change was in the level of accuracy of the average ad. This pattern raises the possibility that the consultants creating the ads responded to the adwatching by engaging in self-correction, tested the waters to see whether adwatching would return, and, finding that it didn't, returned to their earlier practices.

During the health care reform debate, most of the adwatching focused on strategy rather than accuracy. "While the ad plays effectively on many people's fears," notes a "scorecard" in a Sunday *New York Times* (July 17, 1994, 16) of an ad by Citizens for a Sound Economy, "its Darth Vader tone works against it. It has an overblown quality that slips dangerously close to the tone of a spoof. But it closes on a strong point, appealing to viewers' pragmatism with a warning that Congress should just fix what is broken in the health care system instead of embarking on a top-to-bottom overhaul." Such analysis is helpful to readers planning a career in political consulting but useless to those trying to make sense of the controversy over access and choice in the health care debate.

Of equal concern was the fact that two of the four networks that had faithfully employed our adwatch formula in 1992 were now airing ads full screen. Some of the other practices we had argued against in 1988 were back as well. A number of broadcast ads received more free airtime in news than paid time. This lapse might be unimportant if the ads were accurate, but an analysis of 73 broadcast and 125 printed ads revealed that more than half of those aired and more than a quarter of those printed were unfair, misleading, or deceptive (Annenberg Public Policy Center 1995).

We documented the demise of adwatching, the resurrection of strategy-driven coverage, and the escalating inaccuracy of the ads. At a conference sponsored by the University of Pennsylvania's Annenberg Public Policy Center on July 15, 1994, reporters from the major networks and newspapers sat down with us at the National Press Club to talk about reporting on health care and our results. After 1988, changes in press practice were driven by a pervasive belief that both the reporters and the candidates had failed the electorate. No such sense filled discussions of the health-reform debate. As a result, prodding that had worked in 1992 failed in 1994. A column by David Broder urging revival of adwatches on health care ads failed to elicit them.[3] Reports of our findings in the *New York Times* and *Washington Post* and an op-ed in the *Washington Post* also did not prompt a rush of adwatching.

What effect we had occurred on the margins. National Public Radio and the MacNeil-Lehrer *Newshour* did shift from strategy-based reporting on ads to a structure that included analysis of accuracy. And when the Health Insurance Association of America (HIAA) released a new set of "Harry and Louise" ads the week after our conference, our attendees ignored them. Since earlier ads featuring the yuppie couple obsessing about weaknesses in the Clinton plan had garnered almost five and a half free minutes of uncritical national news time and seven hundred press mentions in the previous eleven months, this phenomenon did represent a change. As one of the reporters who attended the conference told us, a tree fell in the woods and no one reported it.

Adwatching in 1996

In late May 1996, the Democrats began broadcasting an ad attacking Bob Dole's Senate departure as "quitting, giving up, leaving behind the gridlock he helped create." Backed by a $1.2 million ad buy in key states, the ad, titled "Empty" by the Democratic campaign, was critiqued in fifty-nine editorials and print articles and on twenty-nine national radio and TV broadcasts. *USA Today* columnist Walter Shapiro called the ad "snarky" (May 29, 1996, 6A). Liberal columnist Mary McGrory observed that the person who created the "quitter" ad should "be reassigned to snipe detail in rural Idaho." She added, "Dole has a long history of sticking to what he does—like 36 years on Capitol Hill—and it's not a term you would slap on an old infantryman on Memorial Day weekend. It's hard to imagine what the audience was for such a low, hard blow" (*Washington Post*, May 28, 1996, A2).

On the *Newshour* (May 28, 1996), Jim Lehrer questioned Hillary Clinton about whether the ad shouldn't be interpreted as an attack on Dole's character and integrity and asked, "Is that clean campaigning?" The

Boston Globe called the ad "terribly bad form," noting, "When Dole announced his decision to step down from the Senate, after nearly three decades of service, the president praised him lavishly: 'You have served your country in so many ways,' Clinton told the Senate majority leader. 'On behalf of a grateful America, I want to thank you.' Now his campaign committee is running ads accusing Dole of dereliction of duty for leaving the Senate" (June 2, 1996, 26). Writing in the *St. Petersburg Times*, Howard Troxler called the ad "a surprisingly mean and desperate attack for a guy who is supposedly 20 points ahead in the polls" (May 31, 1996, 3A). Writing in the *Washington Post*, nationally syndicated columnist David Broder called the charge of "quitting" "a stunningly unseemly choice of words for a man who walked away from his Vietnam-era promise to join the National Guard and from his 1990 campaign promise to Arkansas voters to serve out his four year term" (June 2, 1996, C7). *Newsday* said that airing the ad put Clinton "into the Halloween mode" (June 1, 1996, A18). A Scripps-Howard News Service editorial called the ad "unpresidential" (*Rocky Mountain News*, June 1, 1996, 56A). An editorial in the *St. Louis Post-Dispatch* said of the label *quitter*, "To say this of a man who overcame severe physical disabilities caused by his war wounds is absurd and offensive" (June 1, 1996, 14B). In an adwatch in the *New York Times*, Adam Nagourney also noted that Clinton had not kept his word to Arkansans when he failed to serve out his four-year term as governor (May 25, 1996, 10). Members of Clinton's own party, including some of Dole's Senate colleagues, also criticized the ad.

The "Empty" ad was a response to a Republican ad that was previewed for the press and widely discussed but never aired. That ad, titled "Stripes," pilloried the claim that as commander in chief—and hence on active military duty—Clinton could postpone the Paula Jones sexual-harassment trial. With its pictures of Clinton jogging and biking, that ad also cast Clinton as a slacker. Since one was previewed in the week that the other started airing, commentators paired the two ads, with Democrats as well as Republicans criticizing both. Maine's Senator William Cohen said, "I would like to see a much higher road traveled by both parties" (CNN News, May 28, 1996). Jamieson added, "I think the important thing right now is that a clear message be sent to both candidates and to both parties from the American people, from the journalistic community and from the academic community saying that this is not worthy of us. This was a poor illustration of democracy; let's get on to the substance" (CNN, May 28, 1996). On National Public Radio, Daniel Schorr suggested that the ads might indicate that "there is a mole high up in both campaign organizations committing sabotage of their principals" (May 28, 1996). Columnists and commentators condemned both ads as attacks on the person rather than his policies.

The aftermath of this outpouring of criticism is noteworthy. Saying that a change in the Clinton legal strategy had made the ad irrelevant, the Republicans decided not to air the "Stripes" ad. By the end of the week, the Democratic ad too had disappeared. In public settings Democratic consultants argued that the ad had run its course.[4] In any case, the claims in the ads would not recur in any form in advertising for the two major-party candidates in the next five months. And unlike both of these ads, none of their subsequent ads can be classed as ad hominem attacks. No other ads aired in the 1996 general election presidential campaign would produce a comparable avalanche of disapproval.

There was some other evidence of candidate responsiveness to criticism of ads in 1996. Since it aired late on a Friday evening in the fall of 1996, only insomniacs were likely to have heard an ad for a candidate for president link the practices of his opponents to the preaching of Lenin. But that's just what a Ross Perot infomercial did. Perot "writes his own speeches," said the ad. Pictures of Clinton and Dole then appeared as the female announcer added, "the other two candidates have teams of professional speechwriters to test their speeches with focus groups." And then the zinger. "They are following Lenin's advice, 'Tell the people what they want to hear.'" This instance was one of the few in the 1996 campaign in which adwatching demonstrably made a difference. As part of Jamieson's weekly evaluation of the discourse of the campaign for CNN and in a syndicated op-ed piece, she singled this portion of the infomercial out for condemnation. The next time Perot aired the taped introduction in which it had appeared, the reference to Lenin had been edited out.

Later that fall, a different ad was pulled for factual reasons. The Republicans' first ad on campaign finance, "Riady 1," was reedited (after airing once on CNN) when its first showing elicited thirteen critical articles and adwatching stories. These analyses challenged the veracity of the claim that Clinton had "more investigations, prosecutions and convictions than any administration in two decades." That distinction belonged to the Reagan administration, which was investigated by nine independent counsels; at that point Clinton's administration had been investigated by four. In the Reagan-era Housing and Urban Development and Iran-Contra scandals, twenty-eight people were convicted. At that point, only Webster Hubbell had been convicted on Clinton's watch. The revised version made implicit the comparison that had been explicit, saying, "More investigations, more prosecutions and more convictions, and the list goes on and on."

Other instances in the 1996 general election in which ads were changed suggest the power of media reports of a strong protest from a nationally visible, widely respected group cited in the ad. When Common Cause protested the implication of a Democratic ad that the group was critical of Dole's record on campaign finance reform but not of Clinton's record on the subject, the Democrats stopped airing the piece. The Republicans had a comparable experience. The day after previewing an ad on Medicare that quoted the American Association of Retired Persons (AARP), Dole's campaign responded to media reports of a protest by the AARP and withdrew the ad. The ad had said that "The AARP, the largest and most respected citizen group, said both sides have proposals 'which would slow the rate of growth.'" But it neglected to mention that the AARP had also said that the GOP plan went "far beyond what the program can absorb without jeopardizing quality and access to care."[5] Having withdrawn the first ad, the Republicans then aired a second piece that also drew an AARP objection.

The other lesson of the 1996 corrections is that an ad will be changed if a nationally visible and respected person is offended. So, for example, after Nancy Reagan objected to its use, footage of the Reagan assassination attempt was dropped from a Democratic testimonial ad featuring Jim Brady, who was also injured that day. Noteworthy in the general election of 1996 is the fact that, unlike in 1992, adwatching for accuracy was limited largely to the print press. With the exception of Lehrer's *Newshour* and National Public Radio, there was no regular broadcast adwatching on television. Whereas in 1992 Brooks Jackson had provided regular tests of ads, in 1996 his time was devoted instead to "following the money." In September, for example, only three of the sixteen network evening news stories covering the candidates' ads focused on their accuracy. On ABC Jeff Greenfield corrected a Clinton ad on drug programs by saying, "But one former government official says that, in fact, both parties bear responsibility for brushing aside the key to stopping teenage drug use" (September 9, 1996). On CBS Eric Engberg noted that Clinton had in fact appointed a drug czar but that "He also failed to deliver on the pledge to put far more money into treatment and prevention programs" (September 22, 1996). And on CBS, Sandra Hughes challenged Perot's claim that 76 percent of Americans wanted him in the debates by citing a CBS poll to the contrary (September 22, 1996).

More typical was coverage that commented on the ads' strategic importance, as in this September 20, 1996, example from ABC:

Sam Donaldson: By late today, the Clinton ad team had their response ad shot. [Excerpt from ad.] And that's how it goes in modern campaigns, punch and counterpunch within hours of each other. Whatever the road they take they'll both travel at about ninety miles an hour between now and election day.

The strategic focus of most adwatches is not surprising, since strategy is the primary focus of all campaign coverage (Patterson 1993). Political reporters can view ads and come up with an immediate strategic assessment; campaign strategy is, after all, their area of expertise. To evaluate an ad's accuracy, however, research, including consulting additional sources, may be required. This expends a precious resource, time. In fact, as a content analysis by Bennett (1997) revealed, 70 percent of print adwatches and 100 percent of broadcast adwatches in 1996 focused on campaign strategy. Given that strategy coverage has been shown to elevate cynicism in some cases (Cappella and Jamieson 1997), these figures are particularly troubling.

In addition, both print and broadcast outlets ran far fewer adwatches than they had in 1992. If the campaigns were paying attention, they would have quickly realized that advertising claims were unlikely to be addressed at all; claims that were addressed would be assessed for effectiveness rather than accuracy. Whether the amount of deception in advertising can be directly attributed to the drop in broadcast adwatching is difficult to know, but in 1992, the number of televised ads containing distortions and selective uses of evidence was comparatively small, with 14 percent (seven ads of fifty-one) containing a questionable claim. By contrast, in 1996, 52 percent (thirty-two of sixty-two) of the ads televised after the start of the conventions contained at least one problematic claim.

There is no significant difference in the relative level of deception in the Dole and Clinton ads. The Clinton campaign averaged .8 deceptive claims per ad; the Dole campaign .9 deceptive claims per spot. The most often aired Democratic deception occurred in nine of Clinton's thirty-seven postconvention ads. It said in one form or another that Dole would "slash" Medicare, cutting it $270 billion. What the ad didn't say was that although the Republican plan would have cut the rate more sharply than the Democrats' plan, both the Democrats and the Republicans planned to slow the rate of increase.

The most frequently televised Republican distortion suggested that Clinton's tax increase had fallen most heavily if not entirely on the middle class. Where one ad tied the full Clinton tax increase to pictures of blue-collar workers, three others explicitly claimed that Clinton gave the middle class either a large tax increase or the largest increase in history. In fact, the Clinton tax increase primarily affected the upper 1.2 percent of income earners and high-end Social Security recipients. The increase in the gas tax affected everyone with a car.

One way of surmising that adwatching has not been effective is the reappearance of a claim already shown by adwatchers to be false. The misleading uses of evidence in ads that persisted in the face of press correction included:

- Clinton's claim that Dole was responsible for "900 billion in higher taxes," which appeared in four ads. *Problem:* it failed to credit Dole for his votes to cut taxes.
- Dole's claim that "taxes are the highest in American history" (one ad) and its variant that Clinton gave Americans the "largest tax increase in history" (three ads). *Problem:* Federal taxes were not up. Adjusted for inflation, Clinton's tax increase was the second largest.
- Clinton's claim (in two ads) that under Dole "Women's right to choose [is] gone." *Problem:* Dole said he would permit abortion in cases of incest or rape or when the mother's life was in danger.
- Dole's claim that Clinton cut the Drug Control Office (three ads) and that the president's "own surgeon general even considered legalizing drugs" (two ads). *Problem:* The cuts had been restored, and Elders was speaking hypothetically.
- Clinton's claim that Dole voted against creating a drug czar (two ads). *Problem:* He later voted for it.
- Clinton's claim that there were 10 million new jobs (six ads). *Problem:* That figure counted only jobs gained, not jobs lost; it was not, in other words, a net figure.
- Clinton's claim that Dole opposed vaccines for children (three ads). *Problem:* It was not clear that there was a need for the vaccine program in question.

Despite at least one critique of each of these claims by a reporter, columnist, editorial writer, or academic, these errors persisted in the ads. Most found a home in the candidates' stump speeches as well. By contrast, in 1960, when the accuracy of a Kennedy ad was questioned, the ad was pulled from the air. When a 1968 Nixon ad drew protests, the campaign withdrew it. And when reporters pointed out a misstatement in a Reagan biographical ad, the ad was edited to correct the error.

Why the high level of deception in 1996 but not in 1992? One possibility is that with both broadcast and print coverage as well as public attention down, the consultants may have concluded that the public was not paying enough attention to catch the corrections. And since the best adwatches were done in print, not broadcast, most people in most markets missed them.

One might also hypothesize that the candidates corrected ads that were criticized by large national organizations such as the AARP and Common Cause because those groups have heuristic value for voters. In the absence of such group pressure, the candidates failed to correct when the misleading statement was consistent with party heuristics and hence likely to override a single critical analysis here or there. So, for example, since we assume that Republicans are more eager than Democrats to cut social programs, Clinton continued to imply that the Republicans would cut Medicare despite Dole's assertions to the contrary. Since we assume that Democrats are more likely than Republicans to raise taxes, Dole's ads continued to claim that Clinton's tax increase was the largest in history and that it fell on the middle class. Since Republican Dole was presumed to oppose abortion rights, the notion that he would ban abortion outright functioned as a presumed logical extension of a heuristic inference. Since Republicans oppose federal government intervention, Dole would plausibly oppose appointing a drug czar.

Other problematic claims are natural extensions of the candidate's biography. Would Clinton cut funding for drug programs and appoint a surgeon general who favored legalization of drugs? If he had smoked marijuana, initially deceived the press about it, and protested the war in Vietnam, with all the attendant associations of being an anti-establishment figure—perhaps. The cases of "Empty" and "Stripes" suggest as well that cultural consensus can affect candidate and consultant behavior. When reporters, columnists, scholars, and members of one's own party disapprove of an ad against the opposing candidate, and when the candidate also hears those objections from supporters at campaign events, the signal is probably more powerful than the one delivered by adwatching alone.

A third explanation is more troubling. An October 1996 national survey conducted for the Annenberg Public Policy Center found that 78 percent of respondents felt that candidates tell the public what it wants to hear, not what is best for the country. Thirty-eight percent believed that the candidates deceive the public rather than telling voters what accomplishments the candidates will pursue if they are elected. The candidates' disposition to put the best face on their records and the worst on their opponents' fuels cynicism. So too does press coverage that focuses on strategy rather than substance. And an electorate that pays little attention to conventions, debates, and news is a ready object of manipulation. Perhaps the candidates have concluded that unless the outcry is overwhelming, consistent, and includes objection from one's own party or major groups with high heuristic power, there is no penalty for living up to the low expectations they and we have created.

Research on Adwatches

One factor contributing to the relative infrequency of adwatches in the 1996 election may have been the publication of Steven Ansolabehere and Shanto Iyengar's book *Going Negative* in late 1995, along with an article by the authors in the *Harvard International Journal of Press/Politics* (Ansolabehere and Iyengar 1996). As part of a larger study on the effects of negative political advertising, Ansolabehere and Iyengar conducted an experiment on the effectiveness of adwatches. Their results suggested that adwatches can in some cases produce an increase in support for the candidate in question, which would appear to subvert the adwatch's intent.

The findings received a good deal of press attention. Syndicated columnist David Broder, whose early endorsement of adwatches helped encourage their widespread adoption, recanted. In a column reporting the findings of *Going Negative,* Broder wrote, "one device that we hoped would help—ad watches . . . appear[s] only to reinforce the negative consequences. . . . The evidence is strong. The conclusions strike me as dead right" (1996, 34). In the *New York Times Magazine,* Max Frankel too reported that "Ansolabehere and Iyengar found no redeeming value in the media's attempts to critique and correct those negative ads" (1996, 18). While Broder and Frankel may have overstated the lessons that can be drawn from Ansolabehere and Iyengar's experiment, it seems reasonable to hypothesize that the concurrence of the dean of American political columnists and a respected former editor of the newspaper of record would have affected other editors' and reporters' willingness to conduct adwatches.

While Ansolabehere and Iyengar located a "backfiring" effect of adwatches, other researchers have come to different conclusions. Pfau and Louden (1994) found in one case, but not in another, that adwatches showing ads full screen, contrary to Jamieson's (1992) original recommendation, were more likely to backfire. Unfortunately, many broadcast adwatches do in fact show the ads full screen (Tedesco, McKinnon, and Kaid 1996). O'Sullivan and Geiger (1995) found that adwatches had their intended effect, boosting a candidate's support when the adwatch positively assessed the ad's claims and dampening support when the adwatch was critical. Using boxed adwatches with negative ads, Cappella and Jamieson (1994) found no backfiring; the adwatch did not affect viewers' assessments of the ad's target, although the adwatch did influence whether subjects found the ad to be fair.

The Future of Adwatches

Reporters are caught in a difficult bind. On one hand, focusing primarily on ads that contain inaccuracies and deceptions helps keep campaigns honest; on the other, such a focus may contribute to voter cynicism by encouraging the conclusion that all political ads (and by extension all politicians) lie. An alternative would be to include ads that contain no deception. Praising spots that are accurate and fair might give candidates free advertising time, but doing so would also provide even greater incentive for candidates to hew to the straight and narrow. Even in 1996, when the quantity of deception was relatively high, the majority of claims made in candidate advertising were in fact truthful.

Perhaps journalists should consider themselves neither as ad reviewers (commenting on strategy and effectiveness) nor as ad police. After all, the police go after criminals but do not spend time rewarding acts of virtue. If journalists considered adwatches a system of both punishment and reward, with both harmful and useful discourse highlighted, the multiple goals of influencing candidate behavior, increasing the accuracy of voter information, and dampening cynicism could all be served.

Particularly at a time when candidates are buying larger and larger amounts of airtime, voters will inevitably see more ads than adwatches. It is therefore impossible for news organizations' critiques to forestall the airing or blunt the impact of every deceptive ad. A more achievable goal is to help citizens become more critical viewers of political advertising. Adwatches advance a number of premises, among them that candidate claims are sometimes truthful and sometimes not and that ads should not be taken at face value unless outside confirmation is offered. To keep campaigns honest, adwatches must sanction misbehavior. If they concentrate solely on strategy, adwatches simply reward deception.

NOTES

1. The quotes in this paragraph are from a December 12, 1992, postelection debriefing held at the Annenberg School for Communication at the University of Pennsylvania.

2. A March 1994 *Wall Street Journal*/NBC News poll found that 45 percent of respondents said they opposed the Clinton plan, but when the plan was described without identifying its sponsor, 76 percent said it had "great appeal" ("Many Don't Realize It's Clinton Plan They Like," *Wall Street Journal,* March 10, 1994, B1).

3. David Broder, "Health-Plan Ad Wars Confusing Public," *Houston Chronicle,* February 25, 1994, A22.
4. December 12, 1992, postelection debriefing, Annenberg School.
5. "Dole Ad Is Withdrawn after AARP Complains," *Washington Post,* October 15, 1996, A15.

REFERENCES

Annenberg Public Policy Center. 1995. *Media in the Middle: Fairness and Accuracy in the 1994 Health Care Reform Debate.* Philadelphia: Annenberg Public Policy Center, University of Pennsylvania.

Ansolabehere, Stephen, and Shanto Iyengar. 1995. *Going Negative: How Attack Ads Shrink and Polarize the Electorate.* New York: Free Press.

Ansolabehere, Stephen, and Shanto Iyengar. 1996. "Can the Press Monitor Campaign Advertising? An Experimental Study." *Harvard International Journal of Press/Politics* 1(1):72–86.

Bennett, Courtney. 1997. "Assessing the Impact of Ad Watches on the Strategic Decision-Making Process." *American Behavioral Scientist* 40:1161–82.

Broder, David. 1996. "Negative Ads Translate into Voter Apathy." *Houston Chronicle,* January 12, 34.

Cappella, Joseph N., and Kathleen Hall Jamieson. 1994. "Broadcast Adwatch Effects: A Field Experiment." *Communication Research* 21:342–65.

Cappella, Joseph, and Kathleen Hall Jamieson. 1997. *Spiral of Cynicism: The Press and the Public Good.* New York: Oxford University Press.

Frankel, Max. 1996. "Word and Image: Let Lying Dogs Sleep?" *New York Times Magazine,* January 14, 18.

Jamieson, Kathleen Hall. 1992. *Dirty Politics: Deception, Distraction, and Democracy.* New York: Oxford University Press.

Jamieson, Kathleen Hall, and Joseph Cappella. 1997. "Setting the Record Straight: Do Ad Watches Help or Hurt?" *Harvard International Journal of Press/Politics* 2(1):12–22.

McKinnon, Lori Melton, Lynda Lee Kaid, Janet Murphy, and Cynthia Acree. 1996. "Policing Political Ads: An Analysis of Five Leading Newspapers' Responses to 1992 Political Advertising." *Journalism and Mass Communication Quarterly* 73:66–76.

O'Sullivan, Patrick, and Seth Geiger. 1995. "Does the Watchdog Bite? Newspaper Ad Watch Articles and Political Attack Ads." *Journalism and Mass Communication Quarterly* 72:771–85.

Patterson, Thomas. 1993. *Out of Order.* New York: Knopf.

Pfau, Michael, and Allan Louden. 1994. "Effectiveness of Adwatch Formats in Deflecting Political Attack Ads." *Communication Research* 21:325–41.

Richardson, Glenn. 1998. "Building a Better Ad Watch: Talking Patterns to the American Voter." *Harvard International Journal of Press/Politics* 3(3):76–95.

Tedesco, John, Lori Melton McKinnon, and Lynda Lee Kaid. 1996. "Advertising Watchdogs: A Content Analysis of Print and Broadcast Ad Watches." *Harvard International Journal of Press/Politics* 1(4):76–93.

Times Mirror Center for the People and the Press. 1992. *The Press and Campaign '92: A Self-Assessment.* Los Angeles: Times Mirror.

Chapter 5

Shifting the Balance: Journalist versus Candidate Communication in the 1996 Presidential Campaign

Marion Just, Tami Buhr, and Ann Crigler

Voters need enough information about the candidates, the parties, their records, and their proposals to make instrumental choices and carry out their democratic business. Several researchers using different methods have argued that the political information system is the key to effective democratic citizenship (Sniderman, Brody, and Tetlock 1991; Page and Shapiro 1992; Zaller 1992; Lupia 1994). When radio and television first entered the political arena, scholars were optimistic that easy access to information would empower citizens. The first voting studies were begun in the hope of demonstrating the power of the mass media to inform electoral choice. But the early scholars were disappointed (Lazarsfeld, Berelson, and Gaudet 1944). They found that political party rather than radio was the prime mover in voting. The "Michigan" election studies were undertaken in the era of television (and an increasingly educated electorate) but still found that informed voting was as elusive as ever (Campbell et al. 1960). The decline of partisanship in the electorate and party control of nominations turned scholarly attention to the mass media.

If the electorate is not better informed or more active in the era of electronic communications, perhaps the problem lies with the quality of campaign communication. During the campaign, candidates and journalists exist in uneasy symbiosis. Candidates depend on the news media to take their messages to the people. Journalists depend on candidates to be newsworthy. Journalists, however, do not see their role as merely passing along candidates' messages; the media must select and add value by verifying, investigating, comparing, and contextualizing the candidates' messages.

In this chapter we examine the content of the information environment surrounding the 1996 presidential election campaign and its impact on voters. We extend the focus of past studies by examining a wide range of campaign communications. First, we outline the specific typical criticisms of both journalists' and candidates' contributions to the campaign information environment. Second, we test the validity of these criticisms against a content analysis of the candidates' campaign messages and the media's coverage of the campaign. The number and variety of information sources, particularly those that gave candidates less mediated opportunities to communicate with the audience, continued to expand in 1996. Picking up on a campaign strategy that worked well for Clinton and Perot in 1992, many Republican primary candidates appeared on televised interview programs to present their messages to voters. The major television networks also gave Clinton and Dole free airtime to speak directly to voters as an alternative to short, paid advertising spots. Although only a small number of people used the Internet to learn about the candidates in 1996, for the first time all of the candidates established web sites. Our content analysis compares more traditional forms of communication to these newer information sources to see whether there are significant differences and thus whether one form or another might be more effective at informing and mobilizing the electorate. Finally, we comment on some of the newer information formats and proposed campaign reforms in light of our findings.

Candidates and Journalists: Missions and Incentives

Differences in mission and incentives are reflected in the disparity between candidate and journalist agendas (Patterson 1980). On one level, both candidates and journalists share the goal of informing the electorate, but each has a competing and more pressing goal as well. The candidates' ultimate goal is to persuade citizens to vote for them; the journalist's requirement is to maintain the audience's interest.

Candidates in the Information Environment

Candidate communications try to convince voters to choose particular candidates over their opponents. To persuade citizens, candidates offer various kinds of evidence—past successes, proposed actions if elected, and demonstrations of leadership qualities. In these respects, the candidates' agenda accords well with the kind of evidence that democratic theorists think voters ought to use in making electoral decisions. In the effort to persuade, however, candidates can be faulted for engaging in symbolic politics—making emotional appeals with little substance or relevance to policy issues facing the country. To make the best case, candidates tend to put their records in the most flattering light, to embrace issues where their positions are most popular with the electorate, and to avoid issues that are unpopular. The result can be an unjoined debate in which each candidate talks about a different set of issues. The resulting campaign discourse makes it difficult for voters to compare candidates.

Candidate communication typically focuses on policies, which is the main reason that some observers believe that giving the candidates more control over campaign communication would improve the level of discourse. Patterson (1980, 176–77) maintains, for example, "Candidate-controlled communication comes close to providing voters with useful information. The campaign would probably serve the voters' needs more fully if the candidates had additional opportunities to communicate directly with voters." Fenno (1978) argues that in presenting themselves to the public, candidates naturally focus on issues. But the enthusiasm for candidate speech is not universal or long-standing. For many years, scholars and journalists have decried the lack of substance and integrity of candidate speech, the lack of engagement with policy, and the tendency to attack opponents rather than to explicate their own positions. Journalists who follow the candidates on the campaign trail are especially sensitive to a lack of candidate consistency and to the potential for pandering to different political audiences.

V. O. Key Jr. described the campaign as an "echo chamber." If the candidates speak only platitudes, then the citizens cannot be faulted for basing their electoral decisions on superficialities. Many observers cited the 1988 election campaign as especially empty of substance. The candidates spent a good deal of time claiming to be efficient managers, deploring violent crime, vaunting their patriotism, and reciting the Pledge of Allegiance. At one particularly transparent pseudo-event, one candidate literally wrapped himself in the flag. The 1988 ads were deplored as especially deceptive and manipulative. Ads are generally decried as the format of symbolic politics.[1] Short ads (typically thirty seconds but sometimes as little as ten seconds) reduce policy positions to mere slogans.

Ads often feature attacks on opponents, frequently unaccompanied by a comparison with the advertiser's virtues or policies.[2] The evidence is overwhelming that some candidates use their time primarily to attack their opponents' probity or lineage rather than to engage in serious political debate (Kern 1989). Deception, threats, and outright lies are common when advertising "goes negative" (Jamieson 1992; Ansolabehere et al. 1994).

Journalists in the Information Environment

Journalists seek to maintain or increase the audience for news. Reporters regard the horse race as the narrative hook for the campaign. Indeed, it is difficult to imagine campaign coverage without the metaphor of the game, since the campaign is a contest. Research suggests that the horse-race drama may have the positive consequence of interesting the public in the election process. News that is attention grabbing is most likely to inform audiences that are not highly motivated to attend to the subject matter (Neuman, Just, and Crigler 1992). There is general agreement that the news media do a very good job of tracking candidate support as the campaign progresses. This process used to be the job of campaign beat reporters, who would go out into the country and talk to people along the campaign trail (Lubell 1956). Now, with the advent of media polls, the monitoring of the race depends more on in-house public opinion surveys, with occasional space given to the surveys conducted by other news and polling organizations (Mann and Orren 1992). Tracking the candidates' relative popular support has the characteristics of a good news story. Horse-race stories have high news value because they necessarily involve new facts, uncertain outcomes, and more or less famous people (Gans 1979).

In the years since the publication of T. H. White's *Making of the President* series, and especially after Watergate, journalists have devoted more attention to the strategies of campaigning (Patterson 1993). These stories complement horse-race news by providing an implicit explanation for competing candidates' success or lack thereof. Observers have three main criticisms for news dominated by horse-race and strategy stories. First, the emphasis on the game aspect of the campaign slights substantive coverage. Second, the news takes a cynical analytic stance and gives a negative tone to campaign stories. And third, the increasing focus on journalists' opinions and commentary leaves inadequate opportunities for the public to hear what the candidates have to say.

Critics argue that campaign news is mostly about who is going to win and how (Lippmann 1922; Patterson 1980; Gurevitch and Blumler 1990). Horse-race coverage, however, supplies some important information to voters. In primaries, in particular, voters should be able to weigh whether they should vote for the candidate they prefer most or whether they would be better off voting for a less preferred candidate who has a better chance of winning. A similar voter calculus applies to third-party candidates in the general election. Voters might also want to know if a race is sufficiently close to warrant the effort of turning out to vote. In other words, horse-race coverage can make some significant contribution to the electoral information environment.

Less can be said, however, for news about candidate strategy. For example, in his rigorous study of the 1976 election media, Patterson (1980, 177) concluded, "The political problems facing the country will tend not to be the subjects which prevail in election news. The messages that flow from the media will note the candidates' fates and maneuvers and not the values at stake. The press cannot be expected to organize political information in a meaningful way." Other critics have echoed Patterson's concern about news that focuses on campaign techniques and candidate strategy (Arterton 1984; Clancey and Robinson 1985; Orren and Polsby 1987; Jamieson 1992). Kathleen Hall Jamieson sees the public as ill served by these trends, writing, "the electorate can know who is ahead, why, and what strategies are necessary for each to win without knowing what problems face the country and which candidate can better address them in office" (1992, 186).

Critics lately are also concerned that strategy coverage is not only distracting but also detrimental. Strategy coverage portrays candidates as personally venal and ambitious rather than political leaders attempting to construct governing coalitions. Strategy coverage, therefore, feeds a culture of political cynicism and disdain for the processes of democratic politics (Patterson 1993).

The coverage of candidate strategy as a principal topic of campaign news appears to go hand-in-hand with a snide, negative, cynical tone of reporting. By concentrating on the strategic advantage that candidates gain from taking (or avoiding) policy positions, by seeking the support of particular groups of voters, or by employing particular language, journalists create an impression that personal ambition is politicians' sole motivation. A barrage of cynical stories about politics and politicians is seen as discouraging qualified candidates from entering public life, increasing public distrust of politics (Sabato 1991) and decreasing political participation (Patterson 1993). Lance Bennett argues that the investigative reporting that details what goes on behind the scenes of the campaign may have an unhealthy impact on the electorate: "The ironic result of media attempts to 'deconstruct' candidate images and expose the techniques of news control may be to reinforce public cynicism about the whole process" (1988, 34; see also Patterson 1993, 246).

Several researchers have reported on the decreasing opportunities for candidates to speak and be seen in campaign news. Observers who have compared different kinds of journalism tend to reserve their greatest criticism for television. Recent studies (Adatto 1990; Hallin 1992; Kendall 1995) have expressed concern that television journalism shrinks the candidates, limiting them to trivial nine-second sound bites surrounded by reporter commentary and interpretation. These researchers are implicitly concerned that the potential value of the mass media in bringing candidates closer to the people is undermined by journalists competing for center stage. These scholars also wonder how people can make enthusiastic electoral decisions if the candidates have little or no opportunity to speak or speak only through the critical voice of journalist adversaries.

The remainder of this chapter compares these criticisms of candidate and journalist communication with evidence from content analysis of a wide range of media in the 1996 presidential election campaign. We will find that many, but not all, of these criticisms of the information environment are borne out—especially those characterizing news as cynical and game oriented. Finally, we will take up the prospects for reform of the information environment.

Content Differences in Campaign Media

In the best of all possible democratic worlds, candidates would devote their campaign communications to detailed descriptions of their personal and professional qualifications, policy records, and issue positions. We would expect journalists to spend their time investigating the candidates' personal and professional qualifications and policy records and issue positions and to provide information about the nature and strength of the candidates' support and the progress of the campaign. Media scholarship, as described in the previous section, however, cautions that these democratic expectations are not likely to be met.

Here, we test these expectations against a content analysis of the 1996 campaign information environment. (See the appendix for details regarding the content analysis data.) We examine eleven different information sources: the *New York Times,* a composite of local papers, *Time* magazine, the three major network evening news broadcasts, candidates' appearances on television interviews, the presidential debates, candidates' televised advertisements, candidates' "free" ad spots, Clinton's and Dole's convention speeches, candidates' campaign trail speeches, and candidates' web pages. By looking at different campaign formats (for example, candidates' ads versus speeches or television versus newspaper news) we will be able to see how much the format, as opposed to the source of the communication, determines the quality of the content.

Journalist and Candidate Agendas

Examining the topics of messages in a broad range of media demonstrates a great divide between candidate and journalist communication. Candidates focus on policy issues, while journalists emphasize campaign strategy and the horse race (see figure 1).

The most striking finding is the extent to which policy issues lead all

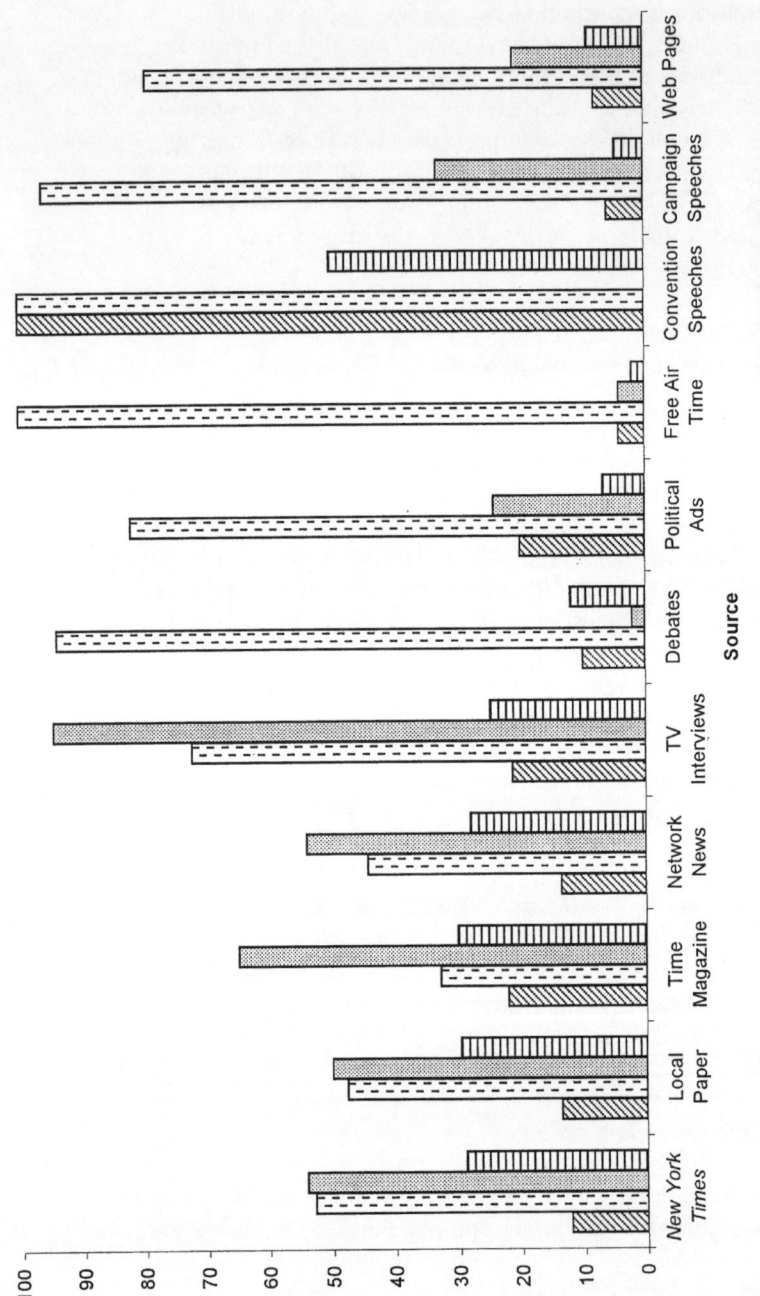

Fig. 1. Topics of campaign communications

other topics in virtually all forms of candidate communication and how little emphasis candidate communication gives to personal and political background. Only convention speeches include roughly the same amount of candidate background and policy information. Fewer than 20 percent of ads mention candidate qualifications, and the mentions are negligible in other formats. The dominance of policy over personal background and professional qualifications suggests that once candidates introduce themselves to the voters (in the early part of the campaign and, especially, at the party conventions) they communicate their messages primarily in policy terms.

Policy was the primary focus for all candidate communication formats, no matter if they were long or short, tightly structured or free flowing. It should come as no surprise that 90 percent of free candidate airtime was spent on policy, since the premise of this format was to restrict candidates to specific issue topics. Likewise, debate questions generally focus on particular issues, records, or proposals. But even campaign speeches and thirty-second political spot advertisements mentioned policy in almost every instance. The research expectations that candidates are more likely than journalists to discuss policy is borne out across a wide range of campaign formats.

Although there is a stark contrast between candidate- and journalist-controlled media, the pattern of attention to various kinds of topics is more consistent among the news or quasi-news outlets than among the diverse formats of candidate media. As others have observed, the professional culture of journalism provides a sturdy set of values that structures the agenda in both elite and popular outlets, print and electronic media, daily and intermittent programming, and long and short formats (Patterson 1980; Just et al. 1996). In our data, all kinds of news coverage leads with horse race and strategy, followed by policy, with attention to the campaign process close behind (slightly outstripping policy in the case of *Time* magazine), and candidate personal and professional background covered least. The similarity of the pattern of coverage across news media is notable in figure 1.

One big disappointment among news media is *Time* magazine. Past researchers (for example, Patterson 1993) have used *Time* as a general indicator of news patterns and journalism values. If anything, its mission as a newsweekly should put it in a leadership position in terms of focusing on the long-term, substantive, and less day-to-day aspects of the campaign. In the 1996 data, the newsmagazine fell far short of the other journalism formats, paying even greater attention to the horse race than did other media—and the least attention to policy.

Given the predictability of the outcome in the 1996 campaign, concentration on long-term issues might have been expected in any news medium. The resilience of horse-race and strategy coverage is, therefore, surprising in this election. Not only were the polls quite flat for months on end, but President Clinton's approach to his reelection campaign was neither unanticipated nor varied. One might think that Senator Dole's vain and public floundering for a winning strategy would not have evoked much news interest by itself. Previous studies, however, have shown that the horse race is the principal script for election news. When the horse race becomes less interesting (as in the period after the primaries or before the fall election heats up), there is less campaign news altogether (Just et al. 1996; Rhee 1996). While there was a clear drop in overall campaign coverage in 1996, the horse race dominated the news presented.

Candidate interviews conformed to journalism's horse-race preoccupation. The interviews in 1996 differed substantially from those in the previous election. In 1992, when the talk show format first became an important outlet for campaign communication, the level of substantive messages in candidate interviews was quite high, and attention to the horse race was low (Just, Crigler, and Buhr 1998). By 1996, however, the interview programs appeared to be among the least substantive of the news media. The reason for the shift in emphasis may reflect the timing of candidate interviews (concentrated during the early nomination contests and at the end of the 1996 campaign rather than during the traditionally slow news period of the late spring and summer, as in 1992). Both Clinton and Dole had reasons to be reluctant to face interviewers in 1996, fearing personal attacks. In addition, the candidates chose shorter programs such as morning news, which tend to focus on the previous day's events, rather than the longer, more wide-ranging interviews, which were more common in the 1992 election. In any case, the 1996 candidate interviews reflected the typical distribution of the journalists' agenda.

Overall, the results of the topic analysis show that while news pays more attention to horse race and strategy than any other topic, policy is not neglected. If record, issue positions, and proposals are not first in news, several media—notably newspapers and network news—mention policy issues more than 40 percent of the time.

Quality

Of course, mentioning policy and saying something of substance are not the same thing. Many journalists and some scholars (Alger 1994) suspect that candidates clothe their appeals in policy while avoiding the potential pitfalls of detail. One might expect that the news media, in their investigative role, would submit the candidates' records, proposals, and issue stands to rigorous scrutiny, while the candidates merely provide the bare outline or worse. To get at the quality of policy coverage in the campaign media, each mention of a candidate's record, proposal, or issue stand was evaluated on four quality dimensions.

- Was the policy extensively discussed (constituting more than a third of the story or speech)?
- Were details provided? For example, was the exact size and nature of the tax cut specified?
- Was the policy presented in some context? For example, in the case of job proposals, was the current rate of unemployment mentioned?
- Was the impact of the policy on society discussed?

Figure 2 presents the percentage of policies mentioned in each medium of candidate or journalist communications that met these various tests. Each block in a stacked bar represents the percentage of policies mentioned in the media that met the respective criterion of substantive discussion. The stacked bar associated with each campaign medium can be viewed as a measure of overall depth of policy discussion in various campaign communications.[3]

There are two clear standouts in this cross-media comparison. The most in-depth policy discussions occurred in long-format candidate communication—debates and party convention speeches. In those formats, policy discussion is strong in all categories but is exceptionally strong in explicating the impact of policy on citizens. Figure 2 also shows that quality does not come from length alone. Televised interviews and campaign speeches, both long formats, pay much less attention to the social context of policy than do convention speeches, debates, or free airtime.

One might imagine that if candidates did not address the impact of their political records or proposals, journalists would leap at the opportunity to do so, but such is not the case. No news format reaches the level of policy discussion found in the richest candidate communications. Whereas 90 percent or more of the convention and debate discussions of policy consider social impact, the next greatest percentage is in another candidate format—free airtime mentions the social impact of policy 60 percent of the time. Figure 1 indicated that free airtime was even more likely than political ads to mention policies. This finding is not surprising, given the networks' requirements that candidates discuss specific policy issues in exchange for the airtime. Figure 2 shows, however, that when policies are mentioned in these two short formats—ads and free airtime—free airtime was far more likely than spot ads to cover issues in depth. Ads score lower than free airtime on all four measures of quality. One explanation may lie

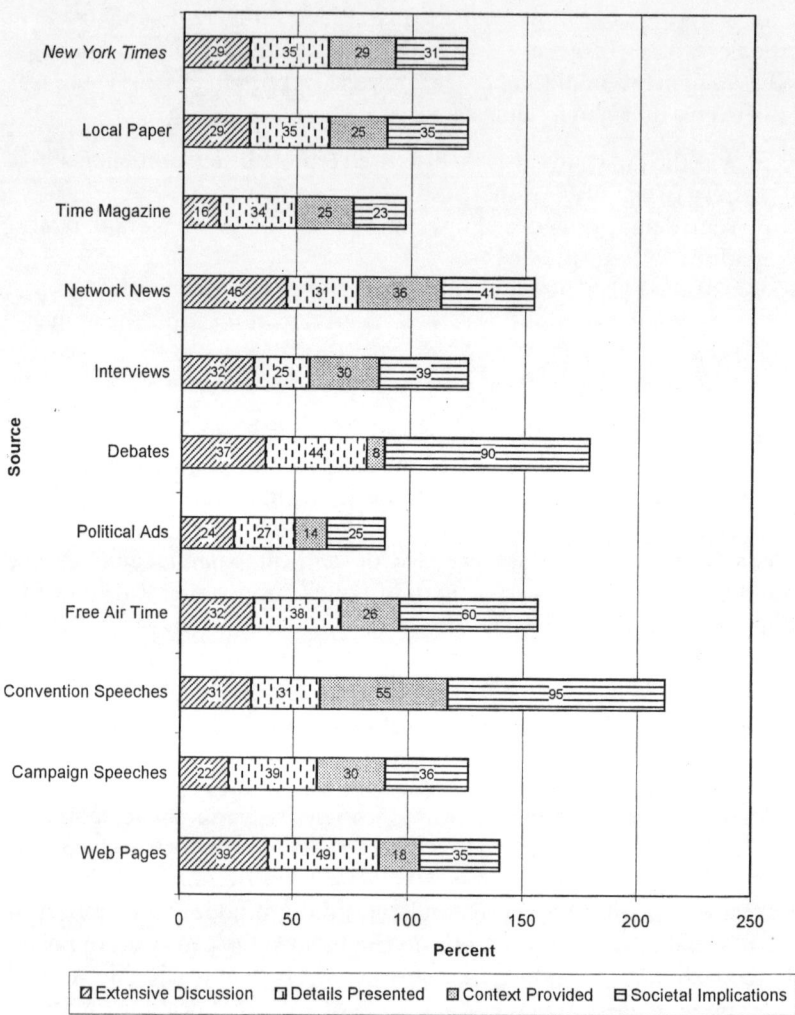

Fig. 2. Quality of discussion of candidates' records, proposals, and issue stands

in the small differences in length between spots and free airtime. Ads are usually thirty seconds long, although they range from ten seconds to a minute. Free airtime in the 1996 election was typically a little longer—one or two minutes, although some segments lasted as long as five minutes. Thirty-second ads may just be too short for any but the most superficial mention of a policy proposal. In addition, candidates may regard that level of policy detail as too dangerous to include in widely viewed persuasive messages.

While the three highest-quality candidate formats scored well above any of the news media, network news (a short format in this comparison) provided the most balanced in-depth discussion of policy, even edging out the best of the newspapers. Forty-six percent of network news stories contained extensive discussion of a policy topic. Of course, the brevity of a network story makes it likely that it will be devoted to a single subject. A policy topic is more than three times as likely to take up a substantial portion of a network news story than a story in *Time* magazine, which typically summarized a week on the campaign trail. Only 15 percent of *Time* magazine stories extensively discussed a single policy issue. In addition, network television news provided a higher degree of contextualization than did any of the print media.

To sum up, the quality of the discussion of policy issues is strongest in some very exceptional candidate media—convention speeches, debates, and free airtime—and to a lesser extent in network television. The main quality attribute that sets these formats apart is the way they contextualize information.

Context

It is fair to ask in what way campaign media contextualize information. Figure 3 categorizes media content more specifically: Are policy questions contextualized in terms of strategy or of impact on citizens? Here again we see a wide discrepancy between candidate and journalist communication. Candidate media concentrate almost exclusively on the way policy choices would affect citizens and society. We would expect nothing less. What would candidates gain from discussing policy in terms of strategy? Surely they would not refer to themselves in terms of strategy, and they would be throwing stones from glass houses if they attacked their opponents in that way (although some candidates have been known to accuse their opponents of pandering to "special interests").

The journalist side of the graph tells a different story. The strategic advantage gained from issue positions not only is mentioned in policy stories but outstrips social impact coverage in all news media. Once again, we see that the pull of journalism values is very strong across all news formats. The emphasis on the political as opposed to the social impact of a candidate's issue positions is similar in a variety of news formats. *Time* magazine's coverage is egregious in this respect, giving three times as much attention to strategy as to social impact. Television interviews, which consist of both the candidate's answers and the journalist-interviewer's ques-

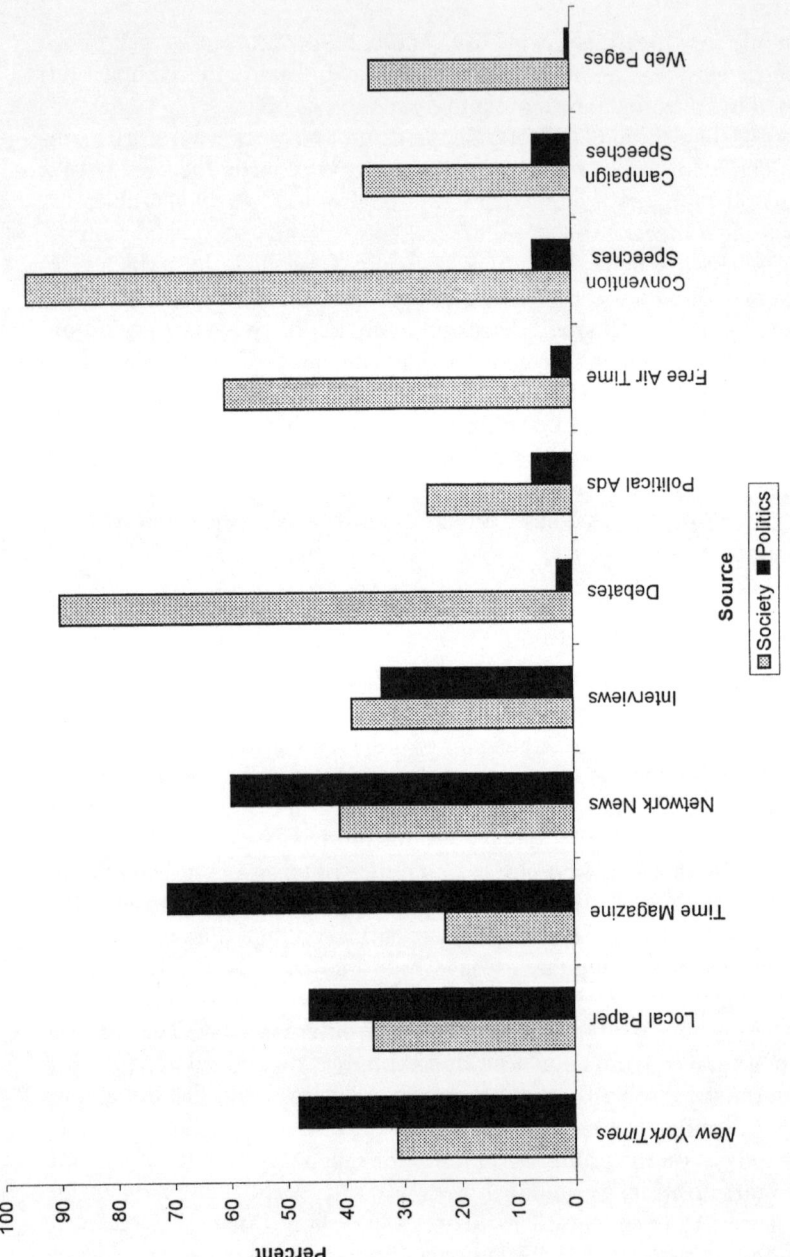

Fig. 3. Implications of candidates' records, proposals, and issue stands

tions, show an expected balance between the incentives of candidates (social impact) and the practices of journalism (political impact). The general pattern across the news media demonstrates the extent to which strategy coverage has become a centerpiece of campaign news.

Lessons of the Content Analysis

Our examination of campaign media confirms what others have argued—that candidate communication is more policy oriented than is news, but that only some types of candidate communication offer depth of substance. Convention speeches, debates, and free airtime are especially information-rich formats. Convention speeches and debates are, of course, one-time events, but free airtime was a continuing (if elusive) format in 1996. News media do not reach the same level of quality of the best forms of candidate communication. What is more, all news media contextualize policies more in terms of strategy and their political implications for candidates than in terms of the policies' social impact on citizens. Therefore, not only in terms of topic but also in terms of contextual richness, candidate communications more closely conform to the citizen's need for instrumental campaign information.

Prospects for Reform

Successful reforms of the campaign information environment must take account of journalists' and candidates' goals and incentives. Candidates already concentrate their communication with the electorate around substantive issues—their records, policies, and new proposals. They do, however, tend to avoid unscripted or shared formats. Reform of candidate communication, therefore, should concentrate on providing more comparative venues or longer formats in which the candidates are required to defend their positions past the point of mere sloganeering.

The task facing reform of journalist communication is more daunting. Research over the past two decades has shown, moreover, that game-oriented news about the campaign is increasing (Patterson 1993). The extent of the journalists' reliance on the horse race is so great that in the 1996 campaign, where the outcome was predictable, there was a steep drop in the total amount of campaign news compared to previous elections. By the end of the 1996 campaign, according to one estimate, network coverage had declined 55 percent and newspaper coverage 40 to 45 percent since 1992.[4]

Journalists appear to be wedded to strategy coverage because it enables voters to, in Adatto's words, peek behind the curtain (1990). Reporters tend to regard strategy coverage as a counterweight to candidates' persuasive speech. Reforms focusing on news coverage should focus on ways that reporters might dramatize news coverage without adding to the voter's cynicism and suspicion of the political process.

Fortunately, reformers do not have to choose between focusing on what the public wants and focusing on what the public needs. Voters want more information about the candidates' background, qualifications, record, experience, and policy positions, and they want to be able to compare the candidates on these dimensions (Just et al. 1996). The trick will be to get the elite players in the information environment—the candidates and the journalists—to provide the needed campaign content. Our analysis shows that party conventions, candidate debates, and free airtime have the capacity to provide the substantive content that is lacking in journalist communications.

New Formats

In a survey we conducted following the 1996 election, respondents were asked to comment on a range of new forms of campaign communication. The choices included a toll-free telephone number that provided nonpartisan information about the candidates (currently offered by Project Vote Smart), free videotapes of the candidates (now offered as advertising by many campaigns), free access to the World Wide Web (available now in hundreds of public libraries around the country), news focusing on how different election outcomes would "affect you" (coded in our content analysis as impact on society), public forums for questioning the candidates (the town hall meeting format, which Clinton popularized in 1992), and time for candidates to speak on television uninterrupted by journalists (that is, free airtime). The interactive town hall meeting format and free airtime received the greatest support among our respondents (one-third thought these types of communication would be "very helpful," and a preponderance thought they would be "helpful"). These data suggest that citizens prefer communication formats with a citizen or candidate agenda rather than a news orientation.[5]

Campaign Reforms

Coupled with voters' stated preferences, the evidence documenting the information-rich nature of conventions and debates supports those campaign reforms that would give candidates more time to put their cases directly to the public. Conventions, candidate debates, town meetings, long interviews, and free airtime are all formats that could be helpful in shifting the balance toward more substantive information in the campaign communication mix.

Conventions and debates are essentially high-profile campaign events, drawing the party faithful in disproportionate numbers. Free airtime does not require that the audience be especially motivated to pay attention, but the exposures are very brief—about a minute. In our 1996 survey, the number of respondents reporting seeing free airtime was less than 5 percent.

Unlike ads, which are also very brief, free airtime spots generally appeared only once on each network. To have an impact similar to ads, the free spots would have to be repeated several times a week. Another way to increase the impact of free airtime would be to move the spots to newsmagazine shows. Television newsmagazines are presently scheduled five days a week on each of the leading networks; short spots could be repeated throughout the week, increasing potential exposure. Television newsmagazines could also accommodate longer free airtime spots (say, five-minute segments), eliminating one of the current defects of free airtime.[6] Televised newsmagazine programs could also accommodate more lengthy and serious interviews.

The town hall meeting, which is frequently employed by ABC's *Nightline* program to debate current issues, could be expanded to other outlets during the campaign. In this format, members of the audience ask questions of public officials, candidates, or experts. Creating more call-in interview programs, like *Larry King Live,* would also respond to the public's expressed interest in interactive formats and lengthy exposure to candidates. These reforms are clearly feasible, since they are already standard practice in some outlets. If reform efforts are to engage more citizens, it is important to concentrate on people who are not already highly motivated to seek out campaign communications. This is the audience for television news and advertising, but it can also be the audience for free airtime or interview segments on popular news and newsmagazine shows.

Incentives for Reform

At the moment, only money (campaign financing) appears to be a reasonably manipulable incentive for candidates. Free candidate airtime is cost-free to candidates (although not to television networks). It is possible that in the future, campaign funds could be tied to candidate agreements to participate in certain designated venues, such as debates, town hall meetings, and structured interviews. While the experience of the 1992 campaign suggested that lengthy interviews would become commonplace in subsequent campaigns, in 1996 the two leading candidates avoided television interviews until quite late because each had good reason to suspect that the interviews would focus on embarrassing personal issues. In the 1996 campaign, interviews were short and more closely resembled other journalism formats in emphasizing personal issues, strategy, and chances for election. One way to improve the incentives for candidates to participate in lengthy television interviews is by providing a structure in which the topics are known in advance to the candidates and the audience, as is presently the case with free airtime. Journalists would give up the chance for a "gotcha" question in exchange for an opportunity to probe candidates on substantive issues. Long structured interviews would not allow candidates to bypass the press and would provide voters with in-depth looks at the candidates, which people seem to appreciate in town hall meetings, conventions, and debates.

Although network news scored high on policy discussion, our content analysis shows that virtually all news sources share a similar agenda. The question remains whether it is possible to shift the journalism agenda in a more substantive direction. The 1996 presidential election provides some hopeful evidence. The outcome was not in doubt for several months before Election Day, and consequently, there was less horse-race news. The Center for Media and Public Affairs (1996) reported a decline in the proportion of horse-race coverage from 58 percent in 1992 and 1988 to 48 percent in 1996. Proportionately more of the 1996 coverage was substantive. There was more innovation, more attention to the views of the public, more pooled coverage of candidates (the "body watch"), and fewer stories from the campaign trail (Just 1997). Since surveys found that the public gave the news media just as high marks as in the past, the 1996 campaign demonstrates that it is possible for journalists to put greater emphasis on substance over the game and still maintain audience approval. It is true that the lack of horse-race suspense resulted in an overall decline in campaign news, but almost no one thought there was too little news (less than 2 percent of the public in our post-election survey).

In attempting to influence the incentive structure for the press, it would help to mount a convincing case that coverage of the horse race and strategy are not especially interesting to the audience and that contextualized policy presentations are interesting. Only then could journalists be convinced to produce more of the latter and less of the former. More research on what keeps audiences interested and involved in the news could provide journalists with the reassurance they need to make important changes in patterns of coverage. In the meantime, increasing candidate voice in the campaign may help shift the balance toward a more substantive campaign discourse.

APPENDIX

Media

The content analysis data reported in this chapter were collected by the Center for Media and Public Affairs under an agreement with the Consortium for Campaign Media Analysis, which was organized in early 1996 to study campaign communication content. The aim was to encompass a broad range of campaign media in an effort to discern differences that would be relevant to the democratic mission of campaigns. From January 1, 1996, through the morning of November 5, 1996, each of the following news media was examined every day: the *New York Times,* one of the thirteen local papers comprising our composite local paper, *Time* magazine (coded weekly), and the three major networks' evening newscasts. For a news story to be coded, it had to contain at least twenty seconds or two printed paragraphs about the 1996 presidential campaign or about Clinton or Dole in their official capacities as president and senator. In addition, candidate appearances on televised interview programs such as *Larry King Live, Meet the Press,* and *Good Morning America* were coded during this same period. The two presidential debates between Clinton and Dole in October 1996 were also coded. The political advertising sample was obtained from the University of Oklahoma's Political Communication Center. All ads produced for the 1996 presidential campaign were coded, so the sample stretches back into 1995. In addition to paid advertisements, the free air spots carried by the major media outlets in September and October were collected and coded. The candidates' speeches from January 1, 1996, through November 4, 1996, were coded. We analyzed Clinton's and Dole's speeches at their respective nominating conventions separately from candidates' campaign trail speeches. The campaign trail speeches were gathered from Lexis-Nexis, CNN, and C-SPAN. The candidates' web pages were retrieved from web archives with the assistance of John Tedesco and Todd Belt.

The unit of analysis varies somewhat across the different formats and depending on the variable coded. In the following description of the variables coded, we often use the term *story* to refer to a single news story, political advertisement, candidate interview, campaign stump speech, or web page.

Topics

Each news story, ad, interview, or speech was assigned one or more topic codes. Since a story could cover more than one topic, multiple codes were often assigned. The unit of analysis was the single news story, ad, speech, or interview. The debates were broken into multiple units based on moderator questions. Web page units were determined by links at a candidate web site. Figure 1 displays the percentage of all units for each information source that mention each topic. For a topic to be coded it must have been discussed "extensively"—that is, the topic must have been the focus of more than twenty seconds of a television news story or interview or more than two paragraphs of a newspaper story or text of a campaign speech. For political advertisements and news stories that are less than sixty seconds or five paragraphs long, an "extensive" discussion is one that accounts for more than one-third of the item.

The twenty-five original topic codes were recoded into the four general categories presented in figure 1. The four categories incorporated the following types of stories:

Personal/Professional Background: discussions of the candidates' personal backgrounds, character, temperaments, qualifications for office, professional experience, leadership abilities, and so forth.

Policy Issues: candidate issue positions, record in office in dealing with a particular issue, details about a particular issue, and so forth.

Campaign Strategy/Horse Race: candidates' campaign conduct, including negative campaigning, campaign tactics and strategy, discussions of candidates' advertisements, poll results, speculation about election results, speculation about choice of running-mates, and so forth.

Campaign Process: the workings of the nomination process, commentary on the performance of the process, debates about the role of the media and interest groups, commentary on the campaign finance system, lamentations about voter apathy, and so forth.

Depth of Discussion of Candidates' Records, Proposals, and Issue Stands

Within a news story, ad, interview, or speech, each separate discussion of a candidate's philosophies, issue positions, specific proposals, and information about his record in public life was coded for the depth of the discussion. A single story could contain multiple issue discussions. Therefore, the unit of analysis is the total number of such discussions across all stories rather than the number of stories. Each issue discussion was coded for the presence of the following variables:

Extent of Discussion: the issue must have been the focus of more than twenty seconds of a television news story, more than two paragraphs of a newspaper item, or more than one-third of an ad, interview, or speech.

Specificity of Discussion: specific details such as dollar amounts, implementation mechanisms, time frames, and so forth, are presented.

Context/Background: the issue is discussed in terms of its broader national context; some information about the scope of the problem or issue is given.

Social Implications: the discussion includes assessments or predictions about the national impact of the candidate's past policies or future proposals.

Political Context/Implications: the issue is discussed in terms of its impact on the candidate's status in the campaign horse race, the candidate's strategic motivations for taking the issue position, or the impact of the position on various groups' support of the candidate.

NOTES

The authors thank The Pew Charitable Trusts, the Ford Foundation, and the National Science Foundation for their generous support for this research.

1. There is some controversy about whether the symbolic campaign is politically empty or is a struggle over values (see Elshtain's essay in Pomper 1989).

2. Several studies (Patterson and McClure 1976; Joslyn 1984; Kern 1989) surprisingly found, however, that there is proportionately more policy information in candidates' ads than in campaign news.

3. The bars sum to more than 100 percent because an issue mention can satisfy more than one measure of quality. Equivalently, we could have given each story, ad, and so forth one point for each measure and computed an average quality score ranging from zero to four.

4. According to the Center for Media and Public Affairs (1996), the amount of coverage on network news averaged twelve minutes per day in 1996, twenty-five in 1992, and seventeen in 1988.

5. A content analysis of talk shows and the citizens' debates in the 1992 election campaign confirms that citizens and candidates put a greater emphasis on proposals and issues and less on strategy and the horse race than do journalists (Just et al. 1996; Just, Crigler, and Buhr 1998).

6. In the 1998 election cycle, the Alliance for Better Campaigns recommended five-minute segments on news programs.

REFERENCES

Adatto, Kiku. 1990. *Sound Bite Democracy: Network Evening News Presidential Campaign Coverage, 1968 and 1988.* Cambridge: Barone Center on the Press, Politics, and Public Policy, Kennedy School of Government, Harvard University.

Alger, Dean. 1994. "The Media in Elections: Evidence on the Role and the Impact." In *Media Power in Politics,* ed. Doris Graber. Washington, DC: CQ Press.

Ansolabehere, Stephen, Shanto Iyengar, Adam Simon, and Nicholas Valentino. 1994. "Does Attack Advertising Demobilize the Electorate?" *American Political Science Review* 88:829–38.

Arterton, F. Christopher. 1984. *Media Politics: The News Strategies of Presidential Campaigns.* Lexington, MA: Lexington Books.

Bennett, W. Lance. 1988. *News: The Politics of Illusion.* 2nd ed. New York: Longman.

Brians, Craig L., and Martin P. Wattenberg. 1995. "The Turnout Effect of Nega-

tive Advertising in a Presidential Campaign." Paper presented at the annual meeting of the American Political Science Association, Chicago.
Brody, Richard A. 1972. "The Assessment of Policy Voting." *American Political Science Review* 66:450–58.
Blumler, Jay, and Dennis McQuail. 1968. *Television in Politics: Its Uses and Influence.* London: Faber.
Campbell, Angus, Philip E. Converse, Warren E. Miller, and Donald E. Stokes. 1960. *The American Voter.* New York: Wiley.
Center for Media and Public Affairs. 1996. *Media Monitor* 10 (November–December).
Clancey, Maura, and Michael Robinson. 1985. "General Election Coverage: Part 1." In *The Mass Media in Campaign '84,* ed. Michael Robinson and Austin Ranney. Washington, DC: American Enterprise Institute.
Fenno, Richard F. 1978. *Home Style: House Members in Their Districts.* New York: HarperCollins.
Gans, Herbert. 1979. *Deciding What's News.* New York: Pantheon.
Graber, Doris A. 1988. *Processing the News: Taming the Information Tide.* New York: Longmans.
Graber, Doris A., ed. 1994. *Media Power in Politics.* Washington, DC: CQ Press.
Gurevitch, Michael, and Jay Blumler. 1990. "Political Communication Systems and Democratic Values." In *Democracy and the Mass Media,* ed. Judith Lichtenberg. New York: Cambridge University Press.
Hallin, Daniel C. 1992. "Sound Bite News: Television Coverage of Elections, 1968–1988." *Journal of Communication* 42:5–25.
Hofstetter, C. Richard, and David Barker, with James T. Smith, Gina M. Zari, and Thomas A. Ingrassia. 1999. "Information, Misinformation, and Political Talk Radio." *Political Research Quarterly* 52:353–70.
Jamieson, Kathleen Hall. 1992. *Dirty Politics.* New York: Oxford University Press.
Joslyn, Richard. 1984. *Mass Media and Elections.* Reading, MA: Addison-Wesley.
Just, Marion R. 1997. "Candidate Strategies and the Media Campaign." In *The Election of 1996: Reports and Interpretations,* ed. Gerald M. Pomper. Chatham, NJ: Chatham House.
Just, Marion R., Ann Crigler, Dean Alger, Timothy Cook, Montague Kern, and Darrell West. 1996. *Crosstalk: Citizens, Candidates, and the Media in a Presidential Campaign.* Chicago: University of Chicago Press.
Just, Marion R., Ann Crigler, and Tami Buhr. 1998. "Voice, Substance, and Cynicism in Presidential Campaign Media." Paper presented at the annual meeting of the Western Political Science Association, Los Angeles.
Just, Marion R., Ann Crigler, and Lori Wallach. 1990. "Thirty Seconds or Thirty Minutes: What Viewers Learn from Spot Advertisements and Candidate Debates." *Journal of Communication* 40:(3):120–33.
Keeter, Scott, and Cliff Zukin. 1983. *Uninformed Choice.* New York: Praeger.
Kendall, Kathleen E. 1995. *Presidential Campaign Discourse: Strategic Communication Problems.* Albany: State University of New York Press.
Kern, Montague. 1989. *30-Second Politics: Political Advertising in the Eighties.* New York: Praeger.

Key, V. O., Jr. 1964. *The Responsible Electorate.* New York: Vintage.
Lazarsfeld, Paul F., Bernard Berelson, and Hazel Gaudet. 1944. *The People's Choice: How the Voter Makes Up His Mind in a Presidential Campaign.* New York: Columbia University Press.
Lippman, Walter. 1922. *Public Opinion.* New York: Harcourt Brace.
Lubell, Samuel. 1956. *The Future of American Politics.* 2d ed. Garden City, NY: Doubleday.
Lupia, Arthur. 1994. "Shortcuts versus Encyclopedias: Information and Voting Behavior in California Insurance Reform Elections." *American Political Science Review* 88:63–76.
MacKuen, Michael. 1984. "Exposure to Information, Belief Integration, and Individual Responsiveness to Agenda Change." *American Political Science Review* 78:372–91.
Mann, Thomas E., and Gary R. Orren, eds. 1992. *Media Polls in American Politics.* Washington, DC: Brookings Institution.
McGuire, William J. 1968. "Personality and Susceptibility to Social Influence." In *Handbook of Personality Theory and Research,* ed. E. F. Borgatta and W. W. Lambert. Chicago: Rand-McNally.
McQuail, Dennis. 1984. "The Influences and Effects of the Mass Media." In *Media Power in Politics,* ed. Doris Graber. Washington, DC: CQ Press.
Neuman, W. Russell. 1986. *The Paradox of Mass Politics.* Cambridge: Harvard University Press.
Neuman, W. Russell, Marion Just, and Ann Crigler. 1992. *Common Knowledge: News and the Construction of Political Meaning.* Chicago: University of Chicago Press.
Orren, Gary R., and Nelson W. Polsby. 1987. *Media and Momentum: The New Hampshire Primary and Nomination Politics.* Chatham, NJ: Chatham House.
Page, Benjamin. 1978. *Choices and Echoes in Presidential Elections.* Chicago: University of Chicago Press.
Page, Benjamin, and Robert Y. Shapiro. 1992. *The Rational Public: Fifty Years of Trends in Americans' Policy Preferences.* Chicago: University of Chicago Press.
Patterson, Thomas E. 1980. *The Mass Media Election: How Americans Choose Their President.* New York: Praeger.
Patterson, Thomas E. 1993. *Out of Order.* New York: Knopf.
Patterson, Thomas E., and Robert D. McClure. 1976. *The Unseeing Eye: The Myth of Television Power in National Elections.* New York: Putnam.
Rahn, Wendy M., John H. Aldrich, and Eugene Borgida. 1994. "Individual and Contextual Variations in Political Candidate Appraisal." *American Political Science Review* 88:193–99.
Rhee, June Wong. 1996. "How Polls Drive Campaign Coverage: The Gallup/CNN/*USA Today* Tracking Poll and *USA Today*'s Coverage of the 1992 Presidential Campaign." *Political Communication* 13:213–29.
Robinson, Michael J., and Margaret A. Sheehan. 1983. *Over the Wire and on TV: CBS and UPI in Campaign '80.* New York: Sage.
Sabato, Larry. 1991. *Feeding Frenzy: How Attack Journalism Has Transformed American Politics.* New York: Free Press.

Sniderman, Paul M., Richard A. Brody, and Philip E. Tetlock. 1991. *Reasoning and Choice: Explorations in Political Psychology.* New York: Cambridge University Press.

Tichenor, Peter, G. Donohue, and Charles Olien. 1970. "Mass Media Flow and Differential Growth in Knowledge." *Public Opinion Quarterly* 53:495–524.

Zaller, John. 1992. *The Nature and Origins of Mass Opinion.* New York: Cambridge University Press.

Chapter 6

Is Reform Really Necessary? A Closer Look at News Media Coverage, Candidate Events, and Presidential Votes

Daron R. Shaw

Introduction

Despite the centrality of presidential election campaigns to the American political process, they are not held in high esteem by political scientists. There are two major reasons for this perception. First, presidential campaigns are thought to be too negative, boring, and nonsubstantive. In particular, candidates, their surrogates, and their advertising are typically believed to be uninteresting and prone to attacking the opposition rather than advancing a positive agenda or clarifying a set of contrasts. Similarly, the news media are thought to contribute to the inadequacy of campaigns. Their coverage is regarded as excessively negative and preoccupied with strategy and candidate standing rather than issues (Jamieson 1996; Lichter and Noyes 1993; Patterson 1980, 1993). As a consequence, one of the main effects of presidential campaigns is to raise public cynicism and mistrust of government without offering a suitable criteria for choosing candidates (Hetherington 1998, 1999).

Empirical research verifying the negative, boring, and nonsubstantive quality of presidential campaigns has been spotty. Negativity does seem to be pervasive among television ads, according to Ansolabehere and Iyengar (1995), Jamieson (1996), and a handful of other content analytical studies. Jamieson correctly observes, however, that political scientists tend to refer to both comparison and attack ads as "negative." In this sense we may be overestimating the deleterious effects of media by conflating a legitimate form of advertising (comparisons) with a less legitimate form (attacks). That campaigns are uninteresting is asserted based on observations of the behavior they are assumed to affect: low turnout, high percentages of Americans claiming to be independent, relatively small audiences for national conventions and debates, and other such aggregate statistics.

Direct evidence of disinterest has been more elusive. Survey data from the National Election Study show oscillations over time in the percentage of Americans saying they are interested or very interested in the presidential election and the percentage saying that they care about the election. These percentages usually exceed 65 percent, however, and there is no discernible trend. As for the charge that campaigns are nonsubstantive, content analyses of television ads, candidate speeches, and news media coverage show past campaigns to have had considerable substance.[1] Furthermore, although nonsubstantive campaigning and campaign coverage has also been found, little effort has been made to link this to subsequent behavior or opinionation.

A second reason for our profession's antipathy is that campaigns are thought to be of secondary importance in explaining election outcomes. Systematic explanations of presidential election outcomes are more often sought in the variations of the macroeconomy, the stability of partisanship, and the power of money and media (Brown and Chappell 1996; Campbell 1992; Campbell and Wink 1990; Fair 1978; Gelman and King 1993; Lewis-Beck and Rice 1992; Rosenstone 1983). Furthermore, those empirical studies that do examine the direct effects of campaigns on presidential election outcomes yield inconsistent results. The dominant, "minimal effects" perspective has garnered continued support from a majority of these studies (Bartels 1992, 1993; Finkel 1993; Markus 1988), although some of the most recent analyses challenge this perspective (Campbell, Cherry, and Wink 1992; Geer 1988; Holbrook 1994, 1996; Shelley and Hwang 1991). The position of the discipline thus seems to be a twist on the Shakespeare quotation: campaigns do not contain enough sound and fury and therefore signify nothing.

But these recent challenges should not be overlooked. Most notably, Holbrook (1994, 1996) finds evidence of presidential campaigning's influence in the 1988, 1992, and 1996 elections that has sparked renewed debate over the minimal-effects claims of the election forecasting literature. These and other challenges not only call into question our understanding of election dynamics but specifically raise the possibility that campaigns serve an important role in the democratic process and are not necessarily in need of reforms designed to increase and rechannel their impact.

In addition to the direct evidence of campaign effects uncovered in the studies mentioned previously, those suspicious of the assumption of campaign irrelevance and the need for reform would find empirical support from studies of the news media's coverage of politics and election campaigns. Numerous analyses have shown that the news media can influence political opinions and behaviors through the favorability of their coverage toward issue positions and candidates (Just et al. 1996; Lichter and Noyes 1993), the subject matter they choose to cover (Iyengar 1991; Iyengar and Kinder 1987; McCombs and Shaw 1972), and their framing of issues and stories (Iyengar 1991; Ansolabehere, Behr, and Iyengar 1993). But this support also points out a weakness in the existing literature: studies of campaign events seldom control for the effects of the favorability of news media coverage when gauging the impact of electioneering (Jamieson 1996).[2]

Empirically Reconsidering Campaigning and Campaign Coverage

In light of this discussion, many elements of campaigns cry out for more detailed, thoughtful analysis. This chapter concentrates on two hypotheses: (1) the news media's campaign coverage is neither unfavorable nor unbalanced, and (2) the attendant effect of campaign event coverage on votes is significant. If news media coverage of campaigns is balanced and favorable, calls for reform made by scholars such as Patterson (1980, 1993) may be undermined. As for the second hypothesis, evidence that electioneering and its attendant coverage affects votes reduces concerns that campaigns do not link candidates and the public. It also somewhat undermines calls by some reformers for more hoopla and entertainment-oriented campaigning.

This chapter draws on several theoretical assumptions to frame the analysis of campaigns and news media coverage. First, aggregate levels of candidate support are considered malleable. Although exogenous factors like partisan identification and economic conditions constrain voters' preferences, exposure to the campaign can change the distribution of support through either mobilization or persuasion (Gelman and King 1993; Iyengar and Petrocik 1998). Second, campaign events are taken as the fundamental expression of campaigning and are assumed to be unlikely to influence candidate support except through the mass media.[3] Put another way, in an electorate of 100 million people, candidates are assumed to be hard-pressed to reach enough voters either personally or through their surrogates to affect changes in aggregate measures of support. I therefore expect that news media coverage of candidate events provides the proximate stimulus for change. Third, the particulars of news media reportage—what gets attention and how it is covered—should impact the malleability of public opinion and (hence) the effectiveness of campaign events. More precisely, and as suggested earlier, this study focuses on the favorability (or unfavorability) of news media coverage of major events, which should be significantly correlated with changes in public opinion. Fourth and finally, I assume that news media coverage is influenced by the nature of the campaign event—that is, blunders or gaffes will draw unfavorable coverage, while policy initiatives will draw more balanced coverage. Note from this example that coverage of some events should always be unfavorable or neutral; conversely, favorable coverage is possible but never guaranteed.

The second of these four assumptions merits elaboration. There is reason to isolate media coverage of campaign events rather than focusing exclusively on media coverage. If, as many studies of public opinion have shown, Americans are not particularly interested in or attentive to politics, it is reasonable to assume that they only tune in during moments of high drama, many of which are produced by the candidates and occur in the last two or three weeks of the campaign. Concurrently, it is also reasonable to believe that news media coverage of these moments is critical to understanding popular reaction. Thus, any study of campaign effects ought to focus on major events and, more to the point, news media coverage of those events. Minor events are unlikely to garner the attention necessary to elicit perceptible changes in the aggregate distribution of candidate support. Similarly, red-letter days in the campaign should be crucial for detecting media effects since small shifts in media favorability on boring days are unlikely to move voters.

Besides these general assumptions, this chapter also posits that two specific factors affect the ability of campaigns and news media coverage to influence voters: (1) how salient is the medium for voters, and (2) how many voters are exposed to the medium? All other things being equal, I expect television coverage to be more important than newspaper coverage because of strong evidence that people find information from television more relevant and because more people rely on television for their political news (see Ansolabehere, Behr, and Iyengar 1993).

This chapter does not offer an explanation for how candidates can garner favorable media coverage, although others have advanced theories ranging from "be ahead in the polls" (Greenfield 1980; Patterson 1993), to "feed them well" and "help them meet their deadlines" (Matalin and Carville 1994), to "advance liberal policy positions" (Sabato 1993). From my perspective, it is important to discern whether favorability matters before expending much energy explaining how it can be earned. This chapter also does not examine the effects of the paid media, which have been explored elsewhere (Ansolabehere and Iyengar 1995). While the recent focus on paid media in presidential elections is not inappropriate, it is incorrect to conclude that the free media are irrelevant. Campaigns are concerned with how their candidate is being covered in the news media and consider it important for voters' perceptions. The presumption here is that the interaction of candidate events and news media favorability is a distinct and worthwhile way of considering campaign effects.

In short, I attempt to empirically engage some of the claims of those advocating campaign reform. Are campaigns too negative? Are campaigning and news media coverage largely ineffective with respect to eliciting preference changes? Although the data gathered and presented here are original, it is on this second claim that this analysis is noteworthy. For while contemporary presidential campaigns rely on the news media to convey messages, and media scholars continue to amass evidence that television and print coverage influence a broad range of political attitudes and behaviors, scholarship on how the media's reportage affects voters has been sparse. Indeed, it may be that much of the recent data attesting to "campaign effects" is really evidence of "media" or "interactive effects." This chapter addresses this central issue of campaign and media impact and should clarify and extend the recent works of Holbrook (1994, 1996) and others.

The following sections present data on media coverage of campaigning and test empirical models of candidate standing. The defining characteristic of the models is a set of independent variables that distinguish between specific manifestations of the campaign (events) and their coverage by the news media, an increasingly important distinction in American elections (see Hetherington 1996). The results show coverage to have been only moderately unfavorable and generally support claims of media favorability effects, though perhaps not as strongly as one might expect.

Data and Design

This chapter studies the 1992 and 1996 U.S. presidential campaigns using daily data from August 1 through November 2. The choice of these election campaigns is purely a practical one: they are the first elections where data have been available to accomplish the analysis undertaken here.

In contrast, the choice of a presidential election is both a practical and a theoretical one. At the practical level, the public opinion, campaigning, and contextual data are available only for presidential elections, making a House or Senate study difficult. At the theoretical level, presidential campaigns provide the most demanding test of whether campaign effects exist. Presidential elections are, arguably, the least susceptible to campaign effects since election laws create approximate financial equity between the two major parties' candidates.[4] Challengers in presidential campaigns are also much more likely to get a substantial amount of coverage than challengers in House and Senate races. Furthermore, both sides have maximal incentives to use their best personnel (pollsters, media consultants, strategists), minimizing the chances that one side will enjoy a technical edge. Finally, the relevant scholarship on campaigning's impact reflects the centrality of presidential elections to this debate, with no one seriously questioning campaign effects at the congressional level (see Ansolabehere, Behr, and Iyengar 1993; Goldenberg and Traugott 1984; Jacobson 1992; Salmore and Salmore 1989).

Candidate Support

I rely on tracking polls to measure voters' presidential preferences. Unlike previous analyses, however, I do not rely on a single tracking poll. Rather, I use the average of three national presidential tracking polls conducted during 1992 (Battleground '92, CNN/*Time*/Gallup, and Market Strategies) and five during 1996 (Battleground '96, CNN/*Time*/Gallup, ABC News, Reuters/Zogby, and Fabrizio and Associates). The aggregation of poll results reduces the instability of the dependent variable and produces a more reliable estimate of campaign effects on voters' preferences.[5]

The dependent variable of choice is the Republican share of the two-party vote. This measure reduces problems associated with amalgamating results from different polling houses by taking third-party support and undecided percentages out of the estimation procedure. This is an especially attractive feature given Perot's candidacy in both years and the significant number of undecided voters throughout the 1992 campaign.

Independent Variables

The explanatory variables roughly sort into three categories: media measures, campaign events, and control variables. Each is described, in turn, in the following sections. The media measures warrant particular attention, both for the richness of the data and their inaugural appearance in empirical models of candidate standing.

News Media Coverage. Daily measures of newspaper and television favorability toward the candidates are used to gauge the nature of coverage and estimate news media effects on candidate standing in the tracking polls. These variables are kept separate because, as discussed earlier, there is reason to believe that television is more powerful because of its larger audience and voters' perception that it is more credible. Both news media favorability and the interaction between coverage and the occurrence of campaign events should positively correlate with fluctuations in candidate support.

For 1992, newspaper coverage data are provided by the Republican National Committee (RNC), which contracted Computer-Aided Research and Media Analysis, International to code newspaper stories during the campaign. For 1996, independent content analyses were conducted for this study. From August 1 through Election Day of both years, thousands of articles were each assigned a rating between zero and one hundred. These scores were based on tone, placement, and source balance, with zero representing the most unfavorable coverage, one hundred representing the most favorable coverage, and fifty representing neutral coverage.

For television, 1992 coverage data come from the RNC, while 1996 data come from an independent study. Both analyses covered nightly news broadcasts from ABC, CBS, CNN, and NBC, encompassed the final three months of the campaigns, and assigned each article a favorability rating between zero and one hundred. Following the newspaper coding design, the 0–100 ratings result from three component scores—tone, placement, and source balance. The appendix provides an explanation of the sample and content analytic design for both the newspaper and television analyses.[6]

The favorability ratings allow the study to track news media coverage across the campaigns and to measure its aggregate effect on candidate standing. It is important to emphasize that the media data estimate each story's average favorability. Other researchers, including those at the Center for Media and Public Affairs, use binary coding schemes, thus focusing on the proportion of favorable versus unfavorable stories. The average favorability is generally preferable because it takes the degree of favorability into account.

Campaign Events. A central focus of this study obviously is campaign events. Other visible manifestations of the campaign (television ads, direct mail, and so forth) and less visible activities (organization, coalition building) are set aside, although these also clearly have the potential to influence elections. Previous studies occasionally confuse some subset of campaign activities with the whole of campaigning, so this clarification aids our interpretation of the findings. Holbrook (1994, 1996, 1997) has measured the direct correlation between campaign events and candidate standing. The means by which this study identifies campaign events, however, is both different and more theoretically attractive. Campaign events are defined as happenings regarded by the campaigns as consequential for the eventual outcome at the time of their occurrence and whose expected impact is in an unambiguous direction. Campaigns are thus thought to encompass both planned, proactive and unplanned, reactive events. While similar to Holbrook's (1994) strategy of selecting events based on media coverage, this approach is less endogenous; media coverage can make events significant (whence the endogeneity), but campaigns consider events important because of their potential to move voters. For this study, three narrative accounts of the 1992 election (Germond and Witcover 1993; Goldman et al. 1994; Matalin and Carville 1994) and two accounts of 1996 (Thomas et al. 1997; Woodward 1996) were cross-checked, and events were included in the analysis if all narratives for a given year reported that the campaigns treated the events seriously. These events were also cross-checked with actual media coverage of the campaign as reported in the daily political newsletter *Hotline,* which showed that the incidents received varied (but nontrivial) media coverage. Other events (of course) occurred during the campaign, but the examination of *Hotline* revealed that none received more than a day or two of media attention. A complete listing of the events used for the analysis is available on request.[7]

The coding of campaign events, borrowing from Holbrook's approach (1994), assigns +1 or –1 scores, depending on whether events were expected to have a positive or negative impact on the campaign responsible, and then sums across the days of the campaign. This creates a daily cumulative score for campaign events for each of the candidates, bypassing the colinearity and interpretability problems associated with event-specific dummy variables. Once again, the expectation is that campaign events influenced voter behavior but that the magnitude and direction of this influence was determined by the news media's coverage.

Political debates required separate variables because their effects on voters' preferences were not predictable. National conventions are also treated as distinct events—rather than as candidate events—for two reasons. First, it is expected that convention effects were greater than those of other events because of their duration (four days) and the substantial media coverage lavished on them (at least one hour of prime-time network television coverage for each night of the festivities). Second, other contemporary analyses (Holbrook 1994, 1996) use dummy variables for conventions to avoid inflated estimates of more general event effects. This study uses dummy variables scored 1 for the dates of particular conventions or debates (and for each day after) and 0 otherwise.

Control Variables. In addition to the standard campaign variables, it is important to control for the presence of Ross Perot. While many have argued that Perot's support came at the expense of Bush in 1992 (Greenberg 1994, Matalin and Carville 1994) and Dole in 1996 (Woodward 1996), this chapter's approach with respect to the direction of his impact is agnostic. Perot's effect is measured by correlating his standing in the tracking polls for a given date with the Republican share of the major party vote.

Of course Perot was not the only outside factor in these elections. As virtually all election forecasting models have shown, economic conditions in the years preceding an election often have substantial impact on election outcomes. Although this analysis is confined to two general election campaigns and does not cover a sufficiently long period of time to account for much (measured) variation in the macroeconomy, it recognizes that the federal government's release of new economic information often constitutes a distinct campaign event. To control for the effects of such events, a pair of dummy variables were introduced for the joint release of the unemployment rate and the index of leading economic indicators. They were scored 1 for the day this information was released (near the beginning of October in each year) and for every day afterwards and 0 otherwise. Since this information was negative for Bush in 1992 and positive for Clinton in 1996, the expectation is that these dates saw an increase in Clinton's standing for both years. A second set of economic controls is introduced with another pair of dummy variables accounting for third-quarter gross domestic product (GDP) figures, which were released at the end of October. These controls showed fairly robust growth for both years, leading us to expect that they were correlated with increased support for the incumbents.[8]

Results and Analysis

Summary accounts of the variables of interest are followed by the results of the multivariate analysis. The univariate summary was deemed useful in light of our interest in the favorability of media coverage and because of potential concerns about the nature of the unique variables used in the analysis. Summary graphs are presented in figures 1 and 2 along with basic statistics.

Univariate Summary

Figure 1 shows the favorability of newspaper and television coverage toward the candidates across the campaigns. In 1992 the mean favorability of stories fluctuated around the neutral midpoint of fifty; Clinton averaged fifty-one for both television and newspapers, while Bush averaged forty-seven for both. In 1996 the relative favorability of coverage was slightly less advantageous for the Democrats. Clinton averaged fifty-three for television and forty-eight for newspapers, while Dole averaged fifty and forty-six, respectively. Although both media were fairly consistent, newspaper coverage appears to have been more variable and less favorable than television coverage. The variation by medium stands out against the

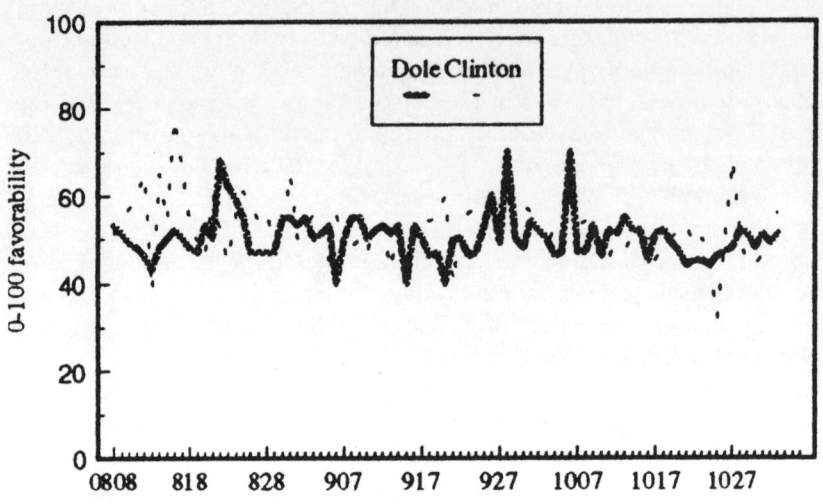

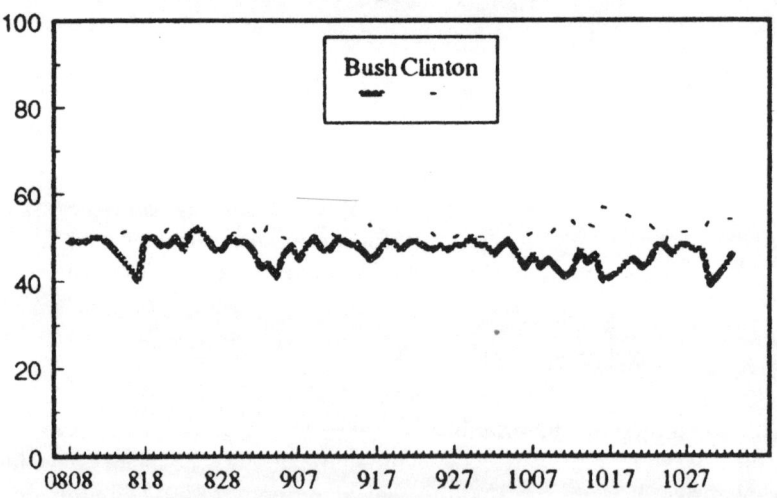

Fig. 1. Media coverage of presidential candidates, 1992–96

	Mean	S.D.
1996		
Clinton TV	52.6	7.2
Dole TV	50.5	5.4
1992		
Clinton TV	50.9	1.8
Bush TV	46.7	2.9

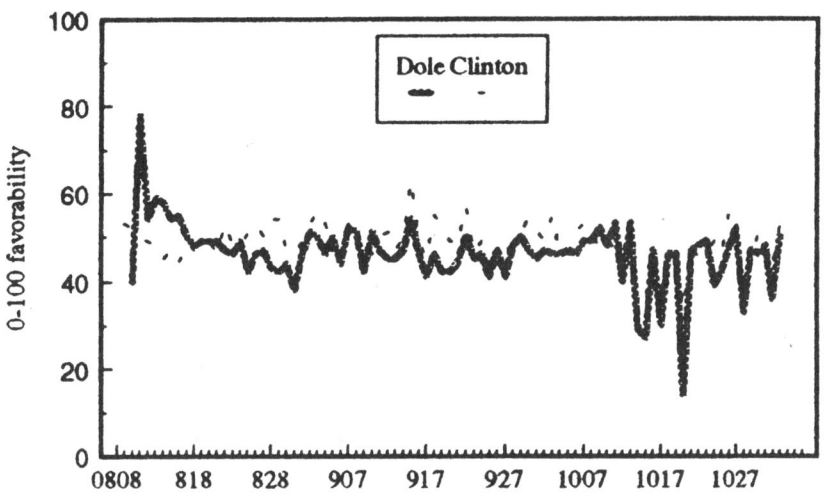

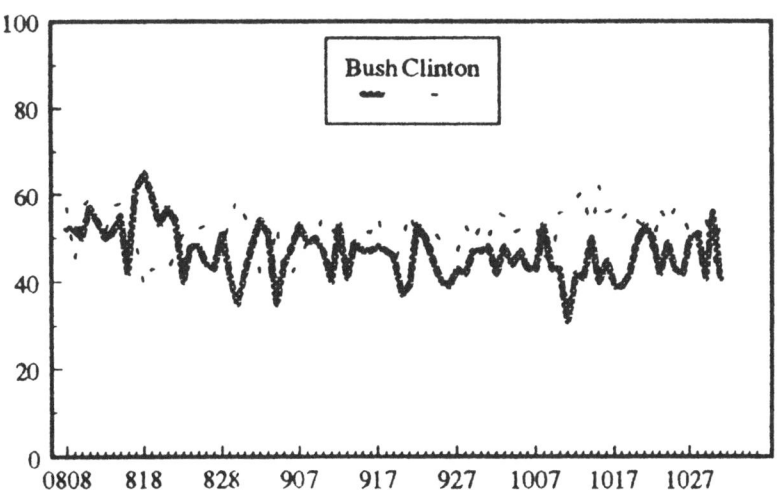

	Mean	S.D.
1996		
Clinton Newspaper	48.4	4.6
Dole Newspaper	46.2	7.5
1992		
Clinton Newspaper	51.2	5.0
Bush Newspaper	46.8	6.2

conventional perception of media coverage as bound together by occupational conventions that promote sameness (Gans 1979; Roshco 1975; Sigal 1973; Wicker 1975), and gives us further reason to keep these variables separate in subsequent analyses. Interestingly, Clinton's media coverage advantage over his Republican opponents seems to have changed in response to red-letter days in the campaign. For example, after the debates, Clinton received much more favorable coverage in the newspapers and, to a lesser extent, on television. Conversely, during the Republican conventions, Bush and Dole received relatively favorable print coverage (but unfavorable television coverage). Thus, we find preliminary support for the idea that there was an interactive relationship between media coverage and campaigning.

What is of particular interest here, however, is the relative balance between the candidates and the general neutrality of coverage. It is true that Democratic candidates fared better than Republicans and that coverage was more unfavorable than favorable. But these tendencies were muted, at best. The favorability of coverage hovered around fifty, across time and for all candidates. As noted previously, the most significant variation in this tendency was by medium, with television coverage having been more balanced and neutral. This finding supports the first hypothesis and undermines those advocating significant reforms in news media coverage of presidential campaigns.

But what of voters' reactions to this coverage? Tracking poll data from the 1992 and 1996 U.S. presidential elections are presented in figure 2. Clearly, 1992 was a more volatile and competitive race. Except for a blip in September, Clinton enjoyed a lead throughout the fall, but it oscillated between a twenty-three-point advantage and a dead heat. Moreover, Perot's presence caused both Clinton and Bush to lose support during October. By contrast, 1996 was largely stable, with Clinton's lead over Dole dipping below double digits only during the Republican convention. In fact, despite the presence of Perot, Clinton and Dole maintained stable shares of the electorate throughout the campaign.

More generally, aside from Bush's mysterious rise in early September 1992, nothing in figure 2 suggests that the data do not reasonably estimate the candidates' standings at any given time during the campaign. Had the Republican vote been estimated at above 50 percent late in either campaign, we would have had reason to question the validity of the polls. The data, however, do not offend reality. More generally, the pattern of variation in tracking polls is consistent with the occurrence of events in the campaign and with the favorability of news media coverage of those events. Still, a more rigorous test of the models can undoubtedly be gained from the results of the multivariate models.

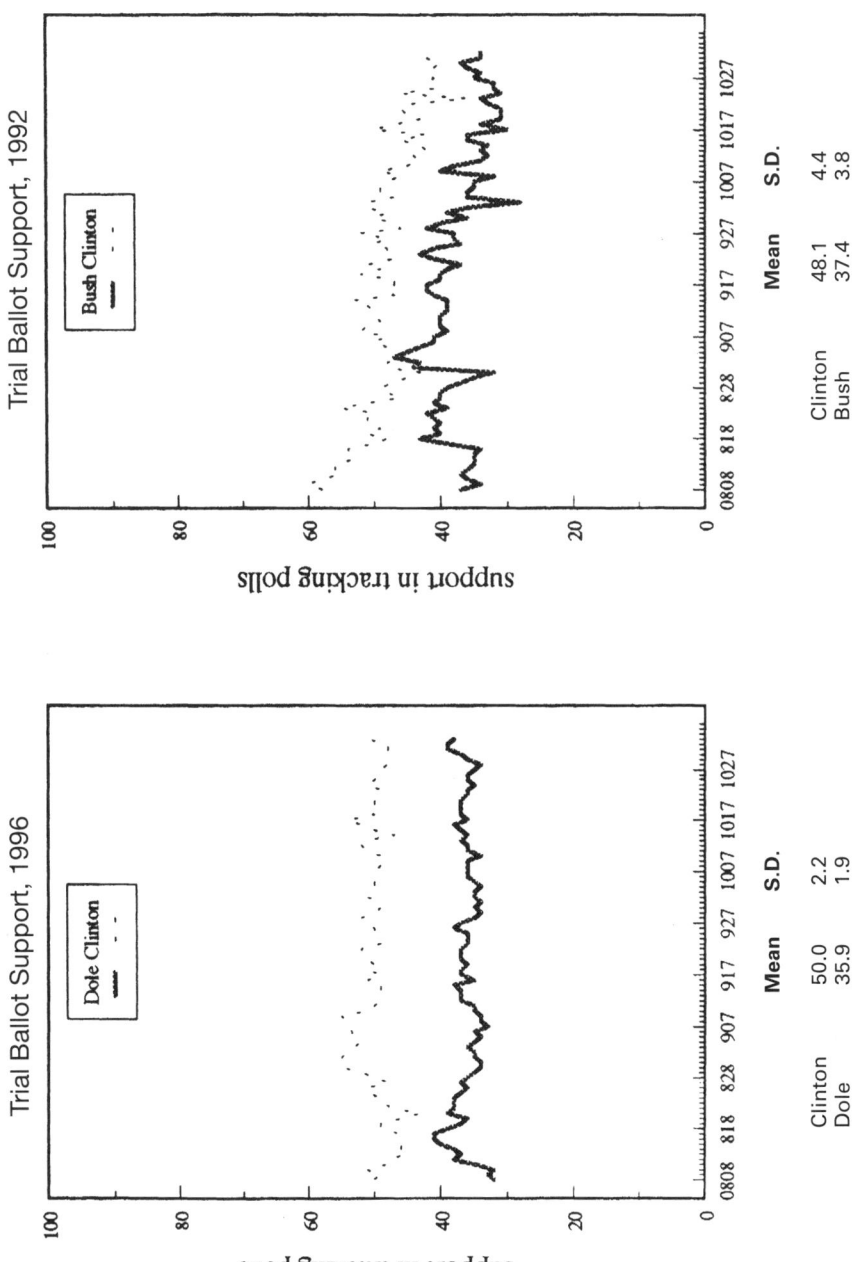

Fig. 2. Presidential candidate support, 1992–96

Multivariate Results

Table 1 shows the ordinary least squares estimations for the models of changes in Republican candidate standing. As explained in detail in the appendix, the data used for these analyses have been differenced to correct some of the troubling properties of the time series. Both models demonstrate modest explanatory power, with adjusted r-squares of .05 and .18 for 1996 and 1992, respectively. This is characteristic of differenced series, however, and at any rate is not the primary analytical focus.

A cursory review of table 1 draws immediate attention to the principal variables of interest—namely, those associated with the interaction between campaign events and media coverage. As expected, the hypothesis of media/campaign effects cannot be falsified. Favorable television coverage of Democratic events reduced the Republican vote, while favorable television coverage of Republican events boosted it. The effects were more pronounced in 1992 (which is not surprising given the closeness and volatility of that election) but managed statistical significance at the .10 confidence level for 1996 as well. On average, a five-point increase in television coverage favorability coupled with one additional event would have produced a 2.5-point increase in the vote.

The interaction between newspaper coverage and events was less influential, reaching marginal levels of statistical significance for 1996 but not for 1992. This finding is somewhat disappointing but fits with the posited relationship between media impact and (1) audience size and (2) perceived credibility. Taken together, the data provide evidence that television coverage of the campaign's major events was probably dominant, at least with respect to public attention, despite the slightly greater direct effects of newspaper coverage for 1996 and the traditional argument that print media influence the tone and agenda of television reportage (e.g., Sigal 1973).[9]

Aside from the media-event interactions, perhaps the most interesting finding is that candidates' campaign events had significant direct effects on support changes. Democratic events were significant in 1992 and 1996, while Republican events were marginally significant in 1992, even when controlling for media favorability. It may be that the events variables are picking up other effects—in particular, media effects—unaccounted for by the interactive variables. That is, agenda setting, framing, and/or priming processes not examined here may influence voters in conjunction with the occurrence of campaign events and therefore be reflected in the significance of these variables.

It is also worth noting that the major events of the campaigns—conventions and debates—generally failed to move voters. Only the first pres-

TABLE 1. OLS Differenced Models of the Republican Vote Share as a Function of Campaign and Media Variables

	Republican Share of the Two-Party Vote			
	1996		1992	
	Parameter estimate	Standard error	Parameter estimate	Standard error
Democratic events × TV coverage	−0.52*	0.27	−0.33***	0.11
Republican events × TV coverage	0.43**	0.19	0.39**	0.19
Democratic events × Newspaper coverage	−0.14	0.09	−0.34	0.35
Republican events × Newspaper coverage	0.09	0.06	0.16	0.14
Democratic TV coverage	−0.11	0.28	−0.03	0.06
Republican TV coverage	0.16	0.14	0.08**	0.03
Democratic Newspaper coverage	−0.11**	0.06	−0.08	0.05
Republican Newspaper coverage	0.12**	0.06	0.09	0.06
Democratic events	−3.19**	1.61	−6.83***	2.33
Republican events	0.75	0.72	1.82*	0.97
Presidential debate #1	−3.81	10.41	−1.34***	0.46
Presidential debate #2	−5.17	11.63	−1.28	1.14
Presidential debate #3	—	—	−1.70*	0.41
Vice presidential debate	2.38	1.86	4.29	4.74
Democratic convention	−2.86*	1.24	—	—
Republican convention	1.75	1.25	1.30	2.27
Perot	−1.45	2.01	1.26*	0.55
Economy #1	−0.41	1.08	−0.59*	0.33
Economy #2	−0.44	1.09	0.61*	0.33
Days until election	−0.23	0.51	0.83	0.85
Intercept	0.32	1.05	−1.77*	1.03
Standard error of regression		0.15		0.42
Adjusted R-squared		.05		.18

Note: There are 84 cases for 1996 and 83 for 1992. All nondummy variables are differenced.

*statistically significant at the .10 level; **statistically significant at the .05 level; ***statistically significant at the .01 level.

idential debate in 1992 (and, to a lesser degree, the third presidential debate of 1992 and the 1996 Democratic convention) meet conventional standards for significance. This result is extremely suspicious, however, given the significance of other campaign events and the well-documented bounces typically associated with conventions and debates (Campbell, Cherry, and Wink 1992, Geer 1988). Of course, a major limitation of the analysis is that the truncated nature of the time series—August through October—precludes examining the July 1992 Democratic National Convention, which, by most accounts, produced the largest bounce since polling data have been available. On a broader level, another explanation for the minimal effects of major events is that (again) media influence occurs through mechanisms besides favorability. This explanation implies that subsequent studies of campaign effects should probably include an even larger array of content analyses accounting for these media dynamics. The present findings therefore cause us to revisit but not to discard the belief that major events are critical for understanding the distribution of presidential candidates' support.[10]

The control variables for Perot and the economy produced mixed results. Perot's share of the vote is strongly and positively correlated with the Republican vote for 1992 but is insignificant for 1996. On the one hand, this finding provides evidence that Perot's 1992 success reduced Clinton's relative advantage over Bush (Goldman et al. 1994). On the other hand, it does little to discredit the opposing hypothesis that Perot's agenda and criticism of Bush's handling of the economy worked to the incumbent's detriment.

Consistent with the expectation drawn from the presidential election forecasting literature, the release of economic information affected the vote in predictable ways in 1992: the release of negative economic indexes hurt Bush, while the report of a rise in third-quarter GDP helped him. In 1996, the magnitude of the relationship diminishes considerably. Clinton appears to have barely benefited from the release of the indexes and the third-quarter GDP, both of which were positive. Information about the state of the economy clearly provided relevant cues to American voters in 1992, but the information conveyed in 1996 was either already factored into voters' preferences or not as clear and salient.

Discussion and Further Analysis

Contrary to the conventional wisdom on the subject, this chapter finds that media coverage of presidential candidates was not especially unbalanced or unfavorable in 1992 or 1996. Tendencies in this direction did exist but were slight. While this finding is, in my view, a blow to the logic underlying the reform argument, some caveats are in order. First, my findings may be driven by methodology. I employed a continuous scale in coding the favorability of news media stories, in contrast to the dichotomous scales used by most other analyses, which may account for my less striking estimation of unfavorability.[11] Although I obviously prefer my approach, the difference almost certainly influences the results. Second, this study does not investigate the subject matter of media coverage and thus cannot address the substance of news media coverage. It is worth noting, however, that preliminary analyses reveal that horse-race stories were most numerous, followed closely by economic, foreign policy, and domestic politics stories. This finding is consistent with both previous research and the assumptions of reformers, although I would point out that the percentage of substantive stories appears to far outpace the percentage of nonsubstantive stories. Moreover, the larger argument persists: there is little evidence from 1992 or 1996 that news media coverage of American presidential election campaigns was unduly negative.

On the second matter of interest, media coverage of campaign events did affect the vote in these elections. Some interesting twists to this story are worth noting, though. First, and as expected, print media coverage was less significant than television coverage, although the differences were small. Second, campaign event variables often had an effect even after controlling for media favorability, indicating that events (and probably their attendant news media coverage) have other mechanisms of influence.

A counterintuitive result of this analysis is that news media favorability toward conventions and debates did not typically change voters' preferences. For a number of reasons, however, this study is skeptical of the broader claim that favorability did not influence the vote. For one thing, my time frame covers only the final three months of the election campaigns; I do not pretend to know how much the media and other factors affected the state of affairs before August (though my two cents worth is that they were quite important). In addition, some campaign endeavors are neutral or seek merely to maintain the status quo, and so to judge news media coverage by its ability to produce a change in the candidates' support misses the point. For example, Clinton's goal in the presidential debates was to reinforce voters' inclination to support him. Thus, an "effective" debate would not change the dynamic of the race because Clinton had almost nowhere to go but down. Similarly, marginally favorable coverage of Clinton's performance would be unlikely to increase his share of the vote. Finally and most importantly, news media coverage of major events was often correlated with changes in voters' preferences, so its insignificance in other cases only confirms the obvious observation that stories sometimes resonate with voters and sometimes do not.

This finding reintroduces the larger question of whether campaign events and media coverage influence election outcomes. The conventional wisdom in political science—and an article of faith among some reformers—is that presidential campaigns activate voters' latent preferences for particular candidates, which depend on exogenous factors like the economy. In this way, campaigns serve to "enlighten" voters by providing information about the candidates, their policy positions, and the general condition of the country but have little independent effect (Bartels 1992, 1997; Gelman and King 1993). Gelman and King argue that the movement evident in public opinion polls is thus understandable as genuine movement toward a predictable aggregate outcome. The authors go on to contend that such movement ought to be greatest in the last few weeks of the campaign, when voters are paying more attention, and results in the convergence of polling trial ballot results with election forecasting models and actual outcomes.[12]

In light of this perspective, the present data provide a useful reality check. According to estimates derived from the 1992 models, one additional positive Bush event garnering a fifty-seven-point favorability score from television network news would have shifted the national electorate by enough votes to have changed the election result. Such was not the case for 1996, when Dole needed much more favorable coverage or many more events to overcome Clinton's eight-point margin of victory. These estimates suggest that campaigns can alter outcomes and should give pause to reformers seeking to increase campaigns' influence and entertainment value.

Of course, the real difficulties in any campaign are (1) accomplishing a major event and (2) eliciting favorable news media coverage. Examples of Bush's last-minute campaign events from 1992 (most notably, his reference to Clinton as "Bozo" and to Gore as "Ozone Man") show activity can be fraught with peril and can even backfire. Perhaps a more important observation is that candidate strategies should take into account the interaction between media favorability and their campaigns. The practical implication is that candidates should adopt flexible strategies whereby their events attempt to capitalize on opportunities for garnering favorable coverage. Bush, for example, might have been better served by undertaking events in connection with the release of favorable third-quarter economic information in 1992. Such strategizing would serve not only the interests of candidates but also the normative concerns of reformers, who prefer system-affirming activities and coverage. This suggestion is, needless to say, not something that would come as great news to campaign consultants, who are constantly trying to stage events that induce a positive media reaction. Still, the significant level of interdependence uncovered here confirms what has previously only been suspected and may be an important reinforcement for existing strategies emphasizing media coverage favorability.

Conclusion

This chapter addresses two questions that have received inadequate scrutiny from advocates of reform and previous studies of presidential campaigning: (1) what is the nature of news media coverage of campaigns, and (2) what is the effect of coverage of candidates' activities on voters? For the first question, this chapter examines the favorability of coverage toward the presidential candidates in dozens of local newspapers and on the four major television news networks. Detailed analysis of favorability scores shows little evidence that news media coverage is as negative and unbalanced as is often asserted. For the second question, the logic animating the chapter is simple. Since a limited number of voters see these events first-hand, it is likely that aggregate effects are largely driven by television and newspaper coverage. Data on news media coverage and campaigning show that television and (to a lesser extent) newspaper coverage had a significant effect on how campaign events influenced voters' preferences. Favorability is not the whole story either, as campaign event variables often had effects on voters' preferences even after controlling for the favorability of media coverage. This finding strongly suggests that other news media processes like agenda setting and framing also influence the impact of campaign events.

All told, the study provides support for skeptics of presidential campaign reforms. The debate over civic journalism and significant media reform appear to have assumed a corrosiveness that is difficult to find in these elections. Ironically, this study is not inconsistent with the work of Patterson (1980, 1993), Iyengar (1991), Jamieson (1996), and others who hold the media accountable for much of the public response to political campaigns. The difference is that these data indicate that media coverage is not all that bad and that the subsequent public response is measured and predictable. While this chapter does not get at the more esoteric dimensions of popular reaction to the campaign (for example, trust or regime support), it does suggest the need for a more balanced, open-minded approach to future inquiry and debate on campaigns.

APPENDIX

Sampling and Coding Newspaper and Television Stories

Newspapers. The newspaper study encompasses front-section and editorial page coverage of each of the newspapers in the sample (local, business, entertainment, and sports sections were not coded). For 1992, newspapers were selected for the sample at the discretion of the RNC, which wished to sample press coverage in as many "battleground" markets as possible. Although the sample is not random, it covers a large proportion of the most important media markets for the 1992 presidential election. Two major newspapers were not included in this study: the *Wall Street Journal* and *USA Today.* Since these newspapers are generally considered both elite and conservative (especially the *Journal*), I am aware that their absence might skew the estimate of the favorability in a liberal direction. Because the analytical focus is on change, however, this concern is minimal. For 1996, a small selection of newspapers were coded, including the *New York Times, Wall Street Journal, Los Angeles Times, Chicago Tribune, Dallas Morning News, USA Today,* and *Washington Post.* This reduction in the scope of the newspapers under analysis resulted from the smaller number of full-time coders available. Nonetheless, an attempt was made to cover the elite newspapers and to gain some semblance of regional diversity.

Most of the newspapers were coded continuously from August 1 through November 2, 1992. In 1992, a few were dropped almost immediately from the sample; others were added later in the campaign. Also in 1992, three coders were used on the "media monitor" project. For 1996, six college undergraduate students were used. For both years, the coders recorded a number of variables for each article, including the newspaper, byline, date, placement, presence/absence of an accompanying photo, primary topic, sources quoted, dominant frame, length of article, and tone. Of primary interest is the "favorability" score, which was calculated as follows:

1. Start at fifty points on the one-hundred-point scale.

2. Using a nine-point scale and moving in increments (or decrements) of five, increase/decrease up to twenty points based on whether the candidate was on the offensive or defensive. This evaluation takes into account the nature of the main topic, whether the candidate is being questioned or is doing the questioning, and the reporter's tone toward the topic. For example, an article about Clinton and the Vietnam draft would qualify as a defensive (unfavorable) article for Clinton. It would be more negative if Clinton were answering allegations. It would be even more negative if the report questioned the veracity of Clinton's comments. More generically, if the article features only favorable impressions of a candidate's event, the rating could rise by as much as twenty points. If opposing views are presented, the rating would be diminished according to the extent of the unfavorable comments.

3. Using a nine-point scale and moving again in increments (or decrements) of five, increase/decrease up to twenty points based on the headline, placement of article (front page, A2, A3, and so forth), and presence and quality of photograph. For example, a front-page *New York Times* article featuring a positive headline with an accompanying photo or graphic would increase an article's favorability by twenty points. If the same story appeared on page A14, conversely, the rating would increase by only ten points. If the same headline appeared over a news brief, the rating would increase by five points.

4. Using a five-point scale and moving in increments (or decrements) of five, increase/decrease up to ten points based on the inclusion of favorable/unfavorable sources (number and extent of favorable and unfavorable comments). In other words, if Bush were quoted and no sources from the other campaigns were included, the rating would rise by ten points. If Bush were quoted and an unfavor-

able source from Clinton's campaign was quoted with countering comments, the rating would remain unchanged. The rating would rise five points if Bush's comments were more extensive or decrease five points if the Clinton source's comments were more extensive. Sources were not weighted (for example, a Bush quote was not given more weight than a quote from Ron Brown), but "man-in-the-street" quotes were not included in the analysis. Perot was treated as an independent source, and the nature of his comments was reflected by the tone component of the overall favorability score.

The resultant favorability scores are thus the composite of three scales—tone (–20 to +20), placement (–20 to +20), and source balance (–10 to +10)—and is constrained to fall between zero and one hundred. This last feature was requested by the RNC so that press coverage could be compared to favorability measures provided by polling data. I reiterate that the favorability measure is not simply an estimate of an article's tone. Rather, it is an estimate of the favorability of that article judged against the whole of the newspaper's daily coverage. This aspect is important because minor stories with a negative tone can otherwise distort our understanding of how a given newspaper is covering politics. It is, in this sense, a measure of anticipated impact that takes into account tone, placement, and balance.

Five percent of all stories were double-coded each week, and discrepancies were resolved through weekly discussions involving all coders. The articles subjected to double-coding were selected randomly and stripped of their newspaper and byline identities to ensure blind coding. The average first-order correlations for the favorability scores involved in the double-coding were 0.83 for 1992 and 0.79 for 1996; this finding is consistent with other studies analyzing media favorability.

Television. The television study is analogous to the newspaper study in many ways. All four major network news broadcasts—ABC's *World News Tonight,* CBS's *Evening News,* NBC's *Nightly News,* and CNN's *Prime News*—were coded every evening from August 1 through November 2. In 1992, the data come from the Republican National Committee, which used two coders. In 1996, six undergraduate students were used. The coders recorded a number of variables for each article, including the network, reporter, date, placement, nature of accompanying video, primary topic, sources quoted, dominant frame, length of story, and tone. Again, the variable of primary interest is the "favorability" score, which was calculated in the same manner as the newspaper favorability score with the exception that placement component of the score reflects the prominence of the story within the context of a half-hour news broadcast rather than a newspaper.

As with the newspaper articles, 5 percent of all stories were double-coded each week, and discrepancies were resolved through weekly discussions. The stories subjected to double-coding were again selected randomly and stripped of their network and reporter identities to ensure blind coding. The average first-order correlations for the favorability scores involved in the double coding were 0.81 for 1992 and 0.82 for 1996. Again, this result is consistent with other studies analyzing media favorability.

Model Specification and Estimation

The data under analysis are time series. The unique properties and problems associated with such data prompt us to view traditional multivariate approaches with skepticism. Simple ordinary least squares techniques, for example, fail to account for possible serial autocorrelation and thus may not produce reliable estimates of multivariate relationships. Including the lagged dependent variable or employing generalized least squares techniques can largely alleviate concerns about serial autocorrelation, but neither addresses a different set of problems associated with nonstationarity (that is, the possibility that stochastic properties vary with respect to time). Unfortunately, the significance of the Durbin-Watson statistic (for serial autocorrelation) and the inability to falsify the null hypothesis of nonstationarity (through augmented Dickey-Fuller tests) argue strongly for a design that accounts for both problems.

The issue of nonstationarity is especially disconcerting, for although I am examining a short, bounded series, DeBoef and Granato (1997) point out that these data often mimic the nonstationary properties of integrated data and require remedy. To achieve stationarity and address concerns about serial autocorrelation, this study differences the noncategorical variables. It should be acknowledged that differencing cointegrated series can lead to erroneous substantive inferences (see, for example, Granger 1990). The practice of differencing is still quite common, however, and many of the particular criticisms leveled at differencing are not an issue for the present series. The study then uses ordinary least squares estimation techniques to gauge daily changes in candidate standing as a function of changes in campaigning and media coverage. Augmented Dickey-Fuller and Durbin-Watson tests, available on request, show the differenced series are stationary and exhibit minimal serial autocorrelation, allowing us to proceed without moving to generalized least squares estimation techniques.

Other Issues. Two additional methodological issues arose in the estimation. First, missing data for media coverage and tracking polls required strategies for interpolation. For the six dates missing either media favorability numbers or trial heat poll numbers, a point estimate of the trend suggested by the most immediate anterior and posterior data points was used.

Second, multicolinearity problems were suggested by correlation matrices, especially among the interactions between candidates' events and media coverage. A closer inspection of the standard errors, variance inflation factors, and principal components analysis strongly indicated that the problem was not as serious as the potential remedies, such as excluding the main effect terms (events and media coverage, respectively), which biases the estimates of the coefficients of the interaction terms (Cohen 1978; Friedrich 1982; Krosnick 1988).

NOTES

Some of the data design and analysis presented here previously appeared in "The Impact of News Media Favorability and Candidate Events in Presidential Campaigns," *Political Communication* 16 (1999):183–202.

1. Jamieson (1996) has conducted extensive analyses of campaign advertising and presents evidence that most ads contain substantive information. Geer offers additional support for this finding in this volume. As for other aspects of the campaign, a comparable result is offered for speeches (Lichter and Noyes 1993) and news media coverage (Just et al. 1996; Shaw and Sparrow 1999).

2. Several studies have demonstrated the news media's tendency to treat some candidates more favorably than others (Efron 1971; Lichter and Noyes 1993; Patterson 1993; Robinson and Sheehan 1983; Sabato 1993). Furthermore, a few recent studies have argued that the media's relatively favorable coverage of Clinton played a particularly influential role in the 1992 presidential election (Hetherington 1996; Patterson 1993; Sabato 1993). But few have actually measured empirically both coverage and its impact on the candidates' support.

3. It could be argued that television advertising is an equally appropriate expression of the campaign. The choice of candidate events is a matter of analytical clarity and convenience. It also has the advantage of being more amenable to examining the interactive effects between candidates' activities and news media coverage.

4. Although soft money and independent expenditures allow for discrepancies in the amount of resources available to the candidates (a study by the Annenberg School of Public Policy estimates that one-third of all spending in federal elections comes in the form of independent expenditures), my total dollar estimates of spending by the 1992 and 1996 Republican and Democratic presidential campaigns show that expenditures were roughly equal. Moreover, funds from these alternative sources are most often spent before September.

5. Recent analyses (e.g., Shaw 1999b) suggest it may halve the error, although doing so depends on the number of polls aggregated and the properties of the individual polls. Even a small reduction is important, however, since the sampling error associated with tracking polls is roughly 2.5 times that typically associated with a benchmark or brush-fire poll (Asher 1998). In addition to sampling error, there are other problems with researchers' traditional reliance on public opinion polls for campaign studies. Polls tend to ask respondents the counterfactual question of how they will vote today when what is really desired is information on how they will vote on Election Day. Thus, strong correlations between preelection preferences and actual votes are only partially reassuring. Furthermore, the use of public opinion data per se has well recognized problems such as question-wording and interviewer effects, the prompting of undecided respondents, and the weighting of data to achieve demographic and political representativeness. Although these matters are always a concern, they do not appear to have been a particular problem for polls of the 1992 and 1996 presidential elections.

6. Because 1992 media coverage data are compiled either for the Republican Party (in the case of newspapers) or by it (in the case of television), there is the pos-

sibility that they invent or overstate a liberal bias. Yet these data appear reliable for several reasons. First, any bias is inconsequential as long as it is constant. Second, the data were for internal use only rather than to "spin" some outside audience. In fact, any error in measuring the favorability of news coverage would have defeated the purpose, which was to estimate media effects. Third, the data are consistent with other studies of media coverage in 1992 (Crigler, Just, and Cook 1994; Just et al. 1996; Lichter and Noyes 1993). Moreover, the data corroborate the myriad of anecdotal accounts of media behavior during that election (Matalin and Carville 1994; Rosenstiel 1993). Finally, the coder reliability scores were reassuring (correlation coefficients of 0.81 for the favorability of television coverage and 0.83 for the favorability of newspaper stories).

7. The main weakness of this approach is that the political reporters and consultants who write these sorts of books have incentives to emphasize certain events and downplay others. Cross-checking only partially ameliorates this concern.

8. Alternative controls for the influence of the economy were explored. Monthly consumer confidence figures were tried, but relationships were weak and difficult to interpret. In a more interesting analysis, news media favorability on economic stories was used to create a continuous measure of economic impact (as seen through the screen of media coverage). Unfortunately, economic coverage was so unfavorable toward Bush in 1992 and (to a lesser extent) favorable toward Clinton in 1996 that these variables did not correlate strongly with oscillations in public opinion. Moreover, they created additional colinearity problems for the models. The analysis therefore relies on dummy variables representing the economic information conveyed by high-profile events to control for the effects of the macroeconomy.

9. A single measure of media favorability, combining television and newspaper coverage, is marginally significant for 1992 and less so for 1996. The interactive effects between this variable and the candidate event variables are mixed but are typically consequential: the Democratic event-media favorability variables are significant at .10 for 1992 and 1996, while the Republican event-media favorability variables are significant at the same level for 1992 but not 1996. While these results are intriguing, this study emphasizes the distinct effects of the newspaper and television favorability measures for reasons discussed earlier in the text.

10. In addition to acknowledging the limits of this study, technical explanations of the convention/debate noneffects merit consideration. Specifically, it is possible that stand-alone measures of news media favorability accounted for much of the variance in the polls and reduced the significance of the convention and debate terms. Indeed, running a short time series around the events in question (which eliminates the need for event-media interaction terms) supports this explanation.

11. Consider one hundred stories, each receiving a favorability score of forty-nine on the zero to one hundred scale. My estimation of favorability would be forty-nine, while a dichotomous scoring system would estimate that 100 percent of the stories are unfavorable.

12. The present data suggest that voters were more responsive to events and event coverage in the waning days of the campaign. While the small number of

cases leads to caution in interpreting the results, they suggest something that may not fit the story delineated by Gelman and King. First, assume that conditions determine the potential for campaigns to move voters. Going into the general election campaigns of 1992 and 1996, Clinton held more of the vote than he should have according to the forecasting models. Voter enlightenment as to the condition of the national economy, one might say, occurred early. Therefore, Clinton should have had difficulty accomplishing campaign events that moved many voters (the relationship should have been zero or even negative). The trouble is that Clinton's events were positively and significantly correlated with his standing in the polls. A second problem is understanding the individual-level psychology behind swings toward the underdog and underachieving Republican candidates. Movement toward the Republican candidates in these elections surely could not have depended on voters receiving information about the state of the economy. A more plausible scenario is that the tide of positive information about the economy was undone by other factors (e.g., information about issue positions or perhaps party identification) as the election neared and candidates made these factors more salient. Still, individual enlightenment that favors the disadvantaged candidate is puzzling, as is the success of Clinton's campaigning in both of these elections.

REFERENCES

Ansolabehere, Stephen, Roy Behr, and Shanto Iyengar. 1993. *The Media Game.* New York: Macmillan.

Ansolabehere, Stephen, and Shanto Iyengar. 1995. *Going Negative.* New York: Free Press.

Asher, Herbert. 1998. *Polling and the Public.* 4th ed. Washington, DC: CQ Press.

Bartels, Larry M. 1992. "Electioneering in the United States." In *Electioneering: A Comparative Study of Continuity and Change,* ed. David Butler and Austin Ranney. Oxford: Clarendon Press.

Bartels, Larry M. 1993. "Messages Received: The Political Impact of Media Exposure." *American Political Science Review* 87:267–85.

Bartels, Larry M. 1997. "How Campaigns Matter." Unpublished manuscript, Princeton University.

Brown, Lloyd B., and Henry W. Chappell Jr. 1996. "Forecasting Presidential Elections in the States." Paper presented at the 1996 annual meeting of the Public Choice Society, Houston.

Campbell, James E. 1992. "Forecasting the Presidential Vote in the States." *American Journal of Political Science* 386–407.

Campbell, James E., Lynne Cherry, and Kenneth Wink. 1992. "The Convention Bump." *American Politics Quarterly* 20:287–307.

Campbell, James E., and Kenneth Wink. 1990. "Trial-Heat Forecasts of the Presidential Vote." *American Politics Quarterly* 18:251–69.

Cohen, Jacob. 1978. "Partialed Products Are Interactions; Partialed Powers Are Curve Components." *Psychological Bulletin* 85:858–66.

Crigler, Ann N., Marion R. Just, and Timothy E. Cook. 1994. "Local News, Network News, and the 1992 Presidential Campaign." Paper presented at the annual meeting of the American Political Science Association, Chicago.

DeBoef, Suzanna, and James Granato. 1997. "Near-Integrated Data and the Analysis of Political Relationships." *American Journal of Political Science* 41:619–40.

Efron, Edith. 1971. *The News Twisters.* Los Angeles: Nash.

Fair, Ray C. 1978. "The Effect of Economic Events on Votes for President." *Review of Economics and Statistics* 60:159–72.

Finkel, Steven E. 1993. "Reexamining the 'Minimal Effects' Model in Recent Presidential Campaigns." *Journal of Politics* 55:1–21.

Friedrich, Robert J. 1982. "In Defense of Multiplicative Terms in Multiple Regression Equations." *American Journal of Political Science* 26:797–833.

Gans, Herbert. 1979. *Deciding What's News.* New York: Pantheon.

Geer, John G. 1988. "The Effects of the Presidential Debates on the Electorate's Preferences for Candidates." *American Politics Quarterly* 16:486–501.

Gelman, Andrew, and Gary King. 1993. "Why Are American Presidential Election Polls So Variable When Votes Are So Predictable?" *British Journal of Political Science* 23:409–51.

Germond, Jack W., and Jules Witcover. 1993. *Mad as Hell: Revolt at the Ballot Box, 1992.* New York: Warner Books.

Goldenberg, Edie N., and Michael W. Traugott. 1984. *Campaigning for Congress.* Washington, DC: CQ Press.

Goldman, Peter, Thomas M. DeFrank, Mark Miller, Andrew Murr, and Tom Mathews. 1994. *Quest for the Presidency, 1992.* College Station: Texas A&M University Press.

Granger, Clive W. 1990. "Seasonal Integration and Cointegration." *Journal of Econometrics* 44:215–39.

Greenberg, Stanley. 1994. *Middle-Class Dreams.* New York: Times Books.

Greenfield, Jeffrey. 1980. *Playing to Win.* New York: Simon and Schuster.

Hetherington, Marc J. 1996. "The Media's Role in Forming Voters' National Economic Evaluations in 1992." *American Journal of Political Science* 40:372–95.

Hetherington, Marc J. 1998. "The Political Relevance of Political Trust." *American Political Science Review* 92:791–808.

Hetherington, Marc J. 1999. "The Effect of Political Trust on the Presidential Vote, 1968–1996." *American Political Science Review* 93:311–26.

Holbrook, Thomas M. 1994. "Campaigns, National Conditions, and U.S. Presidential Elections." *American Journal of Political Science* 38:973–98.

Holbrook, Thomas M. 1996. *Do Campaigns Matter?* Beverly Hills, CA: Sage.

Holbrook, Thomas M. 1997. "Did the Campaign Matter?" Paper presented at the annual meeting of the Midwest Political Science Association, Chicago.

Iyengar, Shanto. 1991. *Is Anyone Responsible?* Chicago: University of Chicago Press.

Iyengar, Shanto, and Donald Kinder. 1987. *News That Matters.* Chicago: University of Chicago Press.

Iyengar, Shanto, and John R. Petrocik. 1998. "'Basic Rule' Voting: The Impact of Campaigns on Party and Approval-Based Voting." Paper presented at the Conference of Political Advertising in Election Campaigns, American University, Washington, DC.

Jacobson, Gary C. 1992. *The Politics of Congressional Elections.* 3d ed. New York: HarperCollins.

Jamieson, Kathleen Hall. 1996. *Packaging the Presidency.* 3d ed. New York: Oxford University Press.

Just, Marion R., Ann N. Crigler, Dean E. Alger, Timothy E. Cook, Montague Kern, and Darrell M. West. 1996. *Crosstalk: Citizens, Candidates, and the Media in a Presidential Campaign.* Chicago: University of Chicago Press.

Krosnick, Jon A. 1988. "The Role of Attitude Importance in Social Evaluation: A Study of Policy Preferences, Presidential Candidate Evaluations, and Voting Behavior." *Journal of Personality and Social Psychology* 55:196–210.

Lewis-Beck, Michael S., and Tom W. Rice. 1992. *Forecasting Elections.* Washington, DC: CQ Press.

Lichter, Robert S., and Richard E. Noyes. 1993. *Good Intentions Make Bad News: Why Americans Hate Campaign Journalism.* Lanham, MD: Rowman and Littlefield.

Markus, Gregory B. 1988. "The Impact of Personal and National Economic Conditions on the Presidential Vote: A Pooled Cross-Sectional Analysis." *American Journal of Political Science* 32:137–54.

Matalin, Mary, and James Carville. 1994. *All's Fair: Love, War, and Running for President.* New York: Random House.

McCombs, Maxwell E., and Donald L. Shaw. 1972. "The Agenda-Setting Function of the Mass Media." *Public Opinion Quarterly* 28:176–87.

Patterson, Thomas E. 1980. *The Mass Media Election.* New York: Praeger.

Patterson, Thomas E. 1993. *Out of Order.* New York: Knopf.

Robinson, Michael J., and Margaret Sheehan. 1983. *Over the Wire and on TV.* New York: Sage.

Rosenstiel, Tom. 1993. *Strange Bedfellows.* New York: Hyperion.

Rosenstone, Steven J. 1983. *Forecasting Presidential Elections.* New Haven: Yale University Press.

Roshco, Bernard. 1975. *Newsmaking.* Chicago: University of Chicago Press.

Sabato, Larry J. 1993. "Is There an Anti-Republican, Anti-Conservative Media Tilt?" *Campaigns and Elections* 14 (September 1993):16–21.

Salmore, Barbara, and Stephen Salmore. 1989. *Candidates, Parties, and Campaigns.* 2d ed. Washington, DC: CQ Press.

Shaw, Daron R. 1999a. "The Impact of News Media Favorability and Candidate Events in Presidential Campaigns." *Political Communication* 16:183–202.

Shaw, Daron R. 1999b. "A Study of Presidential Campaign Effects from 1952–1992." *Journal of Politics* 61:387–422.

Shaw, Daron R., and Bartholomew H. Sparrow. 1999. "From the Inner Ring Out: News Congruence, Cue-Taking, and Campaign Coverage." *Political Research Quarterly* 52:323–51.

Shelley, Mack C., II, and Hwang-Du Hwang. 1991. "The Mass Media and Public Opinion Polls in the 1988 Presidential Election." *American Politics Quarterly* 19:59–79.

Sigal, Leon. 1973. *Reporters and Officials.* Lexington, MA: Heath.

Thomas, Evan, Karen Breslau, Debra Rosenberg, Leslie Kaufman, and Andrew Murr. 1997. *Back from the Dead: How Clinton Survived the Republican Revolution.* New York: Atlantic Monthly Press.

Wicker, Tom. 1975. *On Press.* New York: Viking.

Woodward, Bob. 1996. *The Choice.* New York: Simon and Schuster.

Chapter 7

Regime Support and Campaign Reform

Bruce Buchanan

The Problem: Unsupportive Citizen Attitudes and Behavior

Political discontent with government and its leaders, institutions, and decision-making processes is arguably a latent threat to what David Easton (1975, 444) calls "diffuse regime support," which he defines as "a reservoir of favorable attitudes or good will that helps [citizens] to accept or tolerate outputs to which they are opposed. . . ."

Evidence of discontent of various kinds has mounted substantially in recent decades (see, e.g., Bartels's chapter in this volume; Hunter and Johnson 1997; Hibbing and Theiss-Morse 1995; Luttbeg and Gant 1995; Craig 1993; Lipset and Schneider 1987; A. H. Miller 1974). But the cross-time fortunes of three specific indicators closely related to regime support as I operationalize it here are especially relevant to my argument: voter turnout, trust in government, and faith in elections. Turnout and trust are charted in figures 1 and 2, respectively, of this chapter; faith in elections is charted in figure 9 of Bartels's initial chapter in this volume.

Although the precise meaning of the voter turnout for any particular election is open to argument, it is hard not to interpret the trend line in voting-age population turnout in presidential elections between 1960 (62.8 percent) and 1996 (49 percent) as evidence of increasingly unsupportive citizen behavior (figure 1).[1] (Turnout percentages in charts and tables throughout are from the Federal Election Commission.) Similarly, despite the fact that trust in government has improved significantly since its low point in 1994 (see the trend line based on National Election Study [NES] data in figure 2) it remains the case that in the most recent Pew surveys, conducted in February 1998, a substantial majority remains distrustful:

> Asked for a simple up-or-down assessment—Would you say you basically trust the federal government in Washington or not?—57% say they do not trust the federal government; 39% say they do. Favora-

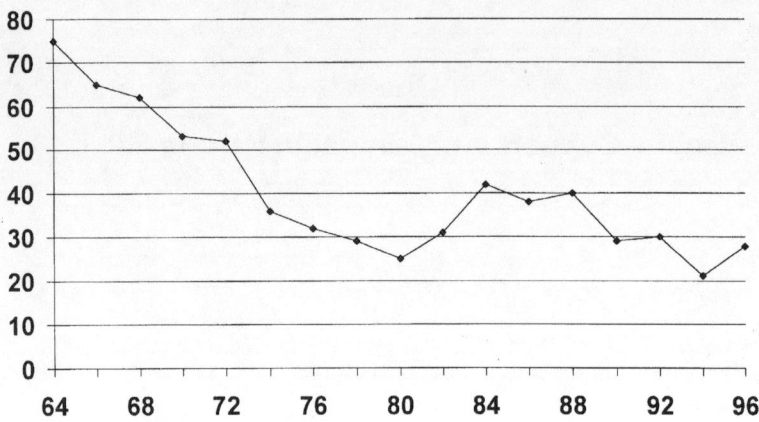

Fig. 1. Voter turnout in presidential elections, 1960–96.
(% = percent of eligible voters. *Source:* Teixeira 1992, 9; U.S. Federal Election Commission.)

bility ratings elicit almost identical responses—59% say they have a very or mostly unfavorable opinion of the federal government; 38% say the opposite. (Pew Research Center 1998, 15)

The long-term trend for faith in elections, as measured by the NES question "How much do you feel that having elections makes the government pay attention to what the people think—a good deal, some, or not much?" is no less revealing. After controlling for related attitudes toward government waste and corruption, Bartels (in this volume) finds that the decline slows after 1984. But the substantial erosion of faith in the electoral process throughout the 1960s and 1970s (Bartels, in this volume, figure 9) leaves it in a comparatively diminished state.

What is the significance of the trends suggested by these and similar data? The answer depends on who is asked. On one side are those who argue that low voter turnout, for example, is either healthy or inconsequential. Berelson, Lazarsfeld, and McPhee (1954) contend that limited citizen participation and apathy contribute stability to the political system by cushioning the shock of disagreement, adjustment, and change. Dahl (1956) extends Berelson by suggesting the possible destabilizing consequences of increasing the participation of society's lower socioeconomic orders.

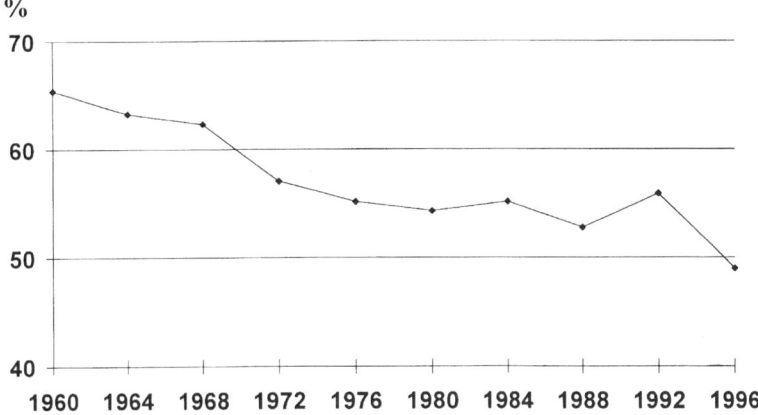

Fig. 2. **Trust in government.**
(Percent who trust just about always/most of the time. *Source:* American National Election Studies, University of Michigan.)

Conversely, others argue that the power of elections to legitimize government via "the consent of the governed" is significantly compromised by low voter turnout, especially turnout that dips below the symbolically significant majority point:

> As fewer and fewer people vote, the extent to which government truly rests on the consent of the governed is eroded. As a result, elected officials may not believe they have sufficient legitimacy to pursue desired policies, and citizens may believe that government is not legitimate enough to merit support. The result of this lack of confidence could be anything from widespread social and political disorganization to the reinforcement of some of the milder social pathologies we already see: gridlocked government and a political culture that turns talented people away from careers in government service. (Teixeira 1992, 3)

As for distrust in government, the authors of the 1998 Pew Research Center report argue that at its current level, majority distrust does not have serious consequences for the system's health, since distrusters are no less likely to vote, no more likely to disobey the law, and no less patriotic than trusters (49). Others, such as Luttbeg and Gant (1995, 162), are less sanguine: "[O]ur findings about change in political trust and alienation do not absolutely refute the notion that contemporary disaffection might render serious damage to our republic." Similarly, Easton (1975, 445) concludes that "if discontent with perceived performance continues over a long enough time, it may gradually erode even the strongest underlying bonds of attachment." And after reviewing the data on trust, faith in elections, and other forms of discontent, Stephen Craig (1993, 17) suggests, "Even though we do not appear to be on the verge of a full-blown system breakdown, it seems reasonable to conclude that the general health of our polity will continue to deteriorate unless the confidence gap is in some way bridged."

Recent increases in trust and the slower erosion of faith in elections are positive signs. Turnout patterns, however, offer less reassurance. Whether or not regime stability and legitimacy are in immediate peril, the long-term trends are disquieting enough to centrist opinion to invite serious attention to this chapter's core question: What can be done to reduce the existing level of estrangement between the mass electorate and the political system, most particularly its electoral process?

My answer—find ways to increase mass learning and voting in presidential elections—may at first seem counterintuitive. Presidential and other election campaigns have recently more often been seen as leading sources of mass political discontent than as potential remedies for it (see, e.g., Dionne 1991). Still, the case can be made that there is no better estrangement-reduction vehicle available than a national campaign and election.

Campaigns as Support-Building Opportunities

The possibility that presidential campaigns and elections can be vehicles not just for seeking candidate support but also for building regime support is rarely considered. Political scientists more commonly think of campaigns and elections as mechanisms for ensuring democratic accountability (e.g., Key 1966; Schattschneider 1960), as devices for achieving some measure of mass political equality (e.g., Verba, Schlozman, and Brady 1995, 12), as occasionally decisive arenas for settling mass partisan alignments and realignments (e.g., Sundquist 1983; Chambers and Burnham 1975), or as problems in predicting who will win and explaining why (e.g., Bartels 1997; Shaw 1995; Lewis-Beck and Rice 1992). While not discounting any of these stances, here I propose that we also think of campaigns and elections as system-maintenance vehicles because they marshal forces able under some circumstances to reinforce and update basic political socialization.

The argument for this view is that election campaigns offer something that is unmatched elsewhere in national civic life: a regularly scheduled opportunity for support-affirming behavior on a mass scale. By support-affirming behavior, I mean not only the opportunity to vote, which is an act fraught with supportive symbolism for any representative democracy, but also the explosion of opportunities campaigns afford to notice, focus, and, most importantly, learn interesting and useful things as the time for voting approaches. Learning and voting both constitute moderately effortful behavior, and I argue that such behavior matters because it represents a kind of "investment" that can prompt the formation and/or reinforcement of associated attitudes, such as those related to support for the political system.

Campaigns are uniquely relevant to the problems associated with discontent because no other institutions—excepting only families and schools—approach the potential of a presidential campaign for influencing mass political attitudes and behavior, including the behaviors and attitudes relevant to regime support. Despite the fact that campaigns rarely feature any explicit effort to do so, there is scattered evidence that they evoke and/or reinforce attitudes supportive of the political system among many citizens. Ginsberg and Weissberg (1978), for example, cite 1968 and 1972 presidential election data showing that participation mobilized citizen support for the regime and for political leaders. Clark and Acock (1989) reach similar conclusions. More recently, Rahn and her colleagues (1993) found that the 1992 presidential election positively affected both economic expectations and trust in government among a small sample of Madison, Wisconsin residents. These authors also cite other evidence suggesting the role of elections in elevating peoples' spirits, including the impact of optimistic election rhetoric on the "spirit of community."

In an analysis of the 1996 election cycle using NES panel data, Rahn, Brehm, and Carlson (1997) tested the ability of four classes of campaign exposure—mobilization, campaign involvement, perceived qualities of the campaign and candidates, and the election ritual—to explain changes in three interrelated, individual-level orientations that represent the "core normative apparatus of democracy": generalized trust in others, trust in government, and external political efficacy (the sense that the political authorities are responsive to citizen demands). The authors found that parts of each campaign exposure had significant impacts on the individual orientations. Thus, one aspect of mobilization—being contacted by a political party—had a modest positive impact on social trust. Similarly, one aspect of campaign involvement—voting—clearly boosted respondents' levels of external efficacy. Those who perceived "multiple positive aspects" about both presidential candidates, Clinton and Dole, became more trusting in government from before to after the election. And exposure to the election ritual increased social trust, especially among those who were the most politically knowledgeable and civically engaged at the start, but also among many with initially distrusting orientations.

Table 1 reports survey data from the Markle Foundation presidential campaign studies of 1988, 1992, and 1996. The campaign season comparisons within each election year, though based on separate random national samples in September and November of each year, reveal differences that are plausibly interpreted as changes brought on by exposure to the campaign. While the magnitude of the changes varies from year to year, all show increases from September to November. (The very large sample sizes in this and other tables insure that all mean differences are statistically significant.)

It is apparent that exposure to these three campaigns—which in practical terms means exposure to media coverage, campaign advertising, and face-to-face exchanges about the campaign, issues, and candidates—sparked a modest increase in the average level of reported interest in the contest and an increase in the percentage of the eligible electorate that followed media coverage of the campaign "very closely."[2] Lynn Vavreck reports similar results in her chapter in this volume, finding that between 1980 and 1992 interested citizens paid more attention to the campaign in the media, even when the campaigns featured attacks.

Interest and media attention matter, of course, because campaigns and elections cannot influence behavior like learning and voting without first attracting attention. Interest measures the motivation to pay attention to the campaign. In other words, interest and associated practices like following media coverage and discussing the campaign with others are both the initial hook and the sustaining force that make learning and voting far more likely.

Exposure to each of the three campaigns in table 1 also appears to have sparked modest increases in reported "personal importance of voting." And in 1996, the only year in which this particular open-ended citizen duty question was asked, the percentage of respondents that identified voting as the most important civic responsibility during a presidential election year moved from 60 to 70 between Labor Day and Election Day.

There is also suggestive Markle survey evidence, not reported in table 1, that "problem voter" subgroups who care least about politics and vote at the lowest rates—young adults, minorities, and those with lower incomes and fewer years of formal education—can be attracted and influenced by some portions of the campaign spectacle. In 1992, for example, some 70 percent reported watching one or more of the presidential and vice presidential debates. While 50 percent of all respondents said the 1992 debates influenced their choice of candidates, the proportion was significantly higher, ranging into the 70s, for the various problem-voter groups (Buchanan 1995). In 1996 the debate audience was much lower for all groups. But lower-income, less educated, younger, and nonwhite groups all still reported being influenced by the debates at significantly greater than average rates.

The Markle and other findings suggest that campaigns have the capacity to attract attention, inspire interest and exert some measure of influence throughout the voting-age population. This potential undoubtedly results from the fact of a regularly scheduled, media-driven, sometimes hotly competitive, and almost always widely discussed national spectacle. These findings imply the potential not only for greater influence but also specifically for support-enhancing influence—but only if the campaign vehicle can somehow be more effectively harnessed to the purpose.

How is such increased campaign influence best achieved? Again, I hypothesize that it is best achieved by finding ways to reliably entice more people to learn and vote. But before looking at theory and data suggesting

TABLE 1. Campaign Influence on Regime-Supportive Attitudes

	1988[a]		1992[b]		1996[c]	
	(1)	(2)	(1)	(2)	(1)	(2)
Voting is important to me[d]	8.9	9.1	8.6	8.8	8.5	8.8
Voting is a citizen duty[e]					60%	70%
Interest in politics[d]	7.1	7.4	7.1	7.5	6.9	7.1
Follow media very closely	16%	25%	22%	38%	20%	24%

[a]Louis Harris & Associates survey 1988: (1) $n = 1,876$, conducted 9/6–9/19/1988; (2) $n = 1,875$, conducted 10/18–11/4/1988.
[b]Princeton Survey Research Associates survey 1992: (1) $n = 1,882$, conducted 9/8–9/21/1992; (2) $n = 1,882$, conducted 10/20–11/02/1992.
[c]Princeton Survey Research Associates survey 1996: (1) $n = 1,923$, conducted 9/6–9/16/1996; (2) $n = 1,881$, conducted 10/21–11/02/1996.
[d]Means on scales of 1 to 10, with 10 being highest.
[e]Open-ended question, 1996 only: "Now, thinking about the responsibilities and duties of being a United States citizen. In your opinion, what are the MOST important responsibilities that citizens have during a presidential election year?"

that learning and voting behavior may independently spark or rekindle interest and other supportive attitudes (which, in turn, can be expected to strengthen the subsequent disposition to learn and vote), it will be helpful to look more closely at the concept of regime support.

The Concept of Regime Support

Easton (1975, 1965) distinguishes specific support (support for the political authorities) from diffuse support (support for the regime) and defines the latter in a way that emphasizes its multidimensionality: "a reservoir of favorable attitudes or good will" (1975, 444). Here I use the word *regime* in a more restrictive sense than Easton, who defines it quite expansively (1965, 190).

The regime in focus here, of course, is the U.S. political system. And for present purposes, I conceive of it primarily in terms of the process that most centrally defines and legitimizes any regime as democratic: national elections. To support a democratic regime is, first and foremost, to support the electoral process. So when I speak of *regime support,* I mean support by the citizenry of the electoral process. This, after all, is what is called into question by declining turnout (figure 1) and diminished faith in elections (Bartels in this volume, figure 9). Conversely, voters who believe elections make the government pay attention to what they and others think are more likely to tolerate what Easton styles as "outputs to which they are opposed" because faith in elections implies the belief that elections can be trusted to make changes in unsatisfying outputs possible and that individual voters can join to force such change.

As the indicators in table 2 show, I conceive and operationalize regime support as a constellation of mutually reinforcing behaviors and attitudes that directly link citizens to the regime via participation in and psychological attachment to its flagship electoral process. A discussion of the support concepts and indicators follows.

Behaviors

The Significance of Voting. Riker nicely captures the larger significance of the act of voting:

[A]ll democratic ideas are focused on the mechanism of voting. All the elements of the democratic method are means to render voting practically effective and politically significant, and all the elements of the democratic ideal are moral extensions and elaborations of the features of the method that make voting work. Voting, therefore, is the central act of democracy. (1982, 6)

More directly to the point here, voting (and attitudes that encourage it) indicate regime support because a high incidence of voting implies and thus confers legitimacy on a representative democracy, and legitimacy is a mainstay of a political system's health.[3]

The Significance of Learning and Knowledge. Like the duty to vote, the normative ideal of a well-informed electorate is a fixture of the democratic tradition. As Rousseau put it (1968, 49), "Born as I was the citizen of a free state and a member of its sovereign body, the very right to vote imposes on me the duty to instruct myself in public affairs, however little influence my voice may have in them." American democratic theorists from Thomas Jefferson to John Dewey to Walter Lippmann to Amy Gutmann and Dennis Thompson have pointed to the informed citizenry ideal while acknowledging that it is rarely achieved and proposing various ways to compensate for the shortfall.

While there are many reasons beyond simply choosing rationally among two or three general election candidates to regard learning and its

TABLE 2.   Regime-Supportive Behavior and Attitudes in Presidential Elections

	1988	1992	1996
Behavior			
Voter Turnout[a]	50.1%	55.2%	48.8%
Issue Knowledge[b]	4	7	1
Attitudes[c]			
Voting is very important to me.	77%	73%	72%
I am very interested in presidential politics.	37%	42%	35%
Citizen duty: vote/register to vote[d]			70%
Citizen duty: stay informed/maintain political awareness[d]			25%

[a]Federal Election Commission
[b]Number of issue positions attributed to candidates correctly by 58%+ of respondents, on a 20-item issue position test.
[c]Sources: 1988, Louis Harris & Associates, 10/18–11/4/88, $n = 1,875$; 1992, Princeton Survey Research Associates, 10/20–11/2/92, $n = 1,882$; 1996, PSRA, 10/21–11/2/96, $n = 1,881$.
[d]Source: PSRA, 1996 only, 10/21/96, $n = 945$. What are the most important responsibilities that citizens have during a presidential election year?

product, knowledge, as important for civic self-protection and regime enhancement (e.g., Delli Carpini and Keeter 1996; Nie, Junn, and Stehlik-Barry 1996), the key feature of learning stressed for present purposes is its potential as one of two key forms of effortful behavioral investment (the other is voting) likely to reinforce supportive attitudes.

The learning portion of the civic investment model subsequently described and illustrated with data uses a three-campaign series of twenty-item issue-position test data from the Markle campaign surveys. Item characterizations are available in Buchanan (1997, forthcoming).

Attitudes

Instilling and sustaining the psychological allegiance of citizens to regimes, as of members to any social organization, is fundamental to system health and survival and thus necessarily a core objective of system maintenance (Buchanan 1974; Katz and Kahn 1972; Easton 1965). No measures of citizen-regime bonding or regime-supportive attitudes known to me fully encompass all the potentially important dimensions of commitment or allegiance of citizens to the regime (see Beiner 1995). But while they obviously do not exhaust the concept, the three attitudinal indicators in table 2—voting importance, political interest, and an open-ended question about citizen duty—clearly tap important dimensions of regime support.

The role of political interest as precursor and stimulus to learning and voting has already been discussed. In the Markle series, political interest is measured by the question, "How interested are you in presidential politics?" The voting importance question, "How important is voting in the November presidential election to you?" taps the extent to which respondents profess that the core regime-supportive act is a personal priority and thus, by implication, a component of self-definition. Citizen duty is measured by an open-ended question: "Now, please think about the responsibilities and duties of being a United States citizen. In your opinion, what are the most important responsibilities that citizens have during a presidential election year? Are there any other important responsibilities that citizens have?" Responses to this question, posed to Markle national samples for the first time in 1996,[4] show what political socialization has instilled in the mass public mind regarding citizens' responsibilities in presidential elections. Registering and voting dominate the self-defined citizen portfolio at 70 percent, with watching and learning a distant and minority-supported second at 25 percent.

Behavior as Attitude-Relevant Investment

The basic proposition of the investment model is that effortful behavior, such as learning and voting across time, represents the kind of tangible personal commitment that tends, when the behavior is regularly repeated and socially reinforced, to solidify or freeze attitudes that are consistent with the behavior, such as interest in politics, the importance of voting, or the civic duty to learn and vote.

The underlying theory, which is most fully specified at the individual level in the cognitive-consistency and behavioral-commitment schools of psychology, is succinctly expressed by Kiesler (1971, 17): "Behavior, if explicit enough, freezes one, in Lewin's terms. Explicit behavior, like an irrevocable decision, provides the pillar around which the cognitive apparatus must be draped. Through behavior, one is *committed.*" Relatedly, normative political theorists have long asserted that various modes of civic participation make the individual more likely to consider the institutions, norms, and values of a given regime morally proper and promote an increase in satisfaction with the system as a whole (e.g., Thompson 1970). Verba (1961) and Almond and Verba (1963) similarly assert that participation increases the tendency to view the regime as legitimate and increases the acceptability of collective decisions and policy outcomes. Supportive empirical evidence is accumulating. Iyengar (1980), for example, finds that voting increases external efficacy, a finding that, as we have seen, is replicated by Rahn, Brehm, and Carlson (1997).

There is also evidence that voting behavior and regime-supportive attitudes reinforce each other. Finkel (1985), for example, tested the proposition that reciprocal causation exists between external efficacy and electoral participation, that the individual who votes or participates develops stronger feelings that the government is responsive, which then makes future participation more likely, whereas nonparticipation reinforces the sense that the government is unresponsive, which encourages nonparticipation. Using the Survey Research Center's 1972–1974–1976 Election Study panel data, and applying a careful statistical procedure for untangling reciprocal effects, he finds evidence of directional influence between voting and external efficacy across the entire sample but especially among less educated citizens, a low turnout group. A partial replication of his U.S. study in then West Germany led Finkel (1987, 461) to conclude that the impact of voting on supportive attitudes "may be a very general process in western democracies."

The hypothesis that learning, like voting, is a form of investment behavior with attitudinal consequences of its own has received less direct research attention. Most relevant studies focus on the relationship of participation and education, learning or knowledge, and do not consider learning variables as potential predictors of supportive attitudes. But in their review of studies showing the strong relationship between participation and knowledge (e.g., Junn 1991; Leighley 1991, and others), Delli Carpini and Keeter (1996, 224) observe, "Knowledge promotes a number of civic attitudes . . . (such as political interest and efficacy) that motivate participation," and conclude that knowledge boosts participation because it promotes an understanding of why politics is relevant. The "knowledge = increased respect for politics = participation" model implicit in their argument is essentially the same "behavior-attitude-behavior" reinforcement dynamic postulated here, and it is suggested (though not confirmed) by the relationships reported in the tables that follow.

The percentage comparisons reported in tables 3 and 4 show that people who report stronger regime-supportive attitudes are more likely to behave supportively (i.e., to report having registered and voted and to demonstrate greater learning). Table 3 shows that significantly greater percentages of those who express interest in presidential politics and attach importance to voting (indicated by ratings between six and ten on a ten-point scale) claim to have voted in 1992 and to have registered in 1996 than of those who express no interest (indicated by ratings between one and four). When the sample is divided into those "very interested" (i.e., those choosing nine or ten), "neutral" (those choosing five) and "not at all interested" (those choosing one or two), it is apparent that the greater the ratings of interest and importance, the greater the tendency to report registering and voting. Conversely, the lower the ratings of interest and importance, the lower the percentages of registrants and voters. Finally, those who identified registering and voting as citizen duties in response to the open-ended question mentioned earlier were far more likely than not to report doing both—three and four times as likely, respectively (not reported in tables).

By the same token, table 4 shows that those expressing higher levels of political interest and ascribing more importance to voting demonstrate more issue learning on the 1996 twenty-item Markle issues test than those who report less interest and attach less importance. For example, the "very important" and "very interested" respondents are more than two and three times as likely, respectively, than the "not at all important, not at all interested" respondents to score in the high knowledge category. And the low supportive-attitude groups are significantly more likely to score in the low knowledge category. On a related note, 70 percent of those who said that citizens should "stay informed and maintain political awareness" in response to the open-ended citizen duty question scored in the high or medium knowledge categories, while only 30 percent achieved low knowledge scores (not reported in tables).

These results add to the weight of available evidence showing a strong positive association between political attitudes and related behavior.[5] Much of it (e.g., Leighley 1991; Finkel 1985, 1987) also demonstrates reciprocal causal effects between attitudinal and behavioral variables. There is good reason to expect, therefore, that regime-supportive attitudes and behavior will be mutually reinforcing and thus that the reform interventions discussed subsequently that target either attitudes or behavior might eventually be expected to influence both.

TABLE 3. Impact of "Interest" and "Importance" on Voting and Voter Registration

How interested are you in presidential politics? Use a 10 to 1 scale where 10 means you are VERY INTERESTED and 1 means you are NOT AT ALL INTERESTED.

	Total Interested (6–10)	Total Not Interested (1–4)	Very Interested (9–10)	Neutral (5)	Not Interested (1–2)
% Who Voted	81	51	86	54	52
% Who Didn't Vote	19	49	14	45	48
% Registered	89	61	92	68	57
% Not Registered	11	39	8	32	43

How important is voting in the NOVEMBER presidential election to you? Use a 10 to 1 scale where 10 means VERY IMPORTANT to you and 1 means NOT AT ALL IMPORTANT to you.

	Total Important (6–10)	Total Not Important (1–4)	Very Important (9–10)	Neutral (5)	Not Important (1–2)
% Who Voted	78	31	82	42	32
% Who Didn't Vote	22	69	18	58	68
% Registered	86	44	90	58	46
% Not Registered	14	56	10	42	54

Source: Princeton Survey Research Associates, 10/21–11/2/96.

186   Campaign Reform

Incentives and Reform

By the line of reasoning I have suggested, those who neither vote nor learn, currently a majority, sidestep the most widely accessible and symbolically charged of the behaviors capable of reinforcing mass civic attachments. How, then, increase the incidence of learning and voting behavior? To interrupt behavior is to stop the attitude-behavior reinforcement cycle. The basic reform strategy, then, is to devise ways to address the behavior disruptors. The primary behavior-prevention suspects can be grouped into four categories:

(a) *Institutional barriers,* such as burdensome registration requirements (e.g., Wolfinger and Rosenstone 1980);
(b) *Off-putting candidate behaviors,* such as attacks, evasions, distortions, and campaign finance abuses (see Ansolabehere and Iyengar 1996; Buchanan 1996; but see also Finkel and Geer 1998);

TABLE 4. Impact of "Interest" and "Importance" on Knowledge

How interested are you in presidential politics? Use a 10 to 1 scale where 10 means you are VERY INTERESTED and 1 means you are NOT AT ALL INTERESTED.

	Total Interested (6–10)	Total Not Interested (1–4)	Very Interested (9–10)	Neutral (5)	Not Interested (1–2)
Knowledge Index					
% Scoring High	24	11	28	8	8
% Scoring Medium	39	30	41	39	30
% Scoring Low	37	59	31	53	62

How important is voting in the NOVEMBER presidential election to you? Use a 10 to 1 scale where 10 means VERY IMPORTANT to you and 1 means NOT AT ALL IMPORTANT to you.

	Total Important (6–10)	Total Not Important (1–4)	Very Important (9–10)	Neutral (5)	Not Important (1–2)
Knowledge Index					
% Scoring High	21	9	23	13	10
% Scoring Medium	38	41	38	32	43
% Scoring Low	41	50	39	54	47

Source: Princeton Survey Research Associates, 10/21–11/2/96.

(c) *The decline of voter mobilization* efforts by parties, campaigns, and social movements (Rosenstone and Hansen 1993, 213); and

(d) *Generational declines in the strength of civic duty* (see Rahn 1998; W. E. Miller and Shanks 1996).

In the case of learning, a somewhat different dynamic is at work. As the citizen duty results in table 2 show, a far smaller percentage of citizens has internalized campaign-related learning norms than voting norms (25 versus 70 percent). Thus—as is also the case with increasing numbers of younger citizens indifferent toward voting—the reform task here is not just removing disincentives but creating incentives.[6]

Interestingly, the most visible recent reforms—both those already adopted and those still under discussion—purport to increase voting and/or learning by reducing institutional barriers (e.g., the motor-voter bill), increasing public confidence in the political process (e.g., campaign finance reform), or increasing the likelihood of an educationally valuable issues debate (e.g., free TV time for candidates). Such reforms have obvious promise but just as obviously leave unaddressed certain disincentives associated with these barriers.

Institutional Barriers

The national "Motor Voter" law passed in 1993 reduced the registration barrier significantly (see chapter 8), but it does not increase incentives to go to the polls once registered. Similarly, former *Washington Post* reporter Paul Taylor's "Free Time for Straight Talk" effort (also described in chapter 8) increased the supply of useful information available to citizens in 1996. But in context, the audience was not large. Audience sizes and impacts of free television programming remain subject to situational fluctuation because, while the reform creates learning opportunities, it does not directly address the usually limited incentive to acquire political information.[7]

Off-Putting Candidate Behavior

Public perceptions that certain candidate practices are distasteful are potential barriers to some voters' participation.[8] Though the evidence is mixed, some of it suggests that practices like attack advertising may shrink the electorate (e.g., Ansolabehere and Iyengar 1995; but note the counterargument in Rosenstone and Hansen 1993 and other caveats in Bartels's initial chapter in this volume and in chapter 8). Attitudes do affect behavior, and potential voters often insist that their distaste for political practices like attack ads is one of the reasons why they "tune out and stay home" (e.g., Brack 1994). Inconclusive research notwithstanding, it is entirely reasonable to expect that a political spectacle that comes to seem either unsavory or irrelevant can erode interest, weaken the sense of civic duty, and discourage the learning and voting behavior associated with each.

Those seeking to increase public confidence and/or political participation therefore should, and usually do, take evidence of public displeasure with any aspect of electoral politics into account.[9] They should also take note of the public's reform priorities. Polls show, for example, that the public supports campaign finance reform, and it is often seen as an essential way to restore public confidence in the political process (as in the Report of the Task Force on Campaign Finance Reform; see Alexander et al. 1997).[10] But campaign finance practices are only one of several features of candidate behavior that troubles citizens and evidently are not the most important.

The final 1996 Markle survey found that campaign finance reform ranked no higher than third in importance to a random national sample on a list of desirable political changes.[11] When asked which two of seven options for changing future campaigns would make the biggest positive differences, respondents put two other changes in candidate behaviors in the top two places: "more honesty and information from the candidates" (57 percent)[12] and "less negative campaigning" (35 percent). Other possible improvements, such as campaign finance reform (25 percent), higher voter turnout (23 percent), a shortened campaign season (19 percent), more informative media coverage (18 percent), and a third party with a real chance to win (20 percent), generated significant but substantially less popular support, as the poll support percentages in parentheses indicate.[13]

The implication of these results for reform is not that campaign finance reform efforts should be abandoned but that additional attention should be directed to those higher-ranking changes that might have even greater short-term impacts on public confidence and thus a greater chance of reducing participation disincentives. Passage of reform legislation along the lines of the McCain-Feingold bill might reduce the influence of monied interests, but it would not address either the candidate evasion or the negativity topping the list of things citizens apparently find most off-putting about campaigns. The First Amendment prevents forcing candidates to be honest, positive, and informative, as citizens want. But if these citizen priorities prove durable, they should motivate greater elite, media, and foundation attention to reform ideas like the voluntary codes of candidate conduct and the candidate accountability, "stand-by-your-ad" proposals currently among the reforms emphasized by the Alliance for Better Campaigns.[14]

Citizen Mobilization

In considering reforms intended to give citizens incentives to learn and vote, I find it useful to distinguish between "situational" and "socialized" incentives. Situational incentives are things that happen, by accident or design, to attract attention, stimulate interest, and thus, at least potentially, increase learning and voting during particular campaign seasons. Voter mobilization is situational in this sense. Voters have often been mobilized in potentially quite significant though unroutinizable and time-bound ways by such attention-getting personalities as John F. Kennedy, Ronald Reagan, Ross Perot, Colin Powell, and Jesse Ventura as well as by anxiety-provoking circumstances like economic crises.

More relevant to reform, though still subject to situational variance, are routinizable events like presidential candidate debates. Debates have been regular features of the landscape since 1976 but still involve campaign-specific decisions (such as the one barring Perot from participation in 1996) that potentially affect the magnitude of learning and voting in particular years. From the standpoint of stimulating interest and possibly participation, barring Perot was arguably a mistake.

Other potentially routinizable events, which are much closer to traditional understandings of mobilization, include the (recently diminished) efforts of political parties, particular candidate campaigns, social movements, and interest groups to mobilize citizens via get-out-the vote and voter-education efforts in particular years. The value of such mobilization was convincingly demonstrated in a recent series of field experiments involving some 30,000 eligible voters in New Haven, Connecticut. Using "mild" nonpartisan exhortations to vote, Gerber and Green (1999) found that face-to-face contacts increased turnout by about 7 percentage points, leaflet distributions generated an increase of 5 percentage points, and a series of mailings yielded an increase of 1.5 percentage points. The value of partisan mobilization techniques was also impressively illustrated by the "unprecedented" and unexpectedly successful labor mobilization of "tens of thousands of union households" that defeated Proposition 226 in the June 1998 California primary (Burkins 1998, A20). (If successful, the proposition would have forced unions to get written permission from their members before spending dues money on politics.) Even some of labor's conservative Republican critics, able practitioners of the same techniques, were said to have been impressed with the effectiveness of a union campaign that featured a massive grassroots mobilization of 659,000 phone calls, contacts by precinct walkers of more than 600,000 union members and their families, visits to 18,000 work sites, more than 500,000 pieces of mail sent to union households, the use of television ads linking the proposition to conservative, antiunion outsiders, and the identification of some 24,000 new activists who were to be used in a campaign to register new voters in union households in the fall campaign.

These examples make the point that both nonpartisan and partisan mobilizations can achieve impressive results. Nonpartisan reformers intent on increasing the American people's civic engagement clearly should make much greater use of mobilization strategies. And their messages should attempt to capitalize on socialized incentives like civic duty.

Civic Duty

If, as public-choice theorists argue, citizens can expect few tangible rewards from investing time and effort in civic activities (see Riker and Ordeshook 1968; Downs 1957), the fact remains that for many the psychic rewards of learning and voting exceed the costs (Fiorina and Peterson 1998, 175). Civic duty, the internalized feeling of obligation to participate that punishes nonparticipation with guilt and rewards participation with relief from guilt or enhanced self-worth from "doing one's duty," is a product of political socialization. It is, in the language introduced previously, a socialized incentive whose intrinsic power to motivate participation (it "delivers" millions of voters to the polls every national Election Day, regardless of situational incentives) can be evoked and potentially strengthened by mobilization.

Table 2 shows that civic duty in the United States is voting centered (70 percent volunteered it as the principal civic duty), with learning far behind at 25 percent.

It is unrealistic to expect presidential campaigns to do the basic work of instilling a sense of political obligation. That is primarily the business of families and schools. But it is clear from evidence introduced earlier that mobilization techniques can increase voter turnout, and it is likely that civic duty sentiment can be more effectively harnessed for this purpose.

The American Citizens Foundation

Virtually all present campaign mobilization efforts that reach a scale grand enough to move the masses are partisan or interest group efforts. Missing is any kind of institutionalized, large-scale, nonpartisan, publicly and/or charitably (i.e., non–special interest or nonpartisan-interest) financed, citizen-and-political system-centered, advertising and mobilization program. Interestingly, Gerber and Green's New Haven mobilization experiments were strictly nonpartisan in character, and many of the people with whom they spoke "expressed pleasant surprise that we were not an advocacy group" (1999, 22).

It is reasonable to expect that routinized civic-duty signals, some packaged like the most effective commercial or political advertising, some in the form of personal and telephone contacts, others involving distribution of leaflets and mass mailings, all sponsored by an established nonpartisan agency able to finance some activities and to solicit volunteer assistance for others (e.g., civic groups like the League of Women Voters for canvassing in local areas), could inspire more supportive behavior than is now almost accidentally evoked by the purely partisan spectacle.

In the aftermath of the 1988 presidential campaign, the Markle Commission on the Media and the Electorate proposed such an entity, the American Citizens Foundation—a permanent, not-for-profit, nonpartisan organization devoted to campaign-related research, education, and mobilization. The commission recommended various techniques to increase public engagement with presidential campaigns and elections (Buchanan 1991, 157–59). Here, I offer my own assessment of how the work of such an entity could be organized to maximum effect.

I envision three distinguishable target groups, each posing different motivational problems, requiring different communication strategies, and representing very different degrees of difficulty and prospects for success.

The first and most promising target for mobilization is the nonvoting fraction of the 70 percent who already recognize the duty to vote and the smaller 25 percent who identify learning as part of citizen duty (only a portion of whom, we may presume, actually bother to inform themselves). Their dutiful sentiment might be tapped, and the incidence of supportive behavior increased, with little more than a regularly scheduled "call to prayer" of the civically faithful and guilty alike, in the form of television spots and other communications that artfully praise those who learn and vote, implicitly stigmatize those who do not, and offer the latter redemption at the polls. Gerber and Green (1999, 21) speculate that nonpartisan appeals like those used in New Haven are effective because they have the credibility of public service messages: "People who believe in the importance of electoral participation are inspired by messages that encourage them to go to the polls, much in the same way that periodic blood donors are inspired by Red Cross appeals." Extrapolating from their own mobilization research expenses and their experimental findings, these authors estimate that using the most cost-effective technology to reach all 150 million registered U.S. voters would cost about $75 million (a tiny fraction of total campaign spending in 1996) and generate an increase of 4 percentage points in voting-age population turnout.

The second and third target groups—disengaged eighteen- to twenty-four-year-olds and older citizens who profess neither voting nor learning as citizen duties—can both be regarded as largely unsocialized and therefore extraordinarily difficult and expensive to mobilize. Yet they are sufficiently dissimilar that very different approaches to attracting their participation are required.

As noted earlier, spectacles like debates spark interest among the young, and unconventional leaders like Minnesota Governor Jesse Ventura have been able to attract unusually large numbers of young voters to the polls (Page 1998). The music industry's 1990 launching of the nonpartisan, nonprofit Rock the Vote organization, which sponsored television ads by such stars as Madonna and Ice-T exhorting young people to register and vote (Harrington 1992), may share some credit with the targeted appeals of the 1992 Clinton-Gore campaign for helping to spark the highest eighteen- to twenty-four-year-old turnout since 1972, 38 percent. But absent compelling issues and novel candidates, youthful turnout dropped back below 30 percent in 1996.

The cost of mobilizing this group in the future will be very high. Gerber and Green found that personal canvassing had far less effect on younger voters than on older voters, resulting in much greater expense per youthful vote ($30.60 versus $8.20). This age group, weakly socialized at best[15] and put off by traditional politics and politicians, is clearly better mobilized by atypical voices and compelling events than by generic exhortations to vote. Recent evidence suggests that their civic impulses tend more toward volunteerism than voting (Crowley 1999). An American Citizens Foundation cannot ignore youthful nonvoters. But their current interests and attitudes suggest that future efforts to engage them could most profitably focus on promoting and publicizing an expanded array of nonpartisan opportunities for community service, whose appeal and value is demonstrated by the success of such ventures as the federal Americorps program. Such an approach may do more in the long run to increase their aggregate civic engagement—including voting—than an immediate expansion of efforts like Rock the Vote.

Finally, chronically disengaged older adults—a group best represented among W. E. Miller and Shanks's (1996, 69) "Post–New Deal generation" that came of age during the turmoil of the 1960s and 1970s and which replaced a much more civically engaged generation that came of age before Franklin Roosevelt and the New Deal—may be the hardest of all to reach. Still, two uses can be made of this group of citizens that might indirectly help to strengthen the civic motivation of others and eventually help to attract a small fraction of middle-aged nonvoters. The first is as an advertised emblem of American democracy's most lamentable recent failure, a nearly forty-year decline in national voter turnout largely attributable to this group, with emphasis on the costs both to these nonparticipants and to the political system. The second is as the focus of a few experimental demonstration projects intended to discover and publicize what works and what it takes to reach and inspire some of the unlikeliest voters in America. We don't presently know how to accomplish either goal, but one mission of an American Citizens Foundation should be to help us learn.

NOTES

1. Rosenstone and Hansen (1993, 150) disagree: "Despite the surface appeal of the idea that Americans have turned off and tuned out of politics, there is in fact no evidence that popular participation in elections constitutes a display of public confidence (or lack of it) in the political system." They attribute turnout decline to lack of mobilization, a point revisited in the reform section. Miller and Shanks (1996, 69) explain declining turnout this way: "[G]enerational differences in voting rates had translated into a continual national decline in turnout because of the demographic machinery of generational replacement." This finding plus abundant parallel evidence of the "steep erosion of support for the American political community among younger generations" (Rahn 1998, 3) strongly suggest the need to redesign civics education and to revitalize other agents of political socialization, such as political campaigns.

2. Interestingly, the 1952–96 NES data plotted by Bartels (figure 8) in this volume appear to contradict these findings. Of the three campaigns surveyed by both Markle and the NES, only in 1992 did both find an increase in interest. Otherwise, Markle found small increases in both 1988 and 1996, while NES data show decreases in those campaign years. Why the discrepancy? One likely reason is question wording. Markle used a simple, ahistorical question: "How interested are you in presidential politics? Use a 10 to 1 scale where 10 means you are very interested, and 1 means you are not at all interested." The NES takes a more complex, campaign-specific, and comparative approach: "Some people don't pay much attention to political campaigns. How about you? Would you say that you have been very much interested, somewhat interested, or not much interested in the political campaigns so far this year?" This measure seems likely to yield lower interest scores for several reasons. First it "legitimizes" not paying attention (i.e., "some people don't pay much attention . . .") and thus may invite expressions of inatten-

tion and disinterest, especially among those at the lower end of the interest scale. Second, by including the "so far this year" language, the NES item implicitly invites the respondent to use subjectively more interesting past campaigns as criteria for assessing interest in the current campaign, which seems more likely than the simpler, ahistorical Markle language to elicit adverse judgments about current campaigns. Finally, the NES three-category response format offers less opportunity to discriminate between lower levels of interest and outright disinterest than the Markle ten-point scale. I consider it likely that virtually any campaign will spark some uptick in interest as Markle measured it, if only because of massive media attention, which is enough to suggest the potential of campaigns as vehicles for addressing regime-support problems, the point made in the text. Clearly, however, the greater the interest, the greater the potential for influencing regime-supportive attitudes and behavior. And the NES data, which show Labor Day to Election Day increases in interest in just four of twelve campaigns since 1952, suggest that however they are measured, big increases in interest after Labor Day are rare. The important question, addressed later in this chapter, is how consistently higher levels of mass public interest might be encouraged.

3. Other requisites of system viability exist as well. For an interesting effort to explicate them, see Lehman 1992.

4. To avoid unintended priming or framing effects, this question preceded in the interview schedule the questions dealing with interest in politics and the importance of voting.

5. Campaigns that are able, like 1992's, to induce more people than usual to vote and to learn (see table 2) reinforce pro-voting and pro-learning attitudes that are intrinsically regime enhancing and supportive. If the theory holds, then several such campaigns in succession should significantly improve the trend lines on the regime-support variables. Table 2 shows that 1992, with higher turnout and a higher incidence of issue position learning than the previous and succeeding campaigns, also generated significantly greater interest than did 1988 and 1996.

6. The irony is that an increasingly well educated population (Holmes 1994; Rosenstone and Hansen 1993, 214) has seemingly erected an invisible psychological fire wall preventing any substantial political learning (Sniderman 1993). For an argument that this phenomenon amounts to a "trained incapacity" rooted in the political culture, see Buchanan 1996, 21–37.

7. The timetables of campaigns and elections do not always perfectly correspond to the ripening and deciding of major public policy questions, which can create at least temporary learning incentives for citizens (e.g., economic anxiety in 1992). In 1996, for example, the most important policy signals emanated from the budget dispute that led to government shutdowns and preceded the presidential campaign. The experience of 1996 teaches that while all campaigns generate many candidate proposals, not every campaign can be expected to produce major policy signals. Maximal public use of an innovation like free TV time is likely to vary with voters' feelings of an urgent '92-style "need to know."

8. Campaigns that some (but not all) individuals find to be irritating, off-putting, or otherwise unsatisfying for whatever reason arguably reduce the expres-

sive or psychic (Fiorina and Peterson 1998, 175) value of participation below its cost, thus discouraging both participation and supportive sentiment. Similarly, issue discussion subjectively perceived as evasive or marginal with respect to urgently felt public priorities may reduce the instrumental value of participation below its costs by sparking either alienation or judgments of irrelevance, thus discouraging it and foreclosing its attitudinal impacts. The alienation factor may well be augmented by media overemphasis on conflict and negativity (see Capella and Jamieson 1997; Lichter and Noyes 1995). The 1996 campaign also illustrates another problem: campaigns not augmented by circumstantial incentives (e.g., economic anxiety, the novelty of a Perot-style candidacy) may strike many people as boring; these campaigns do not alienate but also do not stimulate interest or participation.

9. This is true despite the task force report's general inclination to question the reality of certain publicly perceived failings of the electoral process.

10. A recent *New York Times*/CBS News poll, for example, found that 75 percent of the public believed that "many public officials make or change policy decisions as a result of money they receive from major contributors"; 50 percent believed fundamental changes were needed; and 39 percent felt the system needs to be completely rebuilt (Clines 1997). Interestingly, when asked "Whose attempts to buy influence bother you the most?" the largest plurality, 45 percent, identified foreign governments. Only 25 percent identified "American special interest groups" and just 21 percent selected "wealthy people." Though Americans support reform, in the aggregate they are not as bothered, especially by domestic influence-buying, as many academic, media and political critics seem to be.

11. Survey respondents were asked: "As you think about what you like and dislike about this year's campaign, which ONE of the following changes, if any, do you think would do MOST to make things better in future elections? . . . And which change, if any, would be your second choice?" The question was part of a survey done for the Markle project by Princeton Survey Research Associates between October 21 and November 2, 1996. Thirteen percent did not respond or said they were satisfied with the process as it is (N = 936; margin of error = ± 3 percent; total exceeds 100 percent because of multiple responses).

12. On a related note, an open-ended 1996 Markle survey question asked, "What would you say presidential candidates should do in a campaign to help voters make a good voting choice?" The three most frequent responses were, in order, "be truthful" (30 percent); "avoid mudslinging/negative campaigning" (14 percent); and "explain/clarify stands on issues" (13 percent).

13. Citizen priorities might well differ if people were more fully aware of the nuances and implications of the campaign finance system. But it seems imprudent to ignore the wishes of those whose support can greatly improve the chances for reform. Lack of enthusiastic public support is one important reason why campaign finance reform has languished in Congress.

14. The alliance is a public interest group, directed by Paul Taylor, that seeks to "improve elections by promoting voluntary, realistic standards of campaign conduct, discourse and coverage." (See issue briefs 2 and 3 in the alliance's informa-

tion kit, available at 529 14th Street NW, Suite 320, Washington, DC 20045.) Another interesting effort to combat attack advertising was that of the Annenberg Public Policy Center, University of Pennsylvania, which during the 1998 midterm election campaigns sponsored a series of thirty-second commercials on CNN that amounted to "attack ad[s] against dirty campaigning." The effectiveness of this experiment has not yet been assessed (Stout 1998).

15. The findings and arguments of such scholars as Miller and Shanks (1996) and Rahn (1998) point to a clear generational failure of socialization among younger citizens with respect to voting and learning.

REFERENCES

Alexander, Herbert E., Janet M. Box-Steffensmeier, Anthony J. Corrado, Ruth S. Jones, Jonathan S. Krasno, Michael J. Malbin, Gary Moncrief, Frank J. Sorauf, and John R. Wright. 1997. *New Realities, New Thinking: Report of the Task Force on Campaign Finance Reform.* Citizens' Research Foundation, University of Southern California.

Almond, Gabriel A., and Sidney Verba. 1963. *The Civic Culture: Political Attitudes and Democracy in Five Nations.* Princeton, N.J.: Princeton University Press.

Ansolabehere, Stephen, and Shanto Iyengar. 1995. *Going Negative: How Political Advertisements Shrink and Polarize the Electorate.* New York: Free Press.

Bartels, Larry M. 1996. "Uniformed Votes: Information Effects in Presidential Elections." *American Journal of Political Science* 40:194–230.

Bartels, Larry M. 1997. "How Campaigns Matter." Unpublished manuscript, Princeton University.

Beiner, Ronald, ed. 1995. *Theorizing Citizenship.* Albany: State University of New York Press.

Berelson, Bernard R., Paul F. Lazarsfeld, and William N. McPhee. 1954. *Voting: A Study of Opinion Formation in a Presidential Campaign.* Chicago: University of Chicago Press.

Brack, Reginald K., Jr. 1994. "How to Clean Up Gutter Politics." *New York Times,* December 27, A15.

Brady, Henry E. 1998. "A Review of the Markle Presidential Election Studies." Unpublished manuscript, University of California, Berkeley.

Buchanan, Bruce. 1991. *Electing a President: The Markle Commission Research on Campaign '88.* Austin: University of Texas Press.

Buchanan, Bruce. 1995. "A Tale of Two Campaigns." *Political Psychology* 16:297–319.

Buchanan, Bruce. 1996. *Renewing Presidential Politics: Campaigns, Media, and the Public Interest.* Lanham, MD: Rowman and Littlefield.

Buchanan, Bruce. 1997. "Presidential Campaign Quality: What the Variance Implies." Paper presented at the annual meeting of the American Political Science Association, Washington, DC.

Buchanan, Bruce. Forthcoming. *Presidential Campaigns and American Democracy: Context, Quality, and Change.* Baltimore: Johns Hopkins University Press.

Burkins, Glenn. 1998. "Union Win on California Dues-Notification Issue May Offer Successful Strategy for Fall Elections." *Wall Street Journal,* June 4, A20.

Cappella, Joseph N., and Kathleen Hall Jamieson. 1997. *Spiral of Cynicism: The Press and the Public Good.* New York: Oxford University Press.

Chambers, William Nisbet, and Walter Dean Burnham, eds. 1975. *The American Party System: Stages of Development.* 2nd ed. New York: Oxford University Press.

Clark, Harold D., and Alan C. Acock. 1989. "National Elections and Political Attitudes: The Case of Political Efficacy." *British Journal of Political Science* 19:551–62.

Clines, Francis X. 1997. "Most Doubt a Resolve to Change Campaign Financing, Poll Finds." *New York Times,* April 8, A1.

Converse, Phillip E. 1964. "The Nature of Belief Systems in Mass Publics." In *Ideology and Discontent,* ed. David E. Apter. Glencoe, IL: Free Press.

Craig, Stephen C. 1993. *The Malevolent Leaders: Popular Discontent in America.* Boulder, CO: Westview.

Crowley, Elizabeth. 1999. "More Young People Turn away from Politics and Concentrate Instead on Community Service." *Wall Street Journal,* June 16, A28.

Dahl, Robert A. 1956. *A Preface to Democratic Theory.* Chicago: University of Chicago Press.

Delli Carpini, Michael X., and Scott Keeter. 1996. *What Americans Know about Politics and Why It Matters.* New Haven: Yale University Press.

Dionne, E. J. 1991. *Why Americans Hate Politics.* New York: Simon and Schuster.

Downs, Anthony. 1957. *An Economic Theory of Democracy.* New York: Harper and Row.

Easton, David. 1965. *A Systems Analysis of Political Life.* New York: Wiley.

Easton, David. 1975. "A Re-Assessment of the Concept of Political Support." *British Journal of Political Science* 5:435–57.

Fair, Ray C. 1978. "The Effect of Economic Events on Votes for President." *Review of Economics and Statistics* 60:159–72.

Finkel, Steven E. 1985. "Reciprocal Effects of Participation and Political Efficacy: A Panel Analysis." *American Journal of Political Science* 29:891–913.

Finkel, Steven E. 1987. "The Effects of Participation on Political Efficacy and Political Support: Evidence from a West German Panel." *Journal of Politics* 49:441–64.

Finkel, Steven E., and John G. Geer. 1998. "A Spot Check: Casting Doubt on the Demobilizing Effect of Attack Advertising." *American Journal of Political Science* 42:573–95.

Fiorina, Morris P., and Paul E. Peterson. 1998. *The New American Democracy.* Boston: Allyn and Bacon.

Gerber, Alan, and Donald Green. 1999. "The Effects of Canvassing, Leafleting, and Direct Mail on Voter Turnout: A Field Experiment." Paper presented at the annual meeting of the Midwest Political Science Association, Chicago.

Ginsberg, Benjamin, and R. Weissberg. 1978. "Elections and the Mobilization of Popular Support." *American Journal of Political Science* 22:31–55.

Harrington, Richard. 1992. "Musicians Aim to Rock Youth Apathy at Polls." *Austin (Texas) American-Statesman,* April 27, B8.

Hibbing, John R., and Elizabeth Theiss-Morse. 1995. *Congress as Public Enemy.* New York: Cambridge University Press.

Hibbs, Douglas A. 1982. "President Reagan's Mandate from the 1980 Election: A Shift to the Right?" *American Politics Quarterly* 10:387–420.

Holbrook, Thomas M. 1996. *Do Campaigns Matter?* Thousand Oaks, CA: Sage.

Hunter, James D., and Daniel C. Johnson. 1997. "A State of Disunion?" *Public Perspective* 8:35–38.

Iyengar, Shanto. 1980. "Subjective Efficacy as a Measure of Diffuse Support." *Public Opinion Quarterly* 44:249–56.

Junn, Jane. 1991. "Participation and Political Knowledge." In *Political Participation and American Democracy,* ed. William Crotty. New York: Greenwood Press.

Katz, Joseph, and Robert Kahn. 1978. *The Social Psychology of Organizations.* 2d ed. New York: Wiley.

Key, V. O. 1966. *The Responsible Electorate: Rationality in Presidential Voting, 1936–1960.* Cambridge: Harvard University Press.

Kiesler, Charles A. 1971. *The Psychology of Commitment: Experiments Linking Behavior to Belief.* New York: Academic Press.

Lehman, Edward W. 1992. *The Viable Polity.* Philadelphia: Temple University Press.

Leighley, Jan. 1991. "Participation as a Stimulus of Political Conceptualization." *Journal of Politics* 53:198–211.

Lemann, Nicholas. 1998. "America Right and Left." *Atlantic Monthly,* April, 103.

Lewis-Beck, Michael, and Tom Rice. 1992. *Forecasting Elections.* Washington, DC: CQ Press.

Lichter, S. Robert, and Richard E. Noyes. 1995. *Good Intentions Make Bad News: Why Americans Hate Campaign Journalism.* Lanham, MD: Rowman and Littlefield.

Lijphart, Arend. 1997. "Unequal Participation: Democracy's Unresolved Dilemma." *American Political Science Review* 91:1–14.

Lipset, Seymour M., and William Schneider. 1987. *The Confidence Gap.* Rev. ed. Baltimore: Johns Hopkins University Press.

Luttbeg, Norman R., and Michael M. Gant. 1995. *American Electoral Behavior, 1952–1992.* 2d ed. Itasca, IL: Peacock.

Miller, Arthur H. 1974. "Political Issues and Trust in Government: 1964–1970." *American Political Science Review* 68:951–72.

Miller, Warren E., and J. Merrill Shanks. 1996. *The New American Voter.* Cambridge: Harvard University Press.

Nie, Norman H., Jane Junn, and Kenneth Stehlik-Barry. 1996. *Education and Democratic Citizenship in America.* Chicago: University of Chicago Press.

Page, Clarence. 1998. "An Independent Streak: Generation X Does Vote, but Not Like Mom or Dad." *Austin (Texas) American-Statesman,* November 12, A15.

Patterson, Thomas E. 1993. *Out of Order.* New York: Knopf.

Pew Research Center for the People and the Press. 1998. *Deconstructing Distrust: How Americans View Government.* Washington, DC: Pew Research Center for the People and the Press.

Polsby, Nelson W., and Aaron Wildavsky. 1996. *Presidential Elections.* 8th ed. New York: Free Press.

Princeton Survey Research Associates. 1997. *The 1996 Markle Election Watch Surveys: A Report on the Findings.* Princeton, NJ: Princeton Survey Research Associates.

Rahn, Wendy M. 1998. "Generations and American National Identity: A Data Essay." Paper presented at the Annenberg Center workshop on Communication in the Future of Democracy, Washington, DC.

Rahn, Wendy M., John Brehm, and Neil Carlson. 1997. "National Elections as Institutions for Generating Social Capital." Paper presented at the annual meeting of the American Political Science Association, Washington, DC.

Rahn, Wendy M., Brian Kroeger, and Cynthia Kite. 1993. "The Etiology and Attitudinal Consequences of the Public's Mood." Paper presented at the annual meeting of the International Society of Political Psychology, San Francisco.

Riker, William H. 1982. *Liberalism against Populism.* Prospect Heights, IL: Waveland.

Riker, William H., and Peter C. Ordeshook. 1968. "A Theory of the Calculus of Voting." *American Political Science Review* 62:25–42.

Rosenstone, Steven J., and John Mark Hansen. 1993. *Mobilization, Participation, and Democracy in America.* New York: Macmillan.

Rousseau, Jean-Jacques. 1968. *The Social Contract.* London: Penguin.

Schattschneider, E. E. 1960. *The Semi-Sovereign People: A Realist's View of Democracy in America.* Fort Worth, TX: Harcourt Brace Jovanovich.

Shaw, Daron. 1995. "Strong Persuasion? The Effects of Campaigns in U.S. Presidential Elections." Ph.D. diss., University of California, Los Angeles.

Sniderman, Paul M. 1993. "The New Look in Public Opinion Research." In *Political Science: The State of the Discipline II,* ed. Ada W. Finifter. Washington, DC: American Political Science Association.

Stout, David. 1998. "Group Fights Attack Ads with Its Own." *New York Times,* October 29, A22.

Sundquist, James L. 1983. *Dynamics of the Party System: Alignment and Realignment of Political Parties in the United States.* Rev. ed. Washington, DC: Brookings Institution.

Teixeira, Ruy A. 1992. *The Disappearing American Voter.* Washington, DC: Brookings Institution.

Thompson, Dennis. 1970. *The Democratic Citizen.* Cambridge: Cambridge University Press.

Verba, Sidney. 1961. *Small Groups and Political Behavior.* Princeton: Princeton University Press.
Verba, Sidney, and Norman Nie. 1972. *Participation in America.* New York: Harper and Row.
Verba, Sidney, Kay Lehman Schlozman, and Henry E. Brady. 1995. *Voice and Equality: Civic Voluntarism in American Politics.* Cambridge: Harvard University Press.
Zaller, John R. 1992. *The Nature and Origins of Mass Opinion.* New York: Cambridge University Press.

Chapter 8

Campaign Reform: Insights and Evidence

Report of the Task Force on Campaign Reform

Larry M. Bartels, chair	Marion R. Just
Henry E. Brady	Stanley Kelley, Jr., senior adviser
Bruce Buchanan	Thomas E. Mann
Charles H. Franklin	Samuel L. Popkin
John G. Geer, vice chair	Daron Shaw
Shanto Iyengar	Lynn Vavreck, executive director
Kathleen Hall Jamieson	John R. Zaller

This report presents the views of fourteen scholars in the fields of electoral politics, voting behavior, and political communication about what is wrong with the American campaign process and how to fix it. We write both as scholars and as citizens. As citizens, we share many of the same concerns and aspirations voiced by other participants in the current public debate about campaign reform. Like the vast majority of our fellow citizens, we wish contemporary political campaigns were more informative, more engaging, and more edifying.

At the same time, we believe that our scholarly expertise gives us both a distinctive perspective and a distinctive responsibility. Rather than simply reporting our wishes or prejudices, we aim to build our analysis upon current scholarly understanding of campaigns and elections. In some cases, that scholarly understanding leads us to endorse familiar conclusions in the broader public debate on campaign reform. In other cases, it leads us to revise or even reject conventional assumptions about the nature of contemporary political campaigns or the likely impact of proposed reforms. In still other cases, the scholarly evidence is much less clear—or much less directly relevant to the concrete, practical questions we wish to address; in those cases, we have attempted to provide an honest reading of the available evidence and its implications, pushing our arguments and conclusions as far as the evidence seems to warrant, but no farther.

Despite the diversity of our political views, intellectual perspectives, and professional experiences, we find ourselves in substantial agreement with respect to both diagnoses and prescriptions. We believe that the American electoral process works better than its critics and much of the public seem to recognize. At the same time, we view the manifest dissatisfaction of millions of citizens with contemporary campaign practices as a serious problem for our representative democracy, especially insofar as it may reduce their willingness to participate in the electoral process. Thus, we aim to address both the real failings and the perceived failings of contemporary political campaigns. We are convinced that relatively modest changes in the incentives and behavior of campaigners, journalists, and ordinary citizens could produce appreciable improvements in campaign practice, a better informed and more engaged electorate, and a healthier political system.

Campaigns and the Electoral Process

Whereas many observers seem to imagine that voters wake up on Election Day and mark their ballots for the candidate with the most charisma, the smartest pollster, or the slickest ads, academic research suggests that election outcomes are primarily determined by more substantial factors. In presidential elections—where candidates are invariably well-known, almost always able campaigners, and usually quite conventional representatives of their parties' traditional platforms and interests—voters are powerfully guided by long-standing partisan loyalties, and election outcomes depend mostly upon national economic and political conditions.[1] As one recent summary statement (Zaller 1998, 186) put it, "the public stays focused on a bottom line consisting of peace, prosperity, and moderation." If vote intentions change significantly during the course of a presidential campaign, they are likely to change in ways that reinforce rather than override these basic structural forces (Berelson et al. 1954; Patterson and McClure 1976; Bartels 1992; Finkel 1993; Gelman and King 1993; Holbrook 1996).

At the national level, congressional election outcomes, too, are largely the result of such basic political factors as long-term partisan realignments, erosion in the sitting president's supporting coalition in midterm election years, national economic conditions, and shifts in the ability of incumbents to insulate themselves from these and other national trends (Kramer 1971; Cox and Katz 1996; Jacobson 1997). In many congressional districts (and in many state and local races), incumbents' preexisting advantages with respect to experience, accomplishments, and name recognition are strongly reinforced by the inability of their challengers to attract the attention and money they need to run credible campaigns; but once a credible campaign has been mounted by each side, the election outcome seldom hinges on campaign tactics or technologies.

Of course, to argue that political campaigns seldom determine the outcomes of elections is not to suggest that they are insignificant. For one thing, imbalances in the quantity or quality of campaign effort *are* sometimes decisive, especially in close contests. And even when they are not, the balance resulting from equally vigorous and effective campaign efforts on both sides should not be mistaken for ineffectiveness. In that sense, campaigns certainly do matter.

What is more important, for our purposes, is that campaigns matter in a variety of ways that transcend the immediate efforts of the campaigners themselves to maximize their vote shares. Campaigns provide prospective voters with the information necessary to recognize and interpret the state of the country and the candidates' backgrounds and records—and the motivation necessary to act on that information (Key 1966; Bartels 1988; Popkin 1991; Johnston et al. 1992; Alvarez 1997). They also stimulate democratic deliberation and communication between citizens and their political leaders—and create a record of public commitment and popular legitimation which significantly influences the behavior of winning candidates after they take office (Pomper with Lederman 1976; Fishel 1985; Brady 1988; Budge and Hofferbert 1990). It seems obvious that these functions will be better served by campaigns that are substantive, truthful, and engaging than by campaigns that are vacuous, misleading, and dull.

Even more broadly, campaigns and elections represent the primary contact most ordinary citizens have with the democratic process. Thus, informative, engaging campaigns may play an important role in generating and replenishing interest in and support for the political system more generally. For example, one scholarly study of the social impact of campaigns measured small but significant increases in social trust during the 1996 election season, especially among well-informed citizens and those contacted by one or both political parties during the course of the campaign. Trust in government and political efficacy also increased between the pre- and post-election readings. The authors concluded that improvements in the campaign process, including better candidates and more energetic efforts at partisan mobilization, could lead to "higher levels of political efficacy, more trust in government, and greater social solidarity" (Rahn et al. 1997, 30–31).

The flip side of these potential benefits is that vacuous, distasteful campaigns may contribute to a gradual depletion of interest in and support for the political system more generally (Buchanan 1996). Thus, it is troubling to note that campaigns and the electoral process are currently held in such low public regard. Prospective voters say they are dissatisfied with the candidates offered by the two major parties, and many claim they would prefer a multi-party system, or no parties at all. The proportion of citizens who say elections make the government responsive to their concerns has declined sharply over the past three decades. So has the proportion who bother to turn out to vote.

Our response to these troubling trends is to propose reforms of the campaign process that we believe would elevate the prevailing level of campaign discourse, provide more and better information to prospective voters, and make it easier and more rewarding for citizens to participate in the electoral process. We offer our proposals with some hope that they might increase, ever so slightly, the probability that the best candidate will win. But we offer them also with some hope that better political campaigns might produce a healthier public regard for the American democratic process.

Campaign Participants and Their Goals

Our proposals for reform are directed toward the behavior of three distinct sets of actors in the electoral process: candidates and their staffs and supporters; political journalists, editors, and executives in the print and electronic media; and the broad American public. We believe that campaigners, the media, and the public all bear significant responsibility for the current state of political campaigns, and that successful campaign reform will require changes in the behavior of all three groups. At the same time, we recognize the practical limitations of pious exhortation as a force for change. Thus, our aim is to propose reforms that respect the motivations and incentives that seem to animate the current behavior of each of these actors—or that seem capable of altering existing motivations and incentives in potentially constructive ways.

The primary goal of candidates for political office is and, we believe, always will be to get themselves elected. However much they may be motivated by important political principles—and we do not doubt that most candidates *are* motivated by political principles as well as by personal aims—they can do little to further their political principles *or* their personal aims unless they win access to the levers of political power. Thus, while we see nothing wrong with reminding candidates of their responsibilities to the democratic process, we do not expect such reminders to produce significant changes in their behavior, unless the candidates themselves are convinced that those changes are consistent with their own political interests.

In some cases, we argue that candidates have been mistaken about the nature of the electoral imperatives they face. For example, we can find no rational basis for the conviction of many candidates and campaign consultants that vitriolic attack ads are necessary—or even especially effective—for getting elected. Indeed, we believe that the importance of campaign spending more generally is often greatly exaggerated, and that politicians with a realistic understanding of the role of money among the constellation of factors influencing election outcomes would simply not bother to pursue it with quite the dogged zeal that has offended so many critics of the contemporary political process.

In other cases, we propose changes in regulations or institutions that we believe will produce new, more powerful incentives for candidates to behave responsibly. For example, "ad watches" by journalists and independent observers may encourage candidates to forego misleading advertising by increasing the potential political cost of attempting to deceive the public.

The goals of journalists, editors, and media executives reflect a more complicated mix of economic, political, and professional concerns. Close observation of reporters and editors in their day-to-day working lives suggests that they are animated primarily by professional norms of "newsworthiness"—and by the rewards bestowed upon those whose work is recognized by their peers as good journalism, including prestigious assignments, prominent bylines, and Pulitzer Prizes (Gans 1979; Zaller 1997). The incentives of editors and producers presumably reflect a greater admixture of economic considerations along with journalistic considerations, while publishers and media executives feel even more responsibility to pursue profits along with professional prestige.

Given these goals, the news media should be expected to embrace proposed reforms that promise to enhance—or at least not to diminish—their professional standing and profitability. Here, even more than with candidates, realistic reformers must suggest positive incentives for change, since almost all serious efforts to compel good behavior by the media are likely to be stymied by the legal and cultural protections of the free press enshrined in the First Amendment.[2] Thus, our focus will be on potential changes in media behavior that seem likely to benefit the democratic process while doing little or no damage to the profitability of media enterprises—and that seem broadly consistent with existing journalistic norms.

Fortunately, while journalists' views about the nature of good journalism are elaborately developed and strongly held, they are not entirely impervious to revision or reinterpretation. Thus, we hold out some hope of persuading the reporters, editors, and producers who cover political campaigns to reconsider certain aspects of their current practice. For example, the corrosive cynicism of much press coverage of the electoral process serves no important journalistic purpose; neither does the excessive focus of much press coverage on tracking polls, campaign organizations and tactics, and other day-to-day campaign trivia. Political reporters could succeed better, even by the light of their own professed journalistic values, by simply reorienting their coverage to focus more on what one of them once sagely referred to as "the real campaign" (Greenfield 1982).

Individual citizens are, we assume, also animated by a variety of goals—most of which have nothing to do with politics. Would-be campaign reformers sometimes seem to assume that citizens are naturally civic-minded and eager to consume political information which politicians and the mass media somehow fail to supply. We can discern little evidence in support of this view. Instead, we assume that most citizens most of the time are rather uninterested in politics, and that politicians and the mass media must and do adapt their behavior accordingly.

One important implication of this assumption is that reformers' recommendations, too, should be adapted to the way citizens actually gather and use political information. For example, despite the fitfulness of their civic attention, many citizens have well-developed attitudes toward specific public figures, political parties, and social groups, and these attitudes can help them navigate the complexities of the political world—but only if that world is appropriately structured to make intelligible the connections between preexisting attitudes and new information. Thus, we recommend that campaign-related communications should be required to include clear identification of their sponsors, so that citizens can use the credibility of the sponsor as a cue in evaluating the credibility of the message. As Samuel Popkin (1991, 236) put it, "If voters look for information about candidates under streetlights, then that is where candidates must campaign, and the only way to improve elections is to add streetlights. Reforms can only make sense if they are consistent with the gut rationality of voters."[3] This is not to suggest that citizens cannot be led to take a greater interest in the democratic process, or to pay more attention to campaign discourse. Indeed, many of our recommendations are intended to have precisely those effects. Nevertheless, the starting point of our analysis is a realistic conception of the place of politics in contemporary American life, and our criticisms and proposals for change reflect that conception.

Despite the manifest limitations of the public's civic virtue, tens of millions of ordinary citizens do participate in the electoral process in a variety of ways, and for a variety of reasons. Many have internalized a sense of civic duty, and will be motivated to engage in campaign activities (ranging from information-seeking to propagandizing to turning out at the polls) to the extent that those activities are encompassed in their understanding of what it means to be a "good citizen." Many also view campaigns and elections as entertainment, and they will be motivated to engage in campaign activities to the extent that those activities are interesting and fun. Finally, many citizens see the electoral arena as a forum for pursuing substantive political interests by electing "their" candidate or candidates; for these citizens, campaign activities will be attractive insofar as they seem likely to increase the likelihood that the "right" candidates will actually be elected.

The public can affect the incentives of other actors—the mass media and the candidates—by responding to their behavior in positive or negative ways. For example, citizens in their role as consumers might choose to patronize media outlets that provide detailed, truthful, and politically balanced news coverage—either because they find that sort of coverage interesting and entertaining, or because they want to be well-informed when they go to the polls. On the other hand, citizens in their role as voters might punish candidates who engage in illegitimate campaign tactics, if they recognize those tactics and feel moved to discourage them.

In short, candidates want to win elections, journalists want to exercise their craft, media executives want to earn profits, citizens want to be informed and entertained and see the "right" candidate win. It is worth noting that elevating the democratic process doesn't appear anywhere on this list of the primary goals of campaign participants. That is not to suggest that candidates, the media, or ordinary citizens are indifferent to the condition of American democracy. Most candidates, journalists, and citizens no doubt attach great value to our democratic system, and would make heroic sacrifices, if necessary, to preserve it. The problem is that heroic individual sacrifices are seldom necessary. Instead, the reality is that most of us most of the time can make only imperceptible contributions to the collective maintenance of a healthy democratic system. Given that fact, intellectually honest (and politically realistic) would-be reformers must suit their strategies to their circumstances, offering a variety of relatively modest, distinctly unheroic proposals that, taken together, might produce a perceptible improvement in the quality of our electoral process. That is the aim of this report.

Campaign Advertising

Paid advertisements, especially on television, make up the bulk of political discourse in many contemporary election campaigns. Campaign reformers and ordinary citizens sometimes bemoan that fact, regretting the brevity, tone, and apparent vacuousness of campaign ads. While we recognize the limitations of spot ads as a mode of campaign discourse, we also recognize that ads convey a good deal of substantive political information in simple, sometimes powerful terms—especially to citizens who are relatively uninterested in politics and insulated from other modes of political communication.[4] Broadly speaking, academic research suggests that television ads have gotten a bum rap in the debate about campaign reform.

Critics of modern political advertising are especially critical of the "negativity" of many campaign ads. This complaint has become increasingly common in recent years, as campaigners have become increasingly inclined to "go negative."[5] However, academic research suggests that campaigners and critics alike have been seriously confused about what is at stake in the "negativity" of political advertising.

We believe that the focus of critics on the "negativity" of campaign advertising is largely misplaced, reflecting and perpetuating a general conflation of the important distinction between ads that are characterized as "negative" because they are contentious and argumentative, challenging claims about the records, characters and platforms of opponents, and ads that are characterized as "negative" because they are nasty, inaccurate, or unfair. Indeed, we believe with Kathleen Jamieson and her colleagues (Jamieson, Waldman, and Sherr 1998) that labeling ads as "positive" or "negative" is more confusing than illuminating, and that journalists and scholars alike would do well to jettison that distinction in favor of a more straightforward categorization of ads as "advocacy" (focusing on the candidate's own qualifications), "attack" (focusing on the opponent's failings), or "contrast" (containing explicit comparisons between the candidate's own qualities, record, or proposals and the opponent's).

Ads that attack political opponents can be high-minded or low-down, blunt or subtle, repulsive or engaging, fair or unfair. And ads that trumpet a candidate's own character, record, or platform can be just as deceptive and illegitimate as those that attack opponents. As Jamieson and her colleagues put it (Jamieson, Waldman, and Sherr 1998, 1), "Most reporters and many scholars mistakenly assume that 'attack' is both 'negative' and 'dirty'. Conflating these terms obscures the important distinction between legitimate and illegitimate attack and minimizes the likelihood that the deceptions found in supposedly 'positive' discourse will be probed."

For their part, campaigners have often seemed to assume that they must "attack each other because that is the best way to maximize their own support" (Ansolabehere and Iyengar 1995, 143). However, a significant body of academic research casts serious doubt upon this conventional wisdom. A recent essay by Richard Lau and Lee Sigelman (1998) provided a comprehensive review of the relevant scholarly findings. Lau and Sigelman analyzed the results of over 40 different studies comparing the effects of what we refer to here as "attack" and "advocacy" ads, including some studies based on survey data and others based on laboratory experiments. Only 15 of the 51 relevant findings from these studies supported the notion that attack ads are more effective than comparable advocacy ads. Twenty-four others produced the opposite conclusion, while 12 showed no clear differences in effectiveness between attack ads and advocacy ads (Lau and Sigelman 1998, 13–14). Thus, taking the scholarly evidence as a whole, there is simply no support for the seemingly widespread and confident belief of candidates and campaign consultants that attack advertising is especially effective. While it is certainly possible to cite dramatic cases in which candidates have "gone negative" and won, many others have "gone negative" and lost, while still others have done as well or better running ads advocating their own qualifications and proposals. In most circumstances, the evidence suggests, candidates could moderate or simply give up vitriolic attack advertising and suffer no real electoral harm.

Should they give it up? The evidence on this point is a good deal less clear. There is little doubt that citizens dislike negative advertising,[6] and some reason to fear that it has deleterious social consequences.[7] However, several careful independent content analyses have shown that attack ads actually contain *more* issue information than advocacy ads, that they are more likely to offer evidence in support of the claims they put forward, and that they are less likely to be misleading (West 1997; Jamieson, Waldman and Sherr 1998; Geer in this volume). Thus, it is by no means clear that reducing "negativity" would make campaigns more substantive, as many critics assume.[8]

In our view, attack ads may be quite legitimate, if they draw attention to genuine, politically relevant weaknesses in an opposing candidate's performance or platform. On the other hand, distortions, exaggerations, and outright lies are never legitimate campaign tactics, whether they focus on a candidate's own supposed strengths or on an opponent's supposed flaws. Thus, campaign reformers should be interested in deterring or neutralizing the impact of misleading ads, regardless of whether those ads are "positive" or "negative" in tone. And journalists and reformers should not add unnecessarily to public cynicism by simplistically equating conflict and contention with "negativity" and "dirty politics."

Candidates, in the business of trying to win elections, may often be tempted to skirt the bounds of truthfulness. By one count, about half of the advertisements in the 1996 presidential campaign contained at least one misleading statement (Jamieson et al. 1996b). We believe that the most effective way to reduce the prevalence of misleading advertising is to increase the perceived cost to sponsoring candidates or groups of distortions, exaggerations, and outright lies in campaign ads. That is the aim of "ad watches"—systematic efforts by journalists to monitor and report on the truthfulness of campaign advertising.

"Ad watches" can have two distinct sorts of positive effects. First, and most obviously, prospective voters may attend to press scrutiny of campaign ads and be led to discount misleading claims that they would otherwise have accepted as true. Less obviously, but probably more importantly, ad watches may deter campaigners from sponsoring misleading ads in the first place. If ad watchers are credible and their standards are clear, campaigners may well try to avoid being publicly rebuked for sponsoring "misleading" or "unfair" ads. Thus, even if prospective voters are seldom attentive or responsive enough to be inoculated against specific misleading claims, ad watches may be valuable because they restrain campaigners, inducing them to curb, verify, and condition their claims in anticipation of potentially embarrassing press scrutiny.

There is considerable controversy in the academic literature regarding the actual impact of ad watches on viewers,[9] with some studies reporting positive effects (Cappella and Jamieson 1994; Greer 1997), some reporting negative effects (Ansolabehere and Iyengar 1995, 133–42; O'Sullivan and Geiger 1995), and some reporting mixed results (Pfau and Louden 1994; Just et al. 1996, 125–34). This area should be a high priority for further scholarly research. In the meantime, however, it seems likely to us that careful, clearly presented ad watches *can* mitigate the impact of misleading campaign discourse, especially by deterring campaigners from airing misleading or unfair ads. For that reason, we urge journalists to continue their use of ad watches in national, state, and local campaigns.

Of course, authoritative ad watches cannot be done on the cheap; public accusations of deception should be made with great care, and careful research and reporting on the factual accuracy of ads requires a significant investment of time and expertise. Serious ad watching is especially difficult for small newspapers and broadcast outlets attempting to cover important national, state, and local races with modest reporting staffs. While we recognize this obstacle, we believe that the importance of the task warrants some redirection of journalistic resources away from more traditional political coverage. Some organizational ingenuity may also make it possible for media outlets to use their limited resources more efficiently—for example, by pooling or syndicating ad watches on a nationwide or statewide basis.

We also believe that there is room in the political process for increased scrutiny of candidates' ads and other campaign discourse by independent experts and non-partisan groups, either in conjunction with journalists (for example, as quoted sources in "ad watch" stories) or in their own right (either as watchdogs in predefined issue areas or in response to specific instances of misleading advertising). Obviously, such independent scrutiny will be newsworthy in proportion to the credibility of the source, with nonpartisan experts deserving more attention from the press and the public than generalists and partisans, other things being equal. While it is important for journalists to exercise good news judgment in granting media access to outside "experts," we believe that independent ad watches are a significant untapped resource for hard-pressed news outlets, and for the political process more generally.

In recommending the continued use of ad watches, we urge practitioners to guard against two potentially important pitfalls. First, sustained media attention may inadvertently amplify the impact of misleading campaign ads. Kathleen Jamieson and others have argued that this sort of "boomerang" effect is especially likely when the actual content of an ad is reproduced without being appropriately "contextualized." Jamieson (1992) has suggested a "visual grammar" for televised ad watches utilizing a variety of audio and visual cues (for example, showing the ad playing on a visible television set rather than full-screen, and interrupting the audio and visual tracks to insert the analyst's observations) to impose a critical distance between the audience and the ad. Ansolabehere and Iyengar (1995, 142) have gone even further, urging journalists to refrain completely from showing actual ads in the course of their ad watches. We endorse the use of these precautions in order to minimize the risk of inadvertently amplifying the impact of misleading ads.

Second, there is a very real danger that a relentless focus by the press on inaccuracies in campaign ads will simply reinforce the cynical belief of many citizens that campaigns are "all lies" and politicians are not to be trusted. The most important way to mitigate this danger is for ad watchers to provide an appropriate sense of perspective—distinguishing, for example, between illegitimate, unfair ads and those that are merely critical of an opponent's platform or record, and between significant distortions on one hand and trivial exaggerations and technical inaccuracies on the other.

Another way for journalists to minimize the danger that ad watches will simply generate increasing political cynicism among readers and viewers is to move beyond simple fact-checking box scores to provide broader evaluations and interpretations of ads as the centerpiece of political discourse in many modern campaigns. Too often, when ad watches do go beyond evaluating the veracity of specific claims on a point-by-point basis, they do so by providing what amount to miniature movie reviews or strategic critiques. What we have in mind is a more substantive focus. What is the candidate promising, and to whom?[10] How might he or she fulfill that promise? With what impact on the lives of prospective voters? By asking questions like these, journalists could use ad watches as springboards for broader, more engaging coverage of what is at stake in political campaigns.

In effect, we are arguing that good news coverage of campaign ads should be of a piece with good news coverage of campaign discourse more generally. Journalists should not hesitate to point out when the claims contained in television ads are false or unfair—but they should apply the same standard equally to direct mail appeals, speeches, debates, interviews, and other forms of campaign discourse. Of course, good journalists do scrutinize speeches and debates for accuracy and fairness—but they seldom do so with the force and clarity that distinguish the best examples of the ad watch genre.

On the other hand, no self-respecting news outlet would limit its coverage of a speech or debate to pointing out false or unfair claims. Then why should coverage of advertisements begin and end with fact checking? Our view is that it shouldn't. Instead, ad watches should be one element in a broader effort to report on ads as campaign discourse. By inventing new ways to present such coverage, journalists could significantly improve the quality of the information citizens take into account in casting their votes, while minimizing the danger of exacerbating public cynicism by focusing only on the most questionable or controversial examples of campaign advertising.

Media Coverage

The press serves an indispensable and constitutionally protected role in American politics and society. In political campaigns, print and broadcast news outlets are the primary institutions aspiring to present disinterested information to a mass audience about the candidates, their biographies and dispositions, their records and plans, and the accuracy and implications of their statements in speeches, ads, and debates. Reporters, columnists, and editorial writers help readers make sense of political information by providing analysis and interpretation of the strategies and motives of political actors. The press also performs an important watchdog role in the political process, uncovering and disseminating information about the powerful that would otherwise be unavailable to ordinary citizens. Because these activities are crucial to the functioning of democracy in a country that is large and diverse, and in which most citizens have many competing demands on their time, it is vitally important that they be performed diligently and well. Often, they are.

Indeed, one important byproduct of the dazzling reach and diversity of the contemporary mass media is that citizens probably have more and better access to political information than at any previous time in American history. C-SPAN provides extensive unmediated coverage of campaign events; *National Journal, Congressional Quarterly,* and other specialized print and electronic publications offer sophisticated news and analysis, as do "The NewsHour" on PBS and national editions of the *New York Times* and the *Wall Street Journal;* anyone with access to the Internet can retrieve an almost unimaginable wealth of information from news outlets, government agencies, campaign organizations, and civic groups. For competent consumers interested in learning about politics and public affairs, this is the best of times.

Unfortunately, times are much less good for citizens who happen to be unwired, uncabled, unsubscribed, or simply unmotivated to seek out political information. Media organizations are not in the business of fostering democracy, and the commercial and professional constraints of the business they *are* in sometimes seem to leave them unwilling or unable to provide political news in a form suited to engaging and informing ordinary citizens.

The most dramatic manifestation of this mismatch between organizational goals and civic ideals is the current state of local television news programs. With newspaper readership and audiences for traditional network news programs both declining markedly, many citizens now get the bulk of their news from local television; but intense competition for ratings has squeezed more and more of the serious news content out of local news programs, leaving public affairs as a minor item between crimes, fires, sports, and weather—and political campaigns all but invisible. Even newspapers and network news programs, keen on surviving their own competitive pressures, have increasingly come to view political news as an unaffordable luxury. Thus, for example, the 1996 presidential campaign received much less network news coverage than previous presidential campaigns, because producers, reporters, and network executives decided that it was too "boring" to boost their ratings (Jamieson et al. 1996b).

Hence, our first and most obvious recommendation for media coverage of political campaigns is that the media should cover political campaigns. Elections are important democratic events, and they deserve significant attention from the mainstream media as well as more specialized media, whether or not they seem likely to boost ratings or circulation.

Having said that, we see two main problems with the campaign coverage the media do provide. First, journalists insert themselves too aggressively between candidates and citizens, prosecuting a professional agenda that is, in some respects, distinctly different from the agendas of these primary actors in the electoral process. Second, and relatedly, journalists focus too much on hoopla, the "horse race," campaign tactics, and the ephemera of day-to-day campaigning, and too little on political substance.

These failings of contemporary campaign coverage are rooted in the professional values and competitive pressures of contemporary journalism. Nevertheless, we believe that they are subject to significant alteration, with little or no harm either to journalistic values or to the economic self-interest of the news industry. On one hand, we doubt that readers and viewers are as enamored of conventional campaign coverage as journalists and news executives seem to suppose; indeed, much of it is coverage that only a journalist could love. On the other hand, we are confident that the news media can find new models of campaign coverage that better reconcile their professional values with the broader needs of the political system.

For one thing, contemporary patterns of campaign news coverage are of fairly recent vintage. As recently as 1960, campaign coverage was a good deal more substantive, with more focus on policy issues and on the candidates' speeches, platforms, and records. However, the dazzling success of Theodore White's inside accounts of "The Making of the President," the rise of television news as a potent social force, and changes in the broader American political culture all contributed to the evolution of a new style of campaign journalism—more independent, more interpretive, and more focused on the mechanics of the campaign process.

The most systematic documentation of these shifts has been provided by Thomas Patterson (1993), who analyzed various aspects of media coverage in presidential campaigns from 1960 through 1992. Patterson's data trace a substantial decline over this period in purely descriptive election coverage, with a corresponding rise in interpretive news stories.[11] They also indicate that the tone of campaign stories has increasingly been set by journalists themselves, rather than by candidates or other partisan news sources (113–14).

One unfortunate byproduct of the movement of journalists to center stage is that the tone of campaign coverage has become increasingly cynical. We respect the aspirations of reporters and media commentators to be (and be seen as) sophisticated interpreters of the political process rather than common carriers of campaign news, and "watchdogs" rather than "lap dogs." However, we believe that too many reporters and commentators have gone beyond skepticism—a healthy journalistic value—to adopt stances of corrosive political cynicism. Campaigns and policy debates are portrayed purely as contests of political self-interest, with little or no room for any broader public purpose, even as a byproduct of political competition. In the words of one recovering veteran of the campaign press corps (Taylor 1996, 40), "Television pundits have become our most powerful explainers of political life, and their deepest message to the masses is that if they wish to be in the know, they too should watch the circus from above, with a smirk and a swagger."

Another byproduct of the growing centrality of journalists in their own campaign coverage is that policy issues have receded from view, while hoopla, controversy, and campaign tactics have become much more prominent. For example, front-page stories in the *New York Times* were twice as likely to frame the election in terms of a "game schema" in 1992 as in 1960, while policy frames declined from more than 50 percent of all campaign stories to less than 20 percent over this period (Patterson 1993, 73–74). At the same time, the issue coverage that does still appear has focused less on enduring policy problems and more on short-term campaign controversies (146–47). As Patterson (1993, 137) put it, "For reporters, controversy is the real issue of campaign politics."

It is not difficult to understand why journalists are attracted to controversy—it has both news value and dramatic value. Stories about Dan Quayle's quarrel with Murphy Brown, a fictional television character, are both easier to produce and more likely to attract public attention than stories about Quayle's positions on proposed legislation affecting the family as a social unit. The problem for journalists is to use campaign controversies as springboards for reporting on the real substance of politics and political careers, rather than treating them as self-contained episodes, entertaining but essentially trivial.[12] In the case of Murphy Brown, some journalists solved that problem very successfully, while others were much less successful in transcending the superficial attention-getting aspects of Quayle's speech and the subsequent controversy.

Verbal gaffes and internal campaign squabbles may also provide attention-getting hooks, but will usually be of little genuine importance in their own right. Journalists should use them as starting points for more general descriptions and assessments of the candidates' platforms and management styles.

By the same token, "horse race" coverage can and should be informative as well as entertaining. We have no desire to rid campaign reporting of attention to strategy, tactics, or polls. But attention to these aspects of the campaign should not displace attention to substantive issues, and substantive issues should not be framed primarily in strategic terms. There is some value simply in telling people which candidate is ahead, especially in multi-candidate races where strategic voting is often required to concentrate support on candidates who are both attractive and electable. Moreover, sophisticated "horse race" coverage can help prospective voters figure out which side they should be on by reporting the composition of the competing candidates' supporting coalitions, and can highlight connections between the campaign and the broader political process by reporting on *why* patterns of candidate support are (or are not) shifting over time. This sort of coverage requires more than superficial reporting of tracking polls and campaign "spin"; but it need be no less entertaining as a result.

Nothing in these suggestions seems to us to conflict with journalists' professional values, rightly understood. Nor do we see any reason to believe that more substantive campaign coverage would be less popular or less profitable than the news media's current fare. Of course, dull rehashes of mind-numbing position papers will do nothing to attract audiences or inform citizens. But intelligent, professional coverage of real politics needn't be like that. The "American Agenda" segments on ABC's "World News Tonight" program offer one useful model of engaging issue coverage within the confines of a conventional news format. "The Choice '96," a two-hour dual biography of candidates Clinton and Dole that aired during the 1996 campaign as part of PBS's "Frontline" series, provides an even more impressive model of political journalism that is both substantive and engaging. By juxtaposing important episodes from both men's lives and careers, "The Choice '96" provided a superb demonstration of the political relevance of candidates' "character," a topic on which conventional journalists have mostly taken their cues from supermarket tabloids; it would have brought professional distinction (and, we suspect, very respectable ratings) to any network news division.[13]

We believe that much of the tedium of conventional campaign coverage reflects the tedium of the situation in which media outlets place their reporters. Many television outlets and major newspapers assign one reporter to each candidate's campaign; these beat reporters travel with "their" candidate, hear him give more or less similar speeches in different locales every day, and gradually learn to see the entire campaign from the perspective of that candidate, his campaign staff, and their fellow reporters. Given these peculiar working conditions, it is hardly surprising that reporters come to attach exaggerated significance to relatively minor campaign events such as verbal gaffes, staff shakeups, and shifting opinion polls.[14]

What is most lacking in this sort of campaign coverage is a sense of perspective—a recognition of the big issues behind the day-to-day events. In order to better develop and convey that sense of perspective, reporters should spend less time traveling with candidates and more time covering other aspects of the campaign, including policy issues, the candidates' records, the roles of parties and interest groups, the flow of campaign money, and the views of ordinary voters. Wire service reports and satellite feeds can provide most of what there is to know about events on the campaign trail, freeing most reporters to spend most of their time on more substantial matters. Reporters with expertise in economics, religion, law enforcement, legislative politics, and many other fields can contribute as much or more than those who have slogged for years through the snows of New Hampshire and the back rooms of local party caucuses.

When reporters do travel with the candidates, their assignments should be rotated frequently. Fresh reporters can bring fresh insights to routine campaign coverage, avoiding the jaded, know-it-all tone that infects too much political news. There is simply not enough scope for candidate-specific expertise to outweigh the disadvantages of "pack journalism" on the campaign beat.

None of this is to suggest that the news media should ignore what candidates have to say in their own behalf. Major news *is* sometimes made on the campaign trail, and when it is, it should be covered accordingly. But that has not been happening even with airplanes full of reporters following the candidates from speech to speech. For example, the average length of presidential candidates' "sound bites" on network television news programs shrunk from 42 seconds in 1968 to less than 10 seconds in 1988 and 1992 (Adatto 1990; Hallin 1994, chap. 7), and the *total* speaking time allotted to each of the major candidates in 1992 by each network's evening news program amounted to only about 20 minutes between Labor Day and Election Day (Center for Media and Public Affairs 1992).

The air time that used to be devoted to presenting the candidates in their own words is now primarily filled by the journalists themselves. As Patterson (1993, 75, 77) noted,

> for every minute that the candidates spoke on the evening news in 1988 and 1992, the journalists who were covering them talked 6 minutes. . . . Election news in the 1960s gave candidates the opportunity to present themselves on their own terms to the voters. Today, journalists do most of the candidates' talking for them.

Doing "the candidates' talking for them" may appeal to journalists' sense of professional self-importance, but there is no evidence to suggest that viewers or readers either need or want their political news to be presented in such a heavily digested form. Indeed, careful comparisons of what candidates actually say and what journalists report suggest that the reporting is in some respects distinctly less edifying than the candidates' own campaign discourse. For example, media coverage of what candidates say is dominated much more by attacks on their opponents than are the candidates' own words—and with much less in the way of supporting arguments or evidence (Jamieson et al. 1996a; 1996b). Given propensities like these, it should, perhaps, not be surprising that journalists are one of the few professional groups currently ranked lower in public esteem than politicians!

One other, quite prosaic change in the behavior of journalists might contribute greatly to citizens' comprehension of the campaign: repetition. Too often, crucial information about the candidates' backgrounds, records, and proposals is presented once and then relegated to the void of "old news." Journalists should recognize that *news* need not be *new* in order to be worth reporting. They should compete with each other not only in providing scoops, but also in providing clever, insightful reiterations of crucial background information.

This sort of repetition may strike reporters, editors, and producers as boring and pointless. But what is old news to the political experts who cover campaigns may not be old news even to fairly conscientious readers and viewers. For example, at the height of the 1992 presidential campaign, 36 percent *of regular newspaper readers* (and an even larger fraction of television news viewers) did not know which of the two major political parties was more conservative, 29 percent did not know which party controlled the House of Representatives, 39 percent did not know which of the major presidential candidates favored more government spending and services, and 35 percent did not know which of the major presidential candidates took a more permissive position on abortion.[15] No doubt, these fundamental bits of political information were presented in passing by most major newspapers during the course of the campaign season, along with many other relevant facts. However, because they were less often reiterated than taken for granted, they failed to penetrate the consciousness of millions of ordinary citizens.

The mismatch in information and interests between journalists and their audiences is especially striking in press coverage of presidential campaign debates, which attract millions of viewers who are only casually interested in politics and, for the most part, inattentive to other campaign events. Research suggests that these debates are a significant learning experience for interested and uninterested citizens alike (Jamieson and Adasiewicz 1999). However, the most prominent theme in the news media's debate coverage—absent some dramatic controversy or verbal gaffe—is often that the candidates "said little that was new." Of course, they said much that was new to significant portions of the debate audience—but little that was new to the political reporters and commentators who had spent months following every twist and turn of the campaign.

Like other professional groups (including professors), journalists are often more intent on impressing their professional peers than serving their actual clientele. American democracy would function better if they could overcome this tendency. They might begin by recognizing that the majority of Americans who are not, like them, politics junkies will often require repeated exposure to important information in order to take it in. Here, too, regular rotation of reporters on the campaign beat could facilitate better reporting.

Focus groups in which journalists watched ordinary citizens react to their news reports could also help them recognize more clearly the interests and needs of their mass audience. For example, journalists who justify their emphasis on the "horse race" by arguing that readers and viewers demand it might well find that impression quite mistaken.[16] Having resisted audience research as a dangerous tool of profit-minded owners, journalists have missed the opportunity to adapt it as a tool for bridging the empathy gap that manifestly separates them from their readers and viewers.

By writing for their actual audiences, rather than for their professional colleagues or for an idealized audience of political junkies, journalists could do a great deal to help ordinary citizens make sense of the electoral process. Along the way, they might improve their circulation and ratings—especially if they can succeed in conveying real substance with clarity and style. Would that be an abandonment of journalistic values?

Candidate Debates

Public debates among competing political candidates have deep roots in American political culture—one need only think of the Lincoln-Douglas debates of 1858 or the Kennedy-Nixon debates of 1960. More recently, debates have become a regular feature of presidential campaigns since 1976, and an increasingly common feature of state and local campaigns as well. We believe that debates can and should be an important source of information in every political campaign.

Campaign debates have two key virtues: they tend to attract larger and more diverse audiences than most other campaign events, and they can provide those audiences with an unusual opportunity to observe the candidates thinking and speaking on their feet, without the protective cocoon of speech writers, briefers, and handlers so ubiquitous in modern political campaigns. We believe it is important for debates to be structured in ways that enhance these two virtues, providing as many prospective voters as possible with as much fresh insight as possible into the strengths and weaknesses of the competing candidates.

The most common obstacle to informative campaign debates is the desire of candidates to minimize their exposure to political risks. Unscripted interaction in a very public setting can lead to political disaster if a candidate is caught short on facts, if his mind wanders, if she loses her cool. Not surprisingly, many candidates—and especially front runners and incumbents—prefer to play it safe, avoiding debates entirely or insisting on bland, predictable debate formats that leave as little as possible to chance. In either case, the result is a missed opportunity for prospective voters.

We recommend that debate organizers attempt, as much as possible, to encourage sustained discussion, direct interaction, and spontaneity. It is possible to imagine a wide variety of informative debate formats, and there is no reason to believe that any one format will suit every candidate—much less every citizen.[17] Experimentation with alternative formats should be encouraged for at least three reasons: to learn more about their practical advantages and disadvantages, to tap a variety of strengths (and weaknesses) of the competing candidates in a more or less even-handed way, and to stimulate public interest in the debates by providing an element of novelty and unpredictability. For example, a combination of traditional moderated debates, "town meetings" of the sort introduced in the 1992 presidential campaign, and free-wheeling direct conversations between the candidates might provide an attractive mix of formats within any single race.

How might such debates be organized, despite the natural reluctance of the candidates? One way to increase the probability that informative debates will, in fact, occur is to seek clear commitments to debate from the candidates in the earliest stages of the campaign, before their precise tactical interests are clear; among other things, early agreement can eliminate the distracting "debate about whether there will be debates" which too often absorbs so much news time and space. Another useful mechanism for facilitating effective debates is to lodge significant authority over debate arrangements in a neutral commission or other independent body.

At the presidential level, a bipartisan Commission on Presidential Debates was created in 1987 to provide a coherent administrative apparatus for presidential and vice-presidential debates, replacing a more informal system in which competing debate sponsors were sometimes treated as pawns in the candidates' maneuvers for political advantage. Having a single, special-purpose body designated in advance to organize the debates gives that body added legitimacy, and thus added leverage in negotiating debate arrangements with potentially recalcitrant candidates. Unfortunately, the public legitimacy of the Commission's deliberations has been significantly hampered by a widespread perception that it has been dominated by the interests of the established major parties, rather than providing fair representation for individuals and views from all parts of the political spectrum.[18] Thus, we recommend that the existing Commission be significantly revamped or even replaced by a new, more independent debate organizing body capable not only of maintaining the cooperation of both major parties, but also of representing the interests of the broader public.

Perhaps the most consequential decision that must be made by any debate sponsor is which candidates should be invited to participate. Here, we see a powerful tension between the competing values of inclusiveness and coherence. On one hand, providing access to minor-party and independent candidates may stimulate interest in the campaign and inject new issues and ideas into the debate. That is all to the good. On the other hand, participation by minor candidates may reduce and fragment the time and attention available to the major candidates, diluting their best opportunity to convey their perspectives and proposals to the electorate. The dangers on this side of the balance have been vividly demonstrated in early presidential primary season debates, which sometimes include half-a-dozen or more candidates; the resulting scramble for attention has tended to produce dueling sound bites and mock dramatics better suited to professional wrestling than to political discourse. Thus, it seems clear to us that simply providing equal access to every legally qualified candidate will often not be an attractive option for debate organizers.

In some cases, the competing values of inclusiveness and coherence may be nicely satisfied by organizing a separate public debate for minor-party and independent candidates, giving them access to the public and potential influence on the campaign agenda without intruding on the main face-off between the major-party contenders. We urge debate sponsors and the media to explore the possibility of presenting a single, high-profile, open debate in the early stages of each campaign period, followed by a series of debates limited to the major candidates.

At the same time, we recognize that a third-party or independent candidate may occasionally be a sufficiently popular and serious contender to warrant treatment as a "major" candidate by debate organizers. Given the difficulty and importance of this sort of judgment call, it is especially important that decisions to include or exclude specific candidates be made in accordance with clear and reasonable criteria. At the presidential level, the Commission on Presidential Debates has developed an elaborate set of criteria for debate participation, with ballot access, evidence of national organization, poll standings, and judgments by journalists, political professionals, and political scientists all factored into an assessment of whether any given independent candidate has a "realistic" chance of being elected. While these criteria are certainly not unreasonable, we believe they should be further streamlined to emphasize objective indicators rather than subjective judgments.

Of course, even a prestigious, independent sponsor may have difficulty getting candidates to agree on a satisfactory debate schedule and format. In some cases, legal compulsion may be appropriate. In particular, we believe that participation in public debates should be an explicit condition for receiving public campaign funding, as it already is in New Jersey and some other states. At the presidential level, where most candidates take public matching funds during the primary season and full public funding during the general election campaign, they should be required by law to participate in public debates organized by the Commission on Presidential Debates or its successor, with the commission exercising full control over the timing and format of those debates. If and when public funding is extended to congressional candidates, they should be similarly bound.

Even in the absence of compelling legal authority, informal pressure may go a long way toward encouraging candidates to participate in genuine and effective public debates. The press can and should draw public attention to any efforts by candidates to duck debates or manipulate debate formats. Political opponents and independent citizens can and should do likewise. The potential effectiveness of such efforts is symbolized by the career of "Chicken George," a heckler in a chicken costume whose persistent public ridicule helped soften the intransigent stance of an incumbent president in debate negotiations in the fall of 1992.

As with ad watches, free air time, and campaign funds, the potential value of meaningful candidate debates is especially great in congressional, statewide, and local campaigns, where alternative sources of information about the candidates, their records, and their proposals are likely to be in especially short supply. Simply by providing prospective voters with an opportunity to see the competing candidates side by side, a televised debate may help to transform a one-sided race dominated by incumbency or party affiliation into a two-sided race in which prospective voters recognize real, flesh-and-blood alternatives. Thus, television stations, newspapers, and civic groups should strive to ensure that debates occur in every campaign at every electoral level, and that as many prospective voters as possible have opportunities to see and hear those debates. In addition to broadcasting and rebroadcasting the debates in accessible time slots, the news media should enhance their status as important public events by publicizing, previewing, and recapping them.

A good example of how to conduct an effective state-level debate was provided by the 1998 California gubernatorial primary debate. The debate included all of the major Republican and Democratic candidates, it was broadcast and rebroadcast statewide in both English and Spanish, and it was previewed and recapped in print and broadcast news. The audience for its first airing exceeded the usual audience in its time slot. The questions asked by reporters focused on the substantive issues facing California, and the candidates responded to those questions with detailed answers (Jamieson 1998). While we have no evidence demonstrating that the debate informed the citizens of California or stimulated them to vote in the primary, it cannot have hurt. And in an election year tagged by some observers as the year of the apathetic citizen, turnout in the California primaries was actually up.

Free Air Time

One of the most salient and significant attempts to improve the quality of campaign discourse in the 1996 election cycle was the provision by several broadcasters of "free air time"—television spots offered to candidates without charge to speak directly to prospective voters. As former political journalist Paul Taylor (1996, 41), one of the main proponents of free air time, put it, "the candidates must talk into the camera the whole time. No surrogates. No journalists. No opponent. No unseen narrator. No tricky visuals. Just the candidate talking straight to the citizens—democracy's most sacred transaction."

Taylor and his colleagues in The Free TV for Straight Talk Coalition convinced several broadcasters to provide free air time to presidential candidates on an experimental basis in 1996. For example, the Fox network provided the two major presidential candidates with ten back-to-back one-minute segments in prime time to address specific questions; CBS and NBC provided fewer but longer segments during regular news programs, including *CBS Evening News, CBS This Morning,* and *Dateline;* CNN, PBS, and UPN aired six two-and-a-half-minute statements by each candidate on topics of their own choosing on alternate evenings. While these diverse and rather fragmentary provisions of free air time fell well short of the Coalition's ambitious goal—nightly two- to three-minute segments airing simultaneously on all broadcast channels—they represented a symbolically important precedent, and an opportunity to assess the potential impact of more extensive free time provisions in future election cycles.

An analysis by the Annenberg Public Policy Center (Adasiewicz et al. 1997) found that the actual content of free time presentations mostly satisfied the expectations of free time advocates. Candidates spent about 90 percent of their free time focusing on policy issues, they largely avoided presenting criticisms of their opponents without supporting evidence, and they used less inflammatory language than in their paid advertising. Moreover, available data provide no indication that broadcasters' ratings declined when they aired free time segments. Finally, while the free time experiment generated relatively little press attention or public notice, the 22 percent of registered voters who reported seeing at least one free time segment considered them slightly more informative than either debates or paid ads.

Despite these positive aspects of the 1996 free time experiment, the reactions of campaigners and broadcasters were less than enthusiastic. For example, Dole media consultant Alex Castellanos called free time "fairly inconsequential. It was a distraction, it was insignificant." (Perhaps not surprisingly, Dole did not even bother to use some of his allotted free time.) Meanwhile, CBS news anchorman Dan Rather complained that the candidates "regurgitated sound bites they had been using since last summer. What we got was a lot of waffling and sidestepping. The free time just took up time that otherwise would have been given over to good journalism" (Annenberg Public Policy Center 1997, 14, 17).

The lukewarm response of broadcast executives, campaigners, and journalists to the call for voluntary free air time has led some reformers to propose a more ambitious plan, in which radio and television stations would be required to provide free air time to political candidates as a condition for retaining their licenses to broadcast. In one version of this proposal, broadcasters would simply have to make a fixed amount of free time available to all qualified candidates for offices within their listening or viewing area. An alternative plan (Ornstein et al. 1997) would create a "broadcast bank" to which each broadcast outlet would be required to "donate" two hours of prime advertising time in each two-year election cycle. The Federal Election Commission would issue vouchers to qualifying candidates and parties which could be redeemed for free advertising time on any radio or television station, so long as the ads adhered to specified format restrictions. (Ads would have to be at least one minute in length, and feature the candidate as the sole speaker.) Stations whose free time was oversubscribed would be reimbursed from the broadcast bank at prevailing market rates, while those whose free time went unclaimed would pay into the broadcast bank, again at prevailing market rates.

These and other proposals to impose some of the costs of campaign broadcasting on the owners of radio and television stations seem to reflect three disparate ideas. First, many observers argue that broadcasters have slighted their long-standing obligations under the Communications Act of 1934 to serve the "public interest." Second, the decision by Congress to grant free access to the digital broadcast spectrum to existing broadcasters, rather than auctioning off this multi-billion dollar resource, seems to some to invite additional public interest obligations.[19] Third, frustration at the failure of Congress to pass major campaign finance reforms has led some observers to see free air time—whether imposed by Congress or by the FCC—as an alternative mechanism for reducing the importance of money in political campaigns.

The notion that providing free air time to political candidates would somehow reduce the prevalence or importance of paid political advertising seems dubious to us. Even if broadcasters donated $500 million worth of free air time per election cycle, as the most ambitious plans propose, we see no reason to doubt that candidates would be eager to buy as much additional advertising time as their budgets allowed. In our view, the primary value of free air time would be to supplement the minimal access to the public airwaves currently available to underfunded candidates, not to displace paid political advertising by those candidates who can afford it.

We share the view that broadcasters' public interest obligations under the Communications Act include an obligation to devote significant attention to political campaigns, and that providing direct access for candidates to communicate with citizens is an important part of that obligation. While we recognize the potential value of format restrictions—among other things, as a way to elevate the visibility and civic importance of free air time by distinguishing it from paid ads on one hand and news coverage on the other—we suspect that a more flexible system involving a variety of formats, including statements by candidates, debates, and interviews, would be most likely to appeal to broadcasters, candidates, and citizens. We strongly favor the development and expansion of a flexible system of free air time, either through widespread voluntary efforts by broadcasters or through specific mandates by Congress or the FCC.

Despite their various limitations, the voluntary free air time experiments conducted in 1996 demonstrated a good deal of potential, both in attracting significant cooperation from broadcasters and in providing prospective voters with substantive campaign discourse. We believe that further efforts along the same lines in future election cycles could be even more successful. Free air time can and should become an important routine feature of American political campaigns.

We especially encourage further experimentation with free air time in state and local campaigns. So far, most of the attention of reformers and broadcasters alike has been focused at the presidential level, where the marginal contribution of free air time to the total flow of campaign discourse is likely to be least important.[20] By contrast, free air time in many congressional and local races could significantly augment prospective voters' stores of information about the records and platforms of the competing candidates—especially under-financed challengers who often struggle simply to penetrate the consciousness of the electorate. By providing every qualified candidate with at least minimal access to the public airwaves, free air time could be a real boon to competitiveness in races currently mired below the threshold of sustained public attention.

Campaign Finance

Observers often complain that the American electoral process is dominated by big money. In our view, however, one of the primary problems with the current American system of campaign finance is not too much spending, but too little, especially by relatively unknown challengers in congressional, state, and local elections. Given the dearth of local political news in contemporary America and the high cost of advertising, serious money is necessary to compete for the attention of potential voters bombarded with propaganda from candidates for a wide array of elective offices—not to mention automobile and yogurt salesmen and innumerable other distractions. The inability of many candidates to raise enough money to mount credible campaigns is a major obstacle to ensuring genuine, energetic electoral competition. Thus, a primary aim of campaign finance reform should be to promote competitiveness by providing all serious candidates with enough money to get a fair hearing, rather than to reduce overall levels of campaign spending.

In order to promote competitiveness in congressional elections, we favor the adoption of a system of partial public funding of congressional campaigns comparable in its general outlines to the system in place since 1976 to subsidize presidential primary candidates. Congressional primary candidates would be offered public matching funds in proportion to their success in raising private money in small individual contributions from within their states or districts, while major-party nominees would be offered significant lump sums for their general election campaigns. However, unlike public funding in general elections at the presidential level, these subsidies would serve as "seed money" to help candidates attract additional private funds, rather than providing a ceiling on total campaign spending.[21]

Public funding of political campaigns is sometimes decried as "welfare for politicians." This perception could not be more mistaken, at least if by "politicians" we mean "incumbent politicians." Far from being the primary beneficiaries of public funding proposals, incumbent politicians have for years been the primary opponents of such proposals, precisely because they consider public funding a serious threat to their substantial existing spending advantage. Regardless of the details of the specific proposal, one important effect of almost any public funding system would be to help level the playing field for challengers to current incumbents. Even if it did nothing to limit the spending of most incumbents, such a system would mitigate some of the worst effects of the current system by assuring serious challengers the resources necessary to mount real campaigns. Thus, it is hardly surprising that public funding of congressional elections has never made significant headway in Congress.

What is more surprising, in view of widespread public concerns about the impact of political money, is that there is presently such modest public support for public funding of campaigns. On one hand, 76 percent of the public say it is a major problem that good people are discouraged from running for office by the high cost of campaigns, and 61 percent say it is a major problem that elected officials spend too much of their time raising money for election campaigns. But at the same time, only 26 percent strongly favor "public funding of all congressional and presidential campaigns, at a cost of about $5 a person" (Princeton Survey Research Associates 1997).[22]

We agree with the public that politicians spend too much time raising money—and that some are even discouraged from trying. As Thomas Mann (1999) put it,

> The money chase . . . structures how elected officials allocate their time, where they travel, who they speak with, and how they deploy their legislative energies. White House documents released during the investigations of fundraising practices of the 1996 Clinton reelection campaign provide sobering documentation of the demands on the time of the President and Vice President (by most accounts willingly met) for fundraising. The impact of the money chase on Capitol Hill is even more striking. . . . Personal accounts of former members illustrate the myriad ways in which life in Congress is shaped by the constant quest for campaign funds.

However, we believe that the way to mitigate this problem is not—as many citizens and even some reformers would have it—to make fundraising ever more onerous, by letting the value of maximum contributions erode with inflation and imposing additional restrictions on candidates and contributors. Instead, we advocate a combination of partial public funding, modest increases in basic contribution limits with subsequent indexing for inflation, and new efforts to plug the two most egregious loopholes in the current system of campaign finance: "soft money" and "issue advocacy."

"Soft money" is a category of funds raised by political parties outside the limitations imposed by federal election law; the intended purpose of "soft money" is to pay for general "party-building" activities and state and local campaigning. What began as a modest channel for legitimate organizational activities has mushroomed in recent years into a major loophole, with the two major parties together raising an estimated $263 million in soft money in 1996—about twelve times as much as they had raised only twelve years earlier. Much of that money went to finance the broadcasting of so-called "issue advocacy" ads which were clearly intended to benefit the parties' presidential and congressional candidates, but which did not fall under federal regulation because they did not "expressly advocate" the election or defeat of specific candidates.[23]

The main attraction of soft money from politicians' point of view—and the main complaint of most observers—is that it can be raised without regard to the contribution limits and disclosure requirements that apply to federally regulated campaign money. To politicians, an undocumented six- or seven-figure contribution from a single wealthy individual or corporation is, not surprisingly, a tempting alternative to long evenings spent speaking at chicken dinners or "dialing for dollars" in search of $1000 contributions. At the same time, one can hardly be surprised that such large, unregulated contributions inflame public cynicism about political corruption, whether or not they actually buy undue influence.

One possible solution to this problem—a solution incorporated in the legislation sponsored by Senators McCain and Feingold and Representatives Shays and Meehan in the 105th Congress—would be to ban soft money altogether by prohibiting national parties from financing any of their activities with unregulated funds, prohibiting candidates for federal office from raising unregulated funds for their parties, and prohibiting state parties from raising or spending unregulated funds in any way that would benefit candidates for federal office. We favor a somewhat less radical solution: imposing reasonable ceilings on soft money contributions and on total soft money expenditures. These reforms would alleviate the most pressing concerns about undue influence and uncontrollable soft money "arms races," while retaining some incentive for parties to invest in activities not tied to specific federal candidates or campaigns.

An even more difficult problem for would-be reformers is to stem the flood of "issue advocacy" ads sponsored by dozens of groups outside the direct control of parties or candidates. These ads, too, escape regulation as long as they do not expressly advocate the election or defeat of specific candidates. Because they are not subject to disclosure requirements it is impossible to tell exactly how large a role they play in contemporary campaigns, but there is no doubt that they are significant. One study (Beck et al. 1997) estimated that at least $135 to $150 million was spent on issue advocacy ads in 1996, and they have played an even more prominent role in some subsequent special election campaigns.

Despite the label, "issue advocacy" ads actually contain relatively little issue content, and despite their technical avoidance of "direct advocacy" they prominently feature candidates' names and images (Beck et al. 1997). Indeed, the main thing that distinguishes them from other campaign ads is their lack of accountability. Because they are not subject to federal disclosure requirements, it is often virtually impossible to attach responsibility for specific ads to the individuals or groups who produced them or paid for them.

While we have no desire to restrict the ability of individuals or groups to publicly express their political views, we do believe that disclosure requirements should apply to election-related communications whether they emanate from candidates, parties, or other individuals or groups. For ordinary citizens, a good deal of the information contained in any political message is conveyed by the identity of its sponsor. Is the sponsor credible or biased? A friend or a stranger? These are reasonable and important considerations in interpreting and assessing political communications—and even more important for purportedly "independent" issue advocacy than for candidate- and party-sponsored communications.

The problem here is that applying disclosure requirements to issue advocacy ads would require some relaxation of strictures on the regulation of political speech that does not constitute express advocacy under the courts' current interpretation. A broader definition of express advocacy as communication that "could only be interpreted by a reasonable person as containing advocacy of the election or defeat of one or more clearly identified candidate(s)" was proposed by the Federal Election Commission, but successfully challenged in federal court as too broad and vague to pass constitutional muster. A less vague but even broader approach would simply define as express advocacy any paid communication with the general public within a specified period (say, 30 days or 60 days) prior to an election if that communication used a candidate's name or likeness. While it is possible that such a definition would encompass some political communications that were genuinely unrelated to the upcoming election, we view this as a small price to pay for the significant increase in political accountability that would be provided by requiring effective disclosure of the sponsorship of all campaign-related communications.

The importance we attach to the principle of accountability also leads us to support proposals to require more timely and effective disclosure of political contributions and expenditures. Perhaps the simplest and most important of these would require political committees operating above some modest threshold of activity to file their reports electronically using specially designed software provided by election agencies. Mandatory electronic filing—and automated Internet posting of the resulting data by election agencies—would greatly speed and simplify the efforts of election officials and observers to monitor the flow of money in the political system.

We do not consider full disclosure a panacea for all the ills of the current system of campaign finance. Nor do we believe that the benefits of fuller disclosure would manifest themselves automatically through diligent scrutiny by prospective voters of every candidate's list of contributors. Just as we expect ad watches to work in significant part through the deterrent effect of elite scrutiny, we expect financial disclosure to work best—and perhaps only—when the news media and political activists do most of the hard work of monitoring, disseminating, and interpreting information about the sources of campaign contributions and "independent" expenditures. This is not simply a matter of "following the money," although that is an important first step; it is also a matter of conveying the *significance* of particular patterns of contributions and expenditures. Are a candidate's big contributors local elites or out-of-state interests? What other candidates or causes have they supported in the past? What has an incumbent done (or not done) in Washington to warrant the support or opposition of the NRA, the NEA, the shipping industry, or local businesses? As with other aspects of the campaign, information about contributions and expenditures will be useful to prospective voters only insofar as it sheds light on broader political concerns about the candidates' records, character, and commitments.

Finally, since no regime of campaign finance regulation can be effective without successful implementation and oversight, we strongly favor a significant increase in the administrative capacity and resources of the Federal Election Commission. The FEC has an extremely difficult mission: to enforce a wide variety of laws and regulations governing the collection and expenditure of campaign funds by monitoring the complex financial transactions of more than a thousand separate campaign organizations (many of which are born, live, and die within a single two-year election cycle) and a vastly larger number of politically active organizations and individuals. The Commission's staff and budget are far from adequate to fulfill that mission. As a result, major violations are often identified months or years after they occur—far too late to influence the outcome of the election—and all but the most serious cases are, in the end, ignored for want of investigative attention. American citizens cannot realistically expect even the limited campaign finance regulations currently on the books to be taken seriously by candidates and contributors as long as the FEC remains what one observer (Clines 1997) has called "the orphaned oversight agency of big-money politics."

Information and Engagement

While news coverage, advertisements, and debates are pervasive aspects of modern electioneering, they are far from being the only important channels for campaign discourse. In America's pluralist democracy, many other organizations—ranging from government agencies to interest groups to non-partisan civic associations—use election campaigns as occasions to inform and engage the citizenry. Their activities both reflect and further stimulate the development of a vibrant national political culture. We applaud those activities, and seek to expand upon the most effective of them.

A few states have long traditions of providing informative pamphlets to prospective voters. These voting guides are typically mailed to registered voters a few weeks before Election Day, and include information about candidates for public offices, initiatives, referenda, and policy issues. In some cases, the voting guide includes a facsimile of the actual ballot, allowing voters to familiarize themselves with the layout of the ballot before stepping into the voting booth. We believe these voting guides serve a very useful purpose, providing moderately conscientious voters with a great deal of relevant information in a very convenient form. We encourage all state and local governments to develop and disseminate voter pamphlets, using as models successful examples like those distributed by the California Secretary of State's office.

Voter guides produced by independent interest groups represent a more controversial source of campaign information. Perhaps the most prominent of these is the Christian Coalition Voting Guide, which differs from quasi-official voter pamphlets like California's not only in being produced by a private organization, but also in being mailed to specific targeted voters rather than to the entire electorate. The Christian Coalition voting guide has been criticized for overstepping the boundary of non-partisanship—indeed, a lawsuit was filed against the group alleging that its activities should be treated as in-kind donations to, or independent expenditures on behalf of, the Republican Party.

While we see no reason to attempt to curtail the efforts of activist groups to inform and persuade perspective voters, it is obviously necessary for both practical and legal purposes to distinguish between non-partisan civic education on one hand and endorsements and propaganda on the other. From the ordinary citizen's point of view, what is crucial here, as elsewhere, is that the source of the information be clearly identified, so that she can treat it with an appropriate degree of confidence or skepticism. Thus, we suggest that all campaign-related communications, regardless of the medium by which they are transmitted, be required to identify prominently the individual or organization sponsoring them. In the case of umbrella organizations ("Americans for a Better America"), the identifying information should include a clear identification of the individuals or organizations—be they corporations, trade associations, labor unions, or other membership groups—that are their primary sources of funding.

Recent technological developments have opened some exciting new avenues for campaign communication, making it possible for prospective voters to collect even more—and more personally relevant—information about political candidates and issues. In particular, the evolution of the Internet as a mass medium has facilitated the provision of much more and better-tailored information than could be disseminated even in the best of the traditional printed voter pamphlets. Given the current limitations of Internet access—particularly among older, poorer, and less-educated citizens—these electronic communication channels cannot yet be thought of as satisfactory replacements for more traditional channels. Nevertheless, they deserve to be further developed and more widely utilized as supplementary channels of political communication, and as investments in the democratic technology of the 21st century.

The best-developed and most impressive of these innovative efforts is by Project Vote Smart, a non-profit, non-partisan group that gathers information on over 20,000 candidates and elected officials and provides that information to the public free of charge over the Internet and by telephone using a toll-free hotline. Project Vote Smart provides information on the biographies, voting records, campaign contributions, issue positions, and performance evaluations by interest groups of all federal officeholders, all governors, and some state legislators, as well as contact information for these public officials and information on the backgrounds and platforms of candidates for office. This information is gathered by full-time staff and student interns. The project is funded through foundation grants and individual contributions, and does not accept funding from corporations, interest groups, or organizations that lobby government at any level.

Project Vote Smart is a powerful and flexible information resource for citizens. For example, prospective voters can monitor the performance of specific elected officials, compare the positions of competing candidates on issues of particular interest, and look for endorsements by trusted interest groups. The project also publishes *The Voter's Self-Defense Manual,* which provides information on government offices and elected officials; *The Vote Smart Web Yellow Pages,* which guides voters through Internet pages focusing on politics and public affairs; and a *Reporter's Source Book* and a *Reporter's Resource Guide* to help journalists get information from elected officials and government employees.

Utilization of Project Vote Smart has been widespread. The web site gets approximately 10,000 candidate record requests a day during campaign seasons, while the telephone hotline gets several thousand calls. Hundreds of newspapers print candidate record reports from the project regularly, and many radio stations use information from Project Vote Smart in regular weekly political reports. The project has also distributed over one million copies of the *Voter's Self-Defense Manual* and more than 5,000 copies of the reporter's resource books (Schmid 1996).

Despite this strikingly successful record of accomplishment, we believe that Project Vote Smart has a great deal of still-unrealized potential. On one hand, connections with other sources of political information should be further developed in order to enhance the role of Project Vote Smart as an information clearinghouse. Internet providers, portals, and media sites should be encouraged to point to Project Vote Smart and other voter information sites (such as the Center for Responsive Politics) during election campaigns. Additional resources should be devoted to organizing information in ways that are likely to be useful to citizens and journalists evaluating campaign events in real time, for example, in the form of ad watches or debate watches. Even more importantly, the sheer existence and richness of this information resource should be more broadly publicized, with widespread advertising and other publicity efforts, especially during campaign seasons.

In addition to advocating innovative efforts to provide information to prospective voters, we support broader, long-term efforts to engage citizens in the electoral process. Since scholarly work on political socialization suggests that political identities and roles are largely molded in childhood and adolescence, we believe that efforts aimed at children are especially promising.[24] Renewed attention to early political socialization seems especially appropriate in light of the sharp declines in regime-supportive attitudes and behavior among those in the "post–New Deal" generation that reached voting age between 1968 and 1992 (Miller and Shanks 1996; Rahn 1998). While the reasons for these declines are by no means simple or clear, there is at least a temporal coincidence, and perhaps a causal connection, between the troubling political disengagement of this "baby boom" generation and the shift following World War II in the content of civic education from an emphasis on "nation-building" to an emphasis on "critical thinking" (Janowitz 1983). Thus, we have some reason to hope that a revitalization of political socialization might contribute to stemming or even reversing in the next generation the declines in electoral participation and attachment to the values of citizenship that have been the distinctive "contributions" of the baby boomers to American political culture.

Because elections are salient, participatory, and easy to understand, they provide a splendid occasion for teaching and encouraging young people to learn and care about the political process more generally, and thus to become competent and engaged democratic citizens. One project in particular has enormous reach in this endeavor—Kids Voting USA. This non-profit, non-partisan organization has branch offices in 40 states and activities in 6,000 schools across the United States, and reaches 5 million students ranging in age from kindergarten through high school. The program enables students to visit official polling sites on Election Day, accompanied by parents or guardians, and cast ballots similar in content to the official ballot. An associated curriculum, including family participation and community involvement, stresses the importance of being informed about election choices and the responsibilities of voting.

The Kids Voting USA curriculum includes exercises in gathering information, thinking critically, and making choices. Homework assignments involve using newspapers as information sources, and sometimes include activities or questions for family members. In-class discussions are sometimes led by community business, political, or civic leaders, and are supplemented by community events such as Kids Voting USA Rallies and assemblies. The general lesson of this curriculum is summed up by the Kids Voting USA slogan: "Voters Rule!"

The effects of this program have been documented by a variety of scholars, including Stephen Chaffee, Bruce Merrill, and Jack McLeod.[25] Survey results of participants and non-participants in the Kids Voting USA program suggest that the program stimulates political learning and discussion among students and their parents, and increases parents' rates of electoral participation by 5 to 10 percent. It also seems to reduce the socio-economic gap among students with respect to interest in public affairs and participation in political activities, and the gender gap with respect to social studies learning and performance in the classroom, as well as generating significant increases in newspaper readership among students participating in Kids Voting USA activities.

We urge the continuation and expansion of programs like Kids Voting USA. We especially encourage partnerships between such programs and the media. Newspapers should be strong supporters of programs like Kids Voting USA which, among other effects, socialize young people to become newspapers readers. In addition to participating in such programs through community activities (for example, by sending reporters and editors to speak in classrooms or at rallies or assemblies), media outlets should consider dedicating portions of their election coverage to attracting young readers and viewers, perhaps through explicit tie-ins with Kids Voting USA activities. Lest such tie-ins seem to demean serious political journalism, we note that elements of campaign coverage that make election news easier for young audiences to digest might well appeal to their elders as well, making both groups more engaged and better informed citizens—and, incidentally, more avid consumers of news both in and out of the campaign season.

Citizen Participation

Perhaps the most common—and most damning—indictments of contemporary American electoral politics is that so few citizens even bother to show up at the polls. While turnout rates among those who are actually eligible to vote are surprisingly difficult to ascertain, the standard calculations of turnout as a fraction of the voting-age population make it clear that non-voters now outnumber voters in most American elections (Wolfinger and Rosenstone 1980, Appendix A). This fact, which puts the United States at the low end of electoral participation among contemporary democratic states, is not easy to accept in a nation that, more than any other, has defined itself by its arrangements for self-government.

Of course, the outcomes of elections would not necessarily change if all those eligible to vote actually did so,[26] but this fact should not be overly comforting. The many habitual non-voters are by no means a random sample of the eligible electorate, but are disproportionately young, unschooled, and poor. Moreover, these troubling biases have been exacerbated in the past three decades, as declines in turnout have been noticeably concentrated among groups that were already less likely to participate in the electoral process. The difficulty of getting these citizens to the polls encourages parties and candidates to discount their interests (Bartels 1998). Thus, it is quite possible for non-voters to share the opinions of voters on the issues that happen to be put before the public, while other issues that would be of greater concern to non-voters are simply ignored by candidates for office.

The problem of class bias in turnout is complicated by the fact that those who are most in need of political mobilization often have least access to political information. The poor are a relatively unattractive audience for advertisers, and thus for the traditional commercial media. They are also especially unlikely to have access to cable television news, the Internet, and other potentially rich sources of specialized political information. In many cases, their strongest social ties are to churches, labor unions, neighborhoods, and ethnic groups. Thus, parties and civic groups aiming to engage these least involved citizens may have to rely on old-fashioned methods of personal contact. For example, one recent study of electoral mobilization among Latinos found that only direct contacts by Latino organizations had a significant impact on turnout (Shaw et al. 1998).

One seldom-noticed cause of low turnout is the sheer number of elections in which Americans are expected to participate at the national, state, and local level, including primaries, general elections, and referenda. Whereas a typical democracy might have one round of national elections and one round of local elections in a four-year cycle, a conscientious voter in the United States makes half a dozen or more trips to the polls in four years, and casts dozens of separate votes. The result is to increase considerably the voter's burdens of time and attention, dissipating a finite stock of civic energy. Thus, one careful analysis attributed a significant fraction of the turnout decline in presidential elections since 1960 to the fact that most states have moved their gubernatorial elections to midterm years, losing the potential spillover effects of citizen mobilization produced by competitive gubernatorial campaigns (Rosenstone and Hansen 1993).

A second, even more important cause of low turnout in the United States, by comparison with most other democracies, is the fact that Americans must register to vote rather than simply turning up at the polling place on Election Day (Kelley et al. 1967; Powell 1986). In 1996, more than 50 million otherwise eligible citizens could not vote because they were not registered in advance of the election. Writing in 1980, Raymond Wolfinger and Steven Rosenstone (1980, table 4.2) estimated that easing registration laws in a variety of ways—by eliminating closing dates, allowing registration outside of regular business hours, and the like—would increase national turnout by about nine percentage points.

Some of this potential increase has since been realized, most notably with the passage in 1993 of the National Voter Registration Act, the so-called "Motor Voter" law. The Motor Voter law was intended to reduce bureaucratic obstacles to voting by requiring states to provide uniform registration services through drivers' license offices, public assistance and disability agencies, and mail-in registration. Early evidence suggests that the Motor Voter law did produce a significant increase in voter registration. From 1995 to 1996, the first full year of implementation, more than 20 million citizens were registered to vote or updated their voting addresses—a higher total than in any previous one-year period. Florida and Texas each registered a million *new* voters in 1995–1996; and new registrations in the 18 to 21 year-old category doubled.[27]

The main objections raised against registration reform in the debate leading up to the passage of the Motor Voter law were that it would encourage fraudulent voting and that it would bias election outcomes in favor of Democrats. However, experience with the system so far does not seem to sustain either of those objections. We know of no evidence suggesting that fraudulent voting has increased as a result of simplified registration. Nor is there any evidence of significant partisan bias. Of the 20 million voters who registered under the Motor Voter law in 1995–1996, about half (49 percent) registered as Democrats and about a third (34 percent) registered as Republicans; these proportions are quite consistent with the proportions of party identifiers in contemporaneous surveys of the entire adult population.[28] In a state-by-state analysis, Democratic registrations dropped off slightly in most states using Motor Voter procedures, while Republican registration remained essentially constant (Thompson 1996).

Of course, the main point of easing voter registration is to increase actual turnout on Election Day. Here, the impact of the Motor Voter law is less clear. Some skeptics have argued that the low level of overall turnout in the 1996 elections by comparison with 1992 implies that, in the end, the Motor Voter law had little or no real impact. However, that conclusion seems unwarranted in view of the wide variety of other factors that increase or decrease overall turnout in any given election year. Our view is that further experience, and more careful assessment, will be necessary to gauge the ultimate impact of recent registration reforms.

In the meantime—and in the absence of any convincing evidence of either increased fraud or significant partisan bias—we see every reason to press forward with efforts to make registration and voting as convenient and painless as possible. One avenue worthy of further consideration is a fully automatic registration system, which would presumably have even greater positive effects than those already achieved under the Motor Voter law. Any fully automatic registration system would have to overcome even more substantial concerns about potential fraud and abuse, as well as a variety of logistical hurdles. Nevertheless, we believe that the routine and apparently successful operation of automatic registration systems in many other democracies around the world suggests that the United States, too, should be able to provide automatic access to the ballot for every eligible citizen. Thus, we urge reformers and election officials to explore the logistics of a fully automatic registration system.

Another important way to make electoral participation easier is to give voters more control over when and how they cast their ballots. Some states have liberalized procedures for casting absentee ballots, greatly reducing the difficulty of voting for citizens who are either too immobile to get to the polls (for example, due to illness or infirmity) or too mobile to get to the polls (for example, business travelers and vacationers). In six states, any eligible voter who wants to cast an absentee ballot may do so, producing what is in effect an optional vote-by-mail system; in Oregon all eligible voters in some elections have automatically received mail ballots. Seven other states allow early in-person voting up to three weeks before Election Day.

While these liberalized voting procedures deserve further study, evidence currently available suggests that they do increase turnout, especially when parties and candidates engage in focused mobilizing efforts (Oliver 1996). At the same time, early voting does not appear to produce significant partisan biases or negative effects on the quality of political deliberation.[29] Thus, we view these developments as promising steps toward a less rigid, more inclusive democratic process, and urge states to experiment further with more flexible voting procedures.

One other procedural change that has frequently been suggested to increase turnout is to make Election Day an official holiday, as many other countries do. While we know of no solid evidence regarding the likely benefits or costs of such a proposal, we consider it sufficiently promising to warrant adoption by one or a few states on a trial basis. Aside from whatever direct effect it might have by making electoral participation more convenient for working people, an Election Day holiday would stand as a powerful symbolic recognition of the civic significance of voting.

Combining the Pieces: The Compact Model

Our analysis and recommendations have focused in part upon the structural and legal environment in which American campaigns and elections are conducted, but even more upon the actual conduct of campaigners, the media, and the public. We have, we think, suggested a variety of small but important ways in which each of these major actors could better fulfill its role in the campaign process. While we have attempted to shape our recommendations to take account of their incentives and constraints, we recognize that some of those recommendations will only be practical to the extent that campaigners, the media, and the public are willing to subordinate their immediate self-interest for the sake of a broader social good—a more informative, engaging, and edifying campaign process.

One promising model of cooperative, voluntary reform is provided by the Minnesota Compact, proposed by journalist Tom Hamburger of the *Minneapolis Star and Tribune* in 1995. The Minnesota Compact was sponsored and widely publicized by a coalition of civic, business, media, and academic groups, and was endorsed by 283 candidates for state and local offices in the 1996 election. By setting out clearly the responsibilities of candidates, the news media, and citizens in the electoral process, and by inviting clear commitments to these norms in advance of the campaign, the compact facilitated the enforcement of good campaign behavior on all sides. By casting citizens as responsible partners in the electoral process, its sponsors aimed both to engage and empower them and to mobilize them as a corrective force on the behavior of politicians and the press. Polling data from the senatorial race between Paul Wellstone and Rudy Boschwitz suggest that voters rejected ads aired on Boschwitz's behalf that they perceived as "unfair"; this apparent public backlash was consistent with the spirit of the compact, and may have been facilitated by extensive ad watching conducted by the media as part of their role under the compact. More generally, newspaper coverage of the race avoided an excessive focus on strategy and tactics and provided sustained coverage of issues (Cappella and Brewin 1998; Taylor 1998).

The 1996 Senate race in Massachusetts was notable for two voluntary efforts to improve the quality of the campaign: a series of widely publicized candidate debates hosted by the news media; and an agreement by the two campaigns to limit spending, advertising, and the influence of outside money in the race. The compact in Massachusetts succeeded in all but eliminating outside issue advocacy advertising and independent expenditures. However, the spending agreement broke down in the final weeks of the campaign.

A similar effort was undertaken during the 1997 New Jersey gubernatorial race. A campaign forum sponsored by Rutgers University's Eagleton Institute of Politics brought together campaigners, consultants, academics, and reporters to discuss a variety of efforts to elevate the level of campaign discourse: well-publicized debates; a focus by the news media on information about the candidates, issues, and accuracy in the campaign; and agreements by the candidates to take responsibility for ads by independent groups, appear and speak in ads mentioning their opponents, and avoid running ads distorting the voices or images of their opponents. The Republican and Democratic nominees agreed to participate in two broadcast debates, and to speak in "free time" on the New Jersey public broadcasting station; they also agreed to focus on the issues and avoid personal attacks, and to submit their ads for review by researchers at the Annenberg Public Policy Center. A post-campaign analysis of ads and free time (Waldman 1998) concluded that the campaign was "relatively free of the kinds of harshly 'negative' attacks and distortions that characterized the Senate race in that state the year before."

Obviously, efforts of this sort will be only as successful as campaigners, the media, and the public are willing to make them. Nevertheless, we see some promise in the "compact model," both as a practical mechanism for achieving voluntary cooperation among these various actors and as a potent symbol of their shared responsibility for improving the American campaign process.

NOTES

1. Thus, when the economy is booming, as it was in 1964 and 1984, the incumbent party usually wins in a landslide; when it is weak, as it was in 1980, the incumbent party often gets trounced. Parties held responsible for starting unsuccessful wars (as the Democrats were in 1952 and 1968) suffer significantly as a result; so do parties that nominate candidates who are far from the mainstream of voter opinion (Barry Goldwater, George McGovern). On these and other predictable features of presidential voting patterns and election outcomes, see, for example, Campbell et al. 1960; Rosenstone 1983; Lewis-Beck and Rice 1992; Markus 1992; and Miller and Shanks 1996.

2. The legal responsibilities of broadcasters to serve the public interest under the Communications Act of 1934 present a limited but potentially important exception to this generalization, which we touch on in the subsequent discussion of proposals for free airtime.

3. Other important works on political information and inference include Lupia 1994; Bartels 1996; and Lupia and McCubbins 1998.

4. One pioneering study concluded from an analysis of survey data that campaign advertising had a "truly impressive" impact on voters' knowledge of the candidates' issue positions and "contributed heavily to the political education of the individuals who were least attentive to newspapers" (Patterson and McClure 1976, 116, 125). A more recent study based on experimental data found that "advertising on the issues informs voters about the candidates' positions and makes it more likely that voters will take their own preferences on the issues into account when choosing between the candidates," that "advertising reinforces or 'awakens' latent partisan predispositions," and that "advertising works to level differences between the 'haves' and 'have-nots'" with respect to political information (Ansolabehere and Iyengar 1995, 8–9, 10, 9).

5. For example, one content analysis of presidential campaign spots (Geer 1998) found that the proportion of negative appeals increased from about 22 percent in 1960 to more than half in 1996.

6. "Six of the nine studies found negative political ads being rated as less ethical, less fair, and otherwise less liked than positive political ads, while two studies came to the opposite conclusions and one uncovered no significant differences" (Lau and Sigelman 1998, 15).

7. "Of the 20 relevant findings, 10 report no significant differences and two associate positive outcomes with negative political ads (e.g., higher turnout), but eight report significant negative consequences. . . . Concerns about these possible effects should be treated as genuine, but the jury is still out on them" (Lau and Sigelman 1998, 16–17).

8. For example, moral philosopher Michael Walzer (1997) has argued that there would be more substance in U.S. political discourse if there were fewer attack ads, and political activist Curtis Gans, director of the nonprofit Committee for the Study of the American Electorate, has advocated regulation of political advertising to reduce the prevalence of negativity (Carney 1998).

9. Compare, for example, the conclusions of Ansolabehere and Iyengar 1996 and Jamieson and Cappella 1997.

10. In an era of direct mail, narrowcast cable channels, and e-mail, it is increasingly important—as it was in the era before nationalized mass media—for journalists to monitor the content and consistency of candidates' appeals to various distinct and potentially insulated segments of the electorate.

11. "From 1960 to 1992, the proportion of interpretive election reports on the front page of the *New York Times* increased tenfold, from 8 percent to 80 percent" (Patterson 1993, 81).

12. Richard F. Fenno Jr. provided a forceful case study of the inadequacies of press portrayals of one national candidate's political career in his essay, "Political Scientists and Journalists: The Dan Quayle Experience," in Fenno 1990.

13. "The Choice '96" was one of four specific episodes cited by the jury that awarded "Frontline" the Gold Baton at the 1997 Alfred I. duPont–Columbia University Awards ceremony. The Center for New American Media won a Silver Baton for "Vote for Me," an innovative PBS miniseries profiling local political candidates.

14. One of the first (and most colorful) portrayals of pack journalism on the campaign trail was Crouse's *The Boys on the Bus* (1973).

15. These percentages are based on the 42 percent of the 1992 American National Election Study sample that indicated that they read a newspaper at least five times per week. These percentages overstate somewhat the political knowledge of regular newspaper readers, since with only two possible answers to each question, some respondents presumably arrived at the correct answer through guesswork.

16. One academic study (Just et al. 1996, chap. 6) found that "horse race" news coverage stimulated noticeably less interest and discussion among focus-group participants than either issue coverage (taken from ABC's "American Agenda" series) or direct communication by candidates.

17. In one interesting experiment (Rahn, Aldrich, and Borgida 1994), a team of scholars presented identical information about two hypothetical competing candidates using alternative formats. Some subjects saw a "candidate-centered" video in which each candidate was featured in a continuous seven- to eight-minute profile touching on his personal background, policy positions, and political party membership. Others saw a "debate" in which the same footage was edited to produce alternating statements by the two candidates on their backgrounds, then on their policy positions, then on their political parties. Among politically sophisticated subjects, recalled information and candidate evaluations were more strongly correlated in the candidate-centered format than in the debate format (.49 versus .31), but the reverse was true for relatively unsophisticated subjects (.28 versus .69).

18. The Commission on Presidential Debates has clearly been bipartisan rather than nonpartisan in its operations. Indeed, the organization's founding co-chairmen were Frank J. Fahrenkopf Jr. and Paul G. Kirk Jr., former chairmen of the Republican and Democratic National Committees, respectively.

19. This connection was quasi-officially asserted by Reed Hundt, then chairman of the Federal Communications Commission, in a March 1997 address on "Broadcasters and the Public Interest" (Annenberg Public Policy Center 1997, 30). "The FCC," Hundt pointed out, "is now writing the rules and preparing to grant the broadcast digital television licenses. We intend to make clear that these licenses will be issued subject to concrete and commensurate public interest obligations. Although we will grant these licenses in advance of defining specifically how these obligations will be carried out in the digital age, all broadcasters will take these licenses knowing that they will be subject to such obligations."

20. A notable exception to this generalization is the A. H. Belo Corporation, whose television stations in Dallas, Houston, Norfolk, Sacramento, Seattle, and Tulsa provided free airtime for five-minute statements by seventy-one congressional and gubernatorial candidates in the two weeks leading up to the 1996 election.

21. Some public-funding schemes would offer congressional candidates public money only if they agreed to limit or completely forgo additional private fund-raising. Since congressional candidates could (as presidential candidates can) choose not to accept public funds, relying instead on private contributions raised in accordance with existing regulations, such a system would not violate the prohibition on mandatory spending limits imposed by the Supreme Court's *Buckley v. Valeo* ruling. The majority and minority positions presented in the report of our sister task force on Campaign Finance Reform (Alexander et al. 1997) provide a more detailed discussion of the pros and cons of spending limits.

22. By way of comparison, the same survey found twice as much strong support for minor and largely irrelevant reforms such as banning contributions from noncitizens (56 percent) and requiring congressional candidates to raise a certain proportion of campaign funds in their own states (50 percent) (Princeton Survey Research Associates 1997).

23. The Supreme Court ruled in *Buckley v. Valeo* that federal campaign finance laws could regulate only communication that constituted "express advocacy" of the election or defeat of specific candidates. Subsequent court rulings have interpreted this stricture as ruling out regulation of political communication that does not include specific words such as *elect, defeat,* or *vote for,* regardless of the intent or impact of that communication.

24. Greenstein 1965 and Jennings and Niemi 1974 are representative studies of political socialization. Niemi and Junn 1998 provide contemporary evidence of the potential impact of civics training on political knowledge.

25. Information about the Kids Voting USA program and studies of its effects are available from the organization's website, http//:www.kidsvotingusa.org.

26. Writing in 1980, Wolfinger and Rosenstone (1980, 104) concluded, "For the present, it appears that advocates of both sides of major controversial policy issues

are represented among voters in proportion to their numbers in the general population." Herron 1998a and 1998b presented a more pessimistic assessment.

27. Senator Tom Daschle, news briefing sponsored by U.S. Senate Democratic Policy Committee, May 20, 1996, http://www.senate.gov/comm/dem-policy/general/events/960520.

28. For example, 52 percent of the sample in the 1996 American National Election Study identified themselves as Democrats or said they "leaned" toward the Democrats; 38 percent were Republican identifiers or "leaners."

29. For example, a recent study conducted in Texas (Stein 1998) found that early voters looked and behaved much like the rest of the electorate except that they relied somewhat more heavily on preexisting partisan predispositions.

REFERENCES

Adasiewicz, Christopher, Douglas Rivlin, and Jeffrey Stanger. 1997. "Free Television for Presidential Candidates: The 1996 Experiment." Philadelphia: Annenberg Public Policy Center, University of Pennsylvania, March.

Adatto, Kiku. 1990. "Sound Bite Democracy: Network Evening News Presidential Campaign Coverage, 1968 and 1988." Cambridge: Joan Shorenstein Barone Center, John F. Kennedy School of Government, Harvard University.

Alexander, Herbert E., et al. 1997. "New Realities, New Thinking: Report of the Task Force on Campaign Finance Reform." Citizens' Research Foundation, University of Southern California.

Alvarez, R. Michael. 1997. *Information and Elections.* Ann Arbor: University of Michigan Press.

Annenberg Public Policy Center. 1997. "Free Air Time and Campaign Reform." Philadelphia: Annenberg Public Policy Center, University of Pennsylvania.

Ansolabehere, Stephen, and Shanto Iyengar. 1995. *Going Negative: How Political Advertisements Shrink and Polarize the Electorate.* New York: Free Press.

Ansolabehere, Stephen, and Shanto Iyengar. 1996. "Can the Press Monitor Campaign Advertising?" *Press/Politics* 1:72–86.

Bartels, Larry M. 1988. *Presidential Primaries and the Dynamics of Public Choice.* Princeton: Princeton University Press.

Bartels, Larry M. 1992. "The Impact of Electioneering in the United States." In *Electioneering: A Comparative Study of Continuity and Change,* ed. David Butler and Austin Ranney. Oxford: Clarendon Press.

Bartels, Larry M. 1996. "Uninformed Votes: Information Effects in Presidential Elections." *American Journal of Political Science* 40:194–230.

Bartels, Larry M. 1998. "Where the Ducks Are: Voting Power in a Party System." In *Politicians and Party Politics,* ed. John G. Geer. Baltimore: Johns Hopkins University Press.

Beck, Deborah, Paul Taylor, Jeffrey Stanger, and Douglas Rivlin. 1997. "Issue Advocacy during the 1996 Campaign: A Catalog." Philadelphia: Annenberg Public Policy Center, University of Pennsylvania, September.

Berelson, Bernard R., Paul F. Lazarsfeld, and William N. McPhee. 1954. *Voting: A Study of Opinion Formation in a Presidential Campaign.* Chicago: University of Chicago Press.
Brady, David W. 1988. *Critical Elections and Congressional Policy Making.* Stanford, CA: Stanford University Press.
Buchanan, Bruce. 1996. *Renewing Presidential Politics: Campaigns, Media, and the Public Interest.* Lanham, MD: Rowman and Littlefield.
Budge, Ian, and Richard I. Hofferbert. 1990. "Mandates and Policy Outputs: U.S. Party Platforms and Federal Expenditures." *American Political Science Review* 84:111–31.
Campaign Discourse Mapping Project. 1996. *Assessing the Quality of Campaign Discourse: 1960, 1980, 1988, 1992.* Philadelphia: Annenberg Public Policy Center, University of Pennsylvania.
Campbell, Angus, Philip E. Converse, Warren E. Miller, and Donald E. Stokes. 1960. *The American Voter.* New York: Wiley.
Cappella, Joseph N., and Mark Brewin. 1998. "The Minnesota Compact and the Election of 1996." Philadelphia: Annenberg Public Policy Center, University of Pennsylvania, April.
Cappella, Joseph N., and Kathleen Hall Jamieson. 1994. "Broadcast Adwatch Effects: A Field Experiment." *Communication Research* 21:342–65.
Carney, Eliza Newlin. 1998. "Opting Out of Politics." *National Journal,* January 17, 106–11.
Center for Media and Public Affairs. 1992. "Clinton's the One." *Media Monitor,* November. Center for Media and Public Affairs, Washington, DC.
Clines, Francis X. 1997. "Election Oversight Unit Barely Treading Water." *New York Times,* November 23.
Cox, Gary W., and Jonathan N. Katz. 1996. "Why Did the Incumbency Advantage in U.S. House Elections Grow?" *American Journal of Political Science* 40:478–97.
Crouse, Timothy. 1973. *The Boys on the Bus: Riding with the Campaign Press Corps.* New York: Random House.
Fenno, Richard F. 1990. *Watching Politicians: Essays on Participant Observation.* Berkeley, CA: IGS Press.
Finkel, Steven E. 1993. "Reexamining the 'Minimal Effects' Model in Recent Presidential Campaigns." *Journal of Politics* 55:1–21.
Fishel, Jeff. 1985. *Presidents and Promises.* Washington, DC: CQ Press.
Gans, Herbert J. 1979. *Deciding What's News.* New York: Pantheon.
Geer, John G. 1998. "Campaigns, Party Competition, and Political Advertising." In *Politicians and Party Politics,* ed. John G. Geer. Baltimore: Johns Hopkins University Press.
Gelman, Andrew, and Gary King. 1993. "Why Are American Presidential Election Campaign Polls So Variable When Votes Are So Predictable?" *British Journal of Political Science* 23:409–51.
Greenfield, Jeff. 1982. *The Real Campaign: How the Media Missed the Story of the 1980 Campaign.* New York: Summit Books.

Greenstein, Fred I. 1965. *Children and Politics.* New Haven: Yale University Press.
Greer, Jennifer. 1997. "Newspaper Adwatches and the Less Experienced Voter." Paper presented at the annual meeting of the American Political Science Association, Washington, DC.
Hallin, Daniel C. 1994. *We Keep America on Top of the World: Television Journalism and the Public Sphere.* London: Routledge.
Herron, Michael C. 1998a. "The Presidential Election of 1988: Low Voter Turnout and the Defeat of Michael Dukakis." Unpublished manuscript, Northwestern University.
Herron, Michael C. 1998b. "Voting, Abstention, and Individual Expectations in the 1992 Presidential Election." Paper presented at the annual meeting of the Midwest Political Science Association, Chicago.
Holbrook, Thomas. 1996. *Do Campaigns Matter?* Thousand Oaks, CA: Sage.
Jacobson, Gary C. 1997. *The Politics of Congressional Elections.* 4th ed. Boston: Addison-Wesley.
Jamieson, Kathleen Hall. 1992. *Dirty Politics: Deception, Distraction, and Democracy.* New York: Oxford University Press.
Jamieson, Kathleen Hall. 1998. "The California Case Study." Philadelphia: Annenberg Public Policy Center, University of Pennsylvania, June.
Jamieson, Kathleen Hall, et al. 1996a. "Assessing the Quality of Campaign Discourse—1960, 1980, 1988, and 1992." Annenberg Public Policy Center, University of Pennsylvania, July.
Jamieson, Kathleen Hall, et al. 1996b. "1996: Better or Worse?" Philadelphia: Annenberg Public Policy Center, University of Pennsylvania, November.
Jamieson, Kathleen Hall, and Christopher Adasiewicz. 1999. "Presidential Debates in the U.S." In *Televised Election Debates: An International Comparison,* ed. Stephen Coleman. New York: Macmillan.
Jamieson, Kathleen Hall, and Joseph N. Cappella. 1997. "Setting the Record Straight: Do Ad Watches Help or Hurt?" *Press/Politics* 2:13–22.
Jamieson, Kathleen Hall, Paul Waldman, and Susan Sherr. 1998. "Eliminate the Negative? Defining and Refining Categories of Analysis for Political Advertisements." Paper presented at the American University Conference on Improving Campaign Conduct, Washington, DC.
Janowitz, Morris. 1983. *Reconstructing Patriotism.* Chicago: University of Chicago Press.
Jennings, M. Kent, and Richard G. Niemi. 1974. *The Political Character of Adolescence.* Princeton: Princeton University Press.
Johnston, Richard, André Blais, Henry E. Brady, and Jean Crête. 1992. *Letting the People Decide: Dynamics of a Canadian Election.* Montreal: McGill-Queen's University Press.
Just, Marion, Ann N. Crigler, Dean E. Alger, Timothy E. Cook, Mantague Kern, and Darrell M. West. 1996. *Crosstalk: Citizens, Candidates, and the Media in a Presidential Campaign.* Chicago: University of Chicago Press.
Kelley, Stanley, Jr., Richard E. Ayres, and William G. Bowen. 1967. "Registration

and Voting: Putting First Things First." *American Political Science Review* 61:359–79.
Key, V. O., Jr. 1966. *The Responsible Electorate: Rationality in Presidential Voting, 1936–1960.* Cambridge: Harvard University Press.
Kramer, Gerald H. 1971. "Short-Term Fluctuations in U.S. Voting Behavior, 1896–1964." *American Political Science Review* 65:131–43.
Lau, Richard A., and Lee Sigelman. 1998. "The Effectiveness of Negative Political Advertising: A Literature Review." Paper presented at the American University Conference on Improving Campaign Conduct, Washington, DC.
Lewis-Beck, Michael S., and Tom W. Rice. 1992. *Forecasting Elections.* Washington, DC: CQ Press.
Lupia, Arthur. 1994. "Short Cuts versus Encyclopedias: Information and Voting Behavior in California Insurance Reform Elections." *American Political Science Review* 88:63–76.
Lupia, Arthur, and Mathew D. McCubbins. 1998. *The Democratic Dilemma: Can Citizens Learn What They Need to Know?* New York: Cambridge University Press.
Mann, Thomas E. 1999. "The U.S. Campaign Finance System under Strain: Problems and Prospects for Change." In *Setting National Priorities: 1999,* ed. Robert D. Reischauer and Henry J. Aaron. Washington, DC: Brookings Institution.
Markus, Gregory B. 1992. "The Impact of Personal and National Economic Conditions on Presidential Voting, 1956–1988." *American Journal of Political Science* 36:137–54.
Miller, Warren E., and J. Merrill Shanks. 1996. *The New American Voter.* Cambridge: Harvard University Press.
Niemi, Richard G., and Jane Junn. 1998. *Civic Education: What Makes Students Learn.* New Haven: Yale University Press.
Oliver, J. Eric. 1996. "The Effects of Eligibility Restrictions and Party Activity on Absentee Voting and Overall Turnout." *American Journal of Political Science* 40:498–513.
Ornstein, Norman J., Thomas E. Mann, Paul Taylor, Michael J. Malbin, and Anthony Corrado. 1997. "Reforming Campaign Finance." In *Campaign Finance Reform: A Sourcebook,* ed. Anthony Corrado, Thomas E. Mann, Daniel R. Ortiz, Trevor Potter, and Frank J. Sorauf. Washington, DC: Brookings Institution.
O'Sullivan, P. B., and S. Geiger. 1995. "Does the Watchdog Bite? Newspaper Ad Watch Articles and Political Attack Ads." *Journalism and Mass Communication Quarterly* 72:771–85.
Patterson, Thomas E. 1993. *Out of Order.* New York: Knopf.
Patterson, Thomas E., and Robert D. McClure. 1976. *The Unseeing Eye: The Myth of Television Power in National Elections.* New York: Putnam.
Pfau, Michael, and Allan Louden. 1994. "Effectiveness of Ad Watch Formats in Deflecting Political Attack Ads." *Communication Research* 21:325–41.
Pomper, Gerald, with Susan Lederman. 1976. *Elections in America.* New York: Dodd, Mead.

Popkin, Samuel L. 1991. *The Reasoning Voter: Communication and Persuasion in Presidential Campaigns.* Chicago: University of Chicago Press.
Powell, G. Bingham, Jr. 1986. "American Voter Turnout in Comparative Perspective." *American Political Science Review* 80:17–43.
Princeton Survey Research Associates. 1997. "Money and Politics: A National Survey of the Public's Views on How Money Impacts Our Political System." Washington, DC: Center for Responsive Politics, April–May.
Rahn, Wendy M. 1998. "Generations and American National Identity: A Data Essay." Paper presented at the Annenberg Center workshop on Communication in the Future of Democracy, Washington, DC.
Rahn, Wendy M., John H. Aldrich, and Eugene Borgida. 1994. "Individual and Contextual Variations in Political Candidate Appraisal." *American Political Science Review* 88:193–99.
Rahn, Wendy M., John Brehm, and Neil Carlson. 1997. "National Elections as Institutions for Generating Social Capital." Paper presented at the annual meeting of the American Political Science Association, Washington, DC.
Rosenstone, Steven J. 1983. *Forecasting Presidential Elections.* New Haven: Yale University Press.
Rosenstone, Steven J., and John Mark Hansen. *Mobilization, Participation, and Democracy in America.* New York: Macmillan.
Schmid, Jeff. 1996. "Election '96: Voting Smart with Project Vote Smart." Document at website http//:epicom.com/voices.
Shaw, Daron, Rodolfo de la Garza, and Johngho Lee. 1998. "Explaining Latino Turnout in 1996: A Three State Validated Survey Approach." Paper presented at the annual meeting of the American Political Science Association, Boston.
Stein, Robert M. 1998. "Early Voting." *Public Opinion Quarterly* 62:57–69.
Taylor, Paul. 1996. "Politics in Prime Time." *New Democrat* (September–October): 40.
Taylor, Paul. 1998. *Case Study: The Minnesota Compact.* Washington, DC: Alliance for Better Campaigns.
Thompson, Brent. 1996. "The Motor Voter Boondoggle." *Washington Times,* November 18.
Waldman, Paul. 1998. *Free Time and Advertising: The 1997 New Jersey Governor's Race.* Philadelphia: Annenberg Public Policy Center, University of Pennsylvania, February.
Walzer, Michael. 1997. "Left Alone." *New Republic,* March 24, 27.
West, Darrell. 1997. *Air Wars: Television Advertising in Election Campaigns.* 2d ed. Washington, DC: CQ Press.
Wolfinger, Raymond E., and Steven J. Rosenstone. *Who Votes?* New Haven: Yale University Press.
Zaller, John R. 1997. "A Theory of Media Politics." Unpublished manuscript, University of California, Los Angeles.
Zaller, John R. 1998. "Monica Lewinsky's Contribution to Political Science." *PS: Political Science and Politics* 33:182–89.

Task Force Members

Larry M. Bartels is professor of politics and public affairs and Donald E. Stokes Professor of Public and International Affairs in the Woodrow Wilson School at Princeton University. He is the author of *Presidential Primaries and the Dynamics of Public Choice,* and he served from 1997 to 2000 as chair of the Board of Overseers of the American National Election Studies.

Henry E. Brady is professor of political science and public policy and director of the Survey Research Center at the University of California at Berkeley. He is the coauthor of *Letting the People Decide: Dynamics of a Canadian Election* and *Voice and Equality: Civic Voluntarism in American Politics.*

Bruce Buchanan is professor of government at the University of Texas at Austin. He directed major studies of the media and the electorate in 1988, 1992, and 1996 for the Markle Foundation, and his books *Electing a President* and *Renewing Presidential Politics* are based on those studies.

Charles H. Franklin is associate professor of political science at the University of Wisconsin at Madison. His articles on campaigns, voting behavior, and research methods have appeared in the *American Political Science Review,* the *American Journal of Political Science,* and other leading scholarly journals.

John G. Geer is professor of political science at Vanderbilt University. He is the author of *From Tea Leaves to Opinion Polls: A Theory of Democratic Leadership* and *Nominating Presidents: An Evaluation of Voters and Primaries,* and the editor of *Politicians and Party Politics.*

Shanto Iyengar is professor of communication and political science at Stanford University. His work on the media and political psychology includes *Going Negative: How Political Advertisements Shrink and Polarize the Electorate, Is Anyone Responsible? How Television Frames Political Issues,* and *News That Matters.*

Kathleen Hall Jamieson is dean of the Annenberg School for Communication and director of the Annenberg Public Policy Center at the University of Pennsylvania. She is a leading media commentator on political communication. Her scholarly works include *Spiral of Cynicism, Dirty Politics, Packaging the Presidency,* and *Presidential Debates.*

Marion R. Just is professor of political science at Wellesley College. She led major studies of political communication in the 1992 and 1996 presidential campaigns and is coauthor of *Crosstalk: Citizens, Candidates, and the Media in a Presidential Campaign* and of *Common Knowledge: News and the Construction of Political Meaning.*

Stanley Kelley Jr. is professor of politics, emeritus, at Princeton University. He has published numerous works on political parties and elections, including *Political Campaigning: Problems in Creating an Informed Electorate* and *Interpreting Elections.*

Thomas E. Mann is the W. Averell Harriman Senior Fellow at the Brookings Institution. He is a leading commentator on Washington politics, former executive director of the American Political Science Association, and former director of governmental studies at Brookings. His books include *Unsafe at Any Margin: Interpreting Congressional Elections* and *Campaign Finance Reform: A Sourcebook.*

Samuel L. Popkin is professor of political science at the University of California at San Diego. He has served as a consultant to the CBS News election unit and in the McGovern, Carter, and Clinton presidential campaigns. His books include *The Reasoning Voter: Communication and Persuasion in Presidential Campaigns* and *Candidates, Issues, and Strategies.*

Daron R. Shaw is assistant professor of government at the University of Texas at Austin. He has worked in a variety of Republican campaigns, including the Bush presidential campaign in 1992, and has published studies on the effects of campaign events and political advertising.

Lynn Vavreck is assistant professor of government at Dartmouth College. She served on the Quayle campaign staff in 1992 and has written scholarly articles on campaign effects in the United States and elsewhere.

John R. Zaller is professor of political science at the University of California at Los Angeles. His scholarly works include *The Nature and Origins of Mass Opinion, The American Ethos,* and numerous articles and book chapters on public opinion, attitude change, and media politics.

Index

Acock, Alan C., 177
Adasiewicz, Christopher, 2, 11, 16, 101, 218, 223
Adatto, Kiku, 126, 136, 217
Advertisements: positional, 65, 69–74; substance of, 64–66; traits of, 69; valence, 65, 69–72; 30-second, 69–73; 60-second, 69–73
Advertising, 207–12; distortions in, 115–16, 209; effectiveness of negative, 209; of issues, 64, 129; negative or attack, 10–13, 52–54, 82, 86, 188, 208; and the public bad, 81; and quality of discourse, 131
Adwatch, 2, 210–11, 239; on accuracy, 110–11, 114–15; as a disincentive to lying, 106–8, 115; on "Empty," 112; format of, 110; frequency of, 115; future of, 119; in health care reform debate, 108; lack of effect of, 118; on "Riady1," 113; on strategy, 110–11, 114–15; on "Stripes," 112; in 1988, 106; in 1992, 107; in 1996, 111
Aldrich, John H., 49, 241
Alexander, Herbert E., 188, 242
Alger, Dean E., 3, 58, 66, 129–30, 136, 141, 147, 167–68, 210, 241
Alliance for Better Campaigns, 80, 141, 189
Almond, Gabriel, 183
Alvarez, R. Michael, 203
American Association of Retired Persons, 114, 117
American Citizens Foundation, 191, 193

American National Election Studies, 175
Annenberg Public Policy Center, 76, 107–8, 110–11, 117, 167, 196, 223–24, 239, 242
Ansolabehere, Stephen, 7, 10, 11, 13, 19, 20, 62, 80, 82–83, 118, 124, 145, 147–48, 150, 186, 188, 208, 210–11, 240–41
Arterton, F. Christopher, 126
Asher, Herbert, 167
Ayres, Richard, 236

Bartels, Larry M., 7, 36, 37, 58, 82, 85, 103, 146, 161, 173, 174–76, 180, 193, 202, 203, 235, 240
Bates, Stephen, 66
Beck, Deborah, 228–29
Behr, Roy, 147–48, 150
Beiner, Ronald, 182
Bennett, Courtney, 115
Bennett, W. Lance, 126
Berelson, Bernard R., 30, 76, 89, 122, 174, 202
Blais, André, 203
Blumler, Jay, 125
Boller, Paul F., Jr., 79
Borgida, Eugene, 49, 241
Bowen, William G., 236
Box-Steffensmeier, Janet M., 188
Brack, Reginald K., Jr., 188
Brady, David W., 203
Brady, Henry E., 176, 203
Brehm, John, 177, 183, 203
Breslau, Karen, 152
Brewin, Mark, 239

253

Index

Broadcast bank, 224
Broder, David, 2, 111–12, 118, 120
Brody, Richard A., 122
Brown, Lloyd B., 146
Buchanan, Bruce, 6, 39, 42, 62–63, 66, 99, 182–83, 186, 191, 194, 203
Budge, Ian, 203
Buhr, Tami, 130, 141
Burkins, Glenn, 189
Burnham, Walter Dean, 176
Bush, George, 39, 40, 41, 63, 73, 76, 106–8, 152–54, 156–58, 160, 162, 168

Cain, Bruce, 80
Campaign attention, 84–87, 178; effects of campaign interest and participation on, 88–98
Campaign Code of Conduct/Compact Model, 101, 238; and adwatches, 239; in Massachusetts, 239; and media coverage, 239; in Minnesota, 238; in New Jersey, 239
Campaign Discourse Mapping Project, 5, 16, 76, 80, 82
Campaign effects, 146–50
Campaign events, 147, 151, 155
Campaign Finance Reform, 188, 226; and congressional matching funds, 226; and electronic reporting, 230; increase budget of FEC, 230; and issue advocacy, 227, 229; journalists' role in, 230; to promote competitiveness, 226; and soft money, 227–28
Campaign interest, 20–24, 47, 84–87, 146, 178, 183–84; effects of attention on, 88–92
Campaign quality: in 1988 and 1992, 39–42; in 1996, 42–44
Campaign reform, 2
Campaign tone, 4, 84–85
Campbell, Angus, 30, 89, 122, 240
Campbell, Carroll, 109
Campbell, James E., 146, 159
Candidate discourse, 123; in news, 126–27; on policy, 124, 127–29; quality of, 131
Candidate evaluations, 25–27, 46
Candidate interviews, 130–31
Candidate recruitment, 100
Cappella, Joseph N., 16, 115, 118, 195, 210, 239, 241
Carlson, Neil, 177, 183, 203
Carney, Eliza Newlin, 241
Carville, James, 148, 152, 168
Castellanos, Alex, 224
Center for Global Ethics, 80
Center for Media and Public Affairs, 16, 138–39, 141, 151, 217
Chaffee, Stephen, 234
Chambers, William Nisbet, 176
Chappell, Henry W., Jr., 146
Cherry, Lynne, 146, 159
Chicken George, 222
Christ, C. F., 88
Christian Coalition, 231
Civic duty, 190–91, 206
Civic journalism, 1
Clancey, Maura, 126
Clark, Harold D., 177
Clines, Francis X., 230
Clinton, Bill, 31, 41, 43, 63, 72, 74, 76, 77, 102, 107–17, 123, 130, 139, 153–54, 156–58, 160–62, 167–69, 227
CNN, 107
Cohen, Cathy, 14
Cohen, Jacob, 166
Cohen, William, 112
Commission on Presidential Debates, 220–22, 242
Committee for the Study of the American Electorate, 241
Common Cause, 117
Communication Act of 1934, 224
Consortium for Campaign Media Analysis, 139
Conventions, 136–37, 152, 156, 158, 161
Convention Speeches, 129; quality of discourse, 131
Converse, Philip E., 30, 89, 122, 240

Cook, Timothy E., 3, 58, 66, 129–30, 136, 141, 147, 167–68, 210, 241
Corrado, Anthony J., 188, 224
Cox, Gary W., 202
Craig, Stephen C., 173, 176
Crete, Jean, 203
Crigler, Ann N., 3, 58, 66, 125, 129–30, 136, 141, 147, 167–68, 210, 241
Crowley, Elizabeth, 192
Cues, 35; voter use of, 8
Cynicism, 173, 211

Dahl, Robert A., 174
Dawson, Michael, 14
Debates, 2, 136–37, 152, 158, 161, 219; alternate formats for, 220; as a condition of receiving public funds, 222; differential effects of, 179; impact of, 49; and policy discourse, 129; and quality of discourse, 131; re-broadcasting of, 222; and regime support, 178–79; as socialization mechanism, 189; who participates in, 221
DeBoef, Suzanna, 166
DeFrank, Thomas M., 152, 160
de la Garza, Rodolfo, 236
Deliberative polling, 2
Delli Carpini, Michael X., 182, 184
Democratic National Committee, 109
Diamond, Edwin, 66
Dionne, E. J., 177
Dole, Bob, 31, 57, 77, 109, 111–17, 123, 130, 139, 152, 154, 156–58, 162
Donaldson, Sam, 114–15
Downs, Anthony, 190
Dukakis, Michael, 13, 39, 40, 63, 76, 102, 106
Dulio, David A., 100

Eagleton Institute of Politics, 239
Easton, David, 173, 176, 180, 182
Efron, Edith, 167
Engberg, Eric, 114

Fair, Ray C., 146

Faith in elections, 26–29, 173, 174
Federal Election Commission, 224, 229–30
Fenno, Richard F., 124, 241
Finkel, Steven E., 7, 11, 57, 62, 68, 80, 82–83, 146, 183–86, 202
Fiorina, Morris P., 190, 195
Fishel, Jeff, 203
Fishkin, James S., 2
Forecasting elections, 153, 160
Fournier, Patrick, 38, 55, 58
Frankel, Max, 118
Franklin, Charles H., 13, 45
Free airtime, 2, 100, 127, 137, 187, 223; and "broadcast bank," 224; on CBS, 223; and Communication Act of 1934, 224; and format restrictions, 225; on Fox network, 223; in local elections, 225; on NBC, 223; and paid advertising, 225; on PBS, 223; and policy discourse, 129; and quality of discourse, 131, 223; on UPN, 223; voters' reaction to, 224
Freedman, Paul, 62, 67–68
Free TV for Straight Talk Coalition, The, 223
Friedrich, Robert J., 166
Full Information Maximum Likelihood, 88
Fully informed voting, 36–38

Gans, Curtis, 241
Gans, Herbert J., 125, 156, 205
Gant, Michael M., 173, 175
Gaudet, Hazel, 89, 122
Geer, John G., 5, 11, 12, 17, 46, 47, 56, 57, 58, 64, 67–68, 80, 82–83, 85, 102, 146, 159, 167, 186, 209, 240
Geiger, Seth, 118
Gelman, Andrew, 146–47, 161, 169, 202
Gerber, Alan, 189–92
Germond, Jack W., 39, 152
Ginsberg, Benjamin, 177
Goldenberg, Edie N., 150

Goldman, Peter, 152, 160
Goldstein, Kenneth M., 11, 62, 67–68
Granato, James, 166
Granger, Clive W., 166
Green, Donald, 189–92
Greenberg, Stanley, 152
Greene, William H., 102
Greenfield, Jeff, 4, 114, 148, 206
Greenstein, Fred I., 242
Greer, Jennifer, 210
Grunwald, Mandy, 108–9
Gurevitch, Michael, 125

Hallin, Daniel C., 126, 217
Hamburger, Tom, 238
Hansen, John Mark, 187–88, 193, 194, 236
Harrington, Richard, 192
Harris, Louis, & Associates, 178
Health Insurance Association of America, 111
Herron, Michael C., 243
Hetherington, Marc J., 145, 149, 167
Hibbing, John R., 173
Hofferbert, Richard I., 203
Holbrook, Thomas M., 7, 146, 149, 151–52, 202
Horton, Willie, 13, 14, 39, 40, 106, 108
Hughes, Sandra, 114
Hundt, Reed, 242
Hunter, James D., 173
Hwang, Hwang-Du, 146

Incentives: of candidates, 123–24, 204; of citizens, 106; of journalists, 124–25, 205; for reform, 137
Information, 231; on the Internet, 232; in pamphlets and voting guides, 231; and political socialization, 233–34
Institute for Global Ethics, 99–101
Interest groups, 189
Inter-University Consortium for Political and Social Research, 8
Investment model, 183

Issue advocacy, 228; and disclosure, 229
Issues: ambiguity, 13–14; and learning, 32–37; positional, 65, 69–74; valence, 65, 69–72; voter knowledge of, 8, 30–32, 48
Iyengar, Shanto, 7, 10, 11, 13, 19, 20, 62, 80, 82–83, 118, 124, 145, 147–48, 150, 163, 183, 186, 187, 208, 210–11, 240–41

Jackson, Brooks, 109, 114
Jacobson, Gary C., 150
Jamieson, Kathleen Hall, 2, 4, 5, 11, 14, 58, 62, 63, 65–68, 75, 76, 100, 102, 107, 112–13, 115, 118, 124, 126, 145, 147, 163, 167, 195, 208–11, 213, 217–18, 223, 241
Janowitz, Morris, 233
Jennings, M. Kent, 242
Johnson, Daniel C., 173
Johnson, R. G., 80
Johnson Foundation, Robert Wood, 108
Johnston, Anne, 57, 76
Johnston, Richard, 203
Jones, Ruth S., 188
Joslyn, Richard, 66, 76, 141
Journalists, 213–19; their interests compared to citizens', 219
Junn, Jane, 182, 184, 242
Just, Marion R., 3, 58, 66, 125, 129–30, 136, 138, 147, 167–68, 210, 241

Kahn, Kim Fridkin, 66
Kahn, Robert, 183
Kaid, Lynda Lee, 57, 76, 118, 124
Kanter Political Commercial Archive, 11, 67, 76
Kaplan, Harold, 108
Katz, Jonathan N., 202
Katz, Joseph, 183
Kaufman, Leslie, 152
Keeter, Scott, 182, 184

Kelley, Stanley, Jr., 3, 7, 29, 33, 49, 56, 64–65, 236
Kendall, Kathleen E., 126
Kennedy, John F., 76, 102, 116
Kenney, Patrick, 66
Kern, Montague, 3, 58, 66, 129–30, 136, 141, 147, 167–68, 210, 241
Key, V. O., Jr., 32, 124, 176, 203
Kids Voting USA, 234–35
Kiesler, Charles A., 183
Kinder, Donald, 14, 147
King, Gary, 146–47, 161, 169, 202
Kramer, Gerald H., 202
Krasno, Jonathan S., 188
Krosnick, Jon A., 166

Labor unions, 189–90
Lau, Richard, 11, 67, 80, 82, 208–9, 240
Lazarsfeld, Paul F., 30, 76, 89, 122, 176, 202
League of Women Voters, 80
Learning, 181, 184
Lee, Jongho, 236
Legitimacy, 175–76
Lehman, Edward W., 194
Leighley, Jan, 184–85
Lewis, Jeffrey B., 88
Lewis-Beck, Michael S., 146, 176, 240
Lichter, Robert S., 145, 147, 167–68, 195
Lincoln, Abraham, 79
Lippmann, Walter, 125
Lipset, Seymour M., 173
Louden, Allan, 118, 210
Lubell, Samuel, 125
Luntz, Frank, 66, 80
Lupia, Arthur, 35, 122, 240
Luskin, Robert C., 35
Luttbeg, Norman R., 173, 175

Macdonald, Stuart Elaine, 70
Malbin, Michael J., 188, 224
Mann, Thomas E., 125, 224, 227

Markle Commission on the Media and the Electorate, 191
Markle Foundation Survey, 178–79, 182, 184, 188, 193–94, 195
Markus, Gregory B., 146, 240
Matalin, Mary, 148, 152, 168
Mathews, Tom, 152, 160
Mayer, William G., 11, 82
Mazeika, Erlinda, 11, 80, 82
McAllister, B., 80
McCleod, Jack, 234
McClure, Robert, 66, 141, 240
McCombs, Maxwell E., 147
McCubbins, Mathew D., 240
McGovern, George, 31, 102
McGrory, Mary, 111
McKelvey, Richard D., 35
McKinnon, Lori Melton, 118
McPhee, William N., 30, 76, 176, 202
Mendelberg, Tali, 14
Merrill, Bruce, 234
Miller, A. H., 173
Miller, Mark, 152, 160
Miller, Warren E., 30, 89, 122, 187, 192, 196, 233, 240
Minnesota Compact, 238
Moncrief, Gary, 188
Mondale, Walter, 31
Motor Voter, 187, 236
Motor Voter law [National Voter Registration Act], 236–37
Moynihan, Daniel Patrick, 109
Murr, Andrew, 152, 160
Myers, Lisa, 109

Nagourney, Adam, 112
Negative campaigning, 62; normative appeal of, 63
Nelson, Candice J., 100
Neuman, W. Russell, 125
News coverage, 14, 15, 51–52, 212–29, 239; "Bad News," 17–19; constraints on, 213; of debates, 222; horse-race, 44, 215; negative, 52–54, 86; of policy schema,

News coverage (*continued*)
17–19; quality of, 133, 214; and repetition, 218; and rotating reporters, 217; of strategy/game schema, 17–19, 125–27, 129, 214–15
Newspaper coverage, 153; of events, 155
Nie, Norman H., 182
Niemi, Richard G., 246
Nixon, Richard, 31, 116
Noyes, Richard E., 145, 147, 167–68, 195

Oliver, J. Eric, 238
Ordeshook, Peter C., 35, 190
Ornstein, Norman J., 224
Orren, Gary R., 125–26
O'Sullivan, Patrick, 118, 210

Page, Benjamin I., 13, 35, 122
Page, Clarence, 192
Participation, 84–87, 173, 184, 235; and absentee ballots, 237; and class bias, 235–36; effects of campaign attention on, 93–98; and low turnout in elections, 175–76, 192–93, 235–36; and too many elections, 236; and registration laws, 236; and vote-by-mail, 238
Patterson, Thomas E., 2, 5, 16, 17, 18, 19, 20, 46, 47, 48, 50, 53, 54, 56, 66, 82, 85, 102, 115, 123–26, 129, 135, 141, 145, 147–48, 163, 167, 214–15, 217, 240–41
Perot, Ross, 39, 113–14, 123, 150, 152, 156, 160, 189
Peterson, Paul E., 190, 195
Petrocik, John R., 147
Pew Research Center, 100–101, 174
Pfau, Michael, 118, 210
Policy schema, 17–19
Political Communication Center, University of Oklahoma, 139
Political parties, 189

Political socialization, 233–34
Polsby, Nelson W., 126
Pomper, Gerald, 11, 80, 82, 141; with Susan Lederman, 203
Popkin, Samuel L., 8, 35, 79, 203, 206
Powell, G. Bingham, Jr., 236
Princeton Survey Research Associates, 178, 185–86, 195, 227, 242
Project on Campaign Conduct, 80, 99–101
Project Vote Smart, 136, 232–33
Public opinion, 147
Putnam, Robert D., 80

Quebec, 38

Rabinowitz, George, 70
Rahn, Wendy M., 49, 178, 183, 187, 193, 196, 203, 233, 241
Rather, Dan, 224
Reagan, Ronald, 28, 31, 67, 73, 113, 189
Reform standards, 2, 75, 99
Regime support, 178–81; and voting, 181
Republican National Committee, 151
Rice, Tom W., 146, 177, 240
Riker, William H., 181, 190
Rivlin, Douglas, 2, 11, 16, 101, 223, 228–29
Robinson, Michael J., 126, 167
Rosenberg, Debra, 152
Rosenstiel, Tom, 168
Rosenstone, Steven J., 14, 146, 186–88, 193, 195, 235–36, 240, 242
Roshco, Bernard, 156
Rousseau, Jean-Jacques, 182

Sabato, Larry J., 126, 148, 167
Salmore, Barbara, 150
Salmore, Stephen, 150
Sanders, Lynn, 14
Sargent, Jocelyn, 14
Schattschneider, E. E., 177
Schlozman, Kay Lehman, 177
Schmid, Jeff, 233

Schneider, William, 173
Schorr, Daniel, 112
Shanks, J. Merrill, 187, 192, 196, 233, 240
Shapiro, Robert Y., 35, 122
Shapiro, Walter, 111
Shaw, Daron R., 167, 176, 236
Shaw, Donald L., 147
Sheehan, Margaret, 167
Shelley, Mack C., II, 146
Sherr, Susan, 62, 65, 67–68, 76, 75, 208–9
Sigal, Leon, 156, 158
Sigelman, Lee, 208–9, 240
Simon, Adam, 124
Sniderman, Paul M., 122, 194
Socialization, 188
Soft money, 227; limitations on, 228
Sorauf, Frank J., 188
Sparrow, Bartholomew H., 167
Stand by your ad, 188
Stanger, Jeffrey, 2, 11, 16, 101, 223, 228–29
Stehlik-Barry, Kenneth, 182
Stein, Robert M., 243
Stimson, James, 64, 76
Stokes, Donald E., 30, 65–69, 76, 73, 89, 122, 240
Stout, David, 196
Sundquist, James L., 176

Taylor, Paul, 2, 80, 101, 187, 195, 214, 223–24, 228–29, 239
Tedesco, John, 118
Teixeira, Ruy A., 174, 175
Television coverage, 153; of events, 158
Tetlock, Philip E., 122
Theiss-Morse, Elizabeth, 173

Thomas, Evan, 152
Thompson, Brent, 237
Thompson, Dennis, 183
Thurber, James A., 100
Times Mirror Center, 108
Toner, Robin, 39
Town meetings, 220
Tracking polls, 150
Traits, 69
Traugott, Michael W., 150
Troxler, Howard, 112
Trust in government, 173–76
Tufte, Edward R., 7

Valentino, Nicholas, 124
Vavreck, Lynn, 102, 178
Verba, Sidney, 177, 183
Vote-by-mail, 238

Waldman, Paul, 62, 65, 67–68, 76, 75, 208–9, 239
Walzer, Michael, 241
Weissberg, R., 177
West, Darrel M., 3, 58, 66, 76, 129–30, 136, 141, 147, 167–68, 209, 210, 241
White, T. H., 125
Whitman, Christine Todd, 109
Wicker, Tom, 156
Wink, Kenneth, 146, 159
Witcover, Jules, 39, 152
Wolfinger, Raymond E., 89, 186, 235–36, 242
Woodward, Bob, 152
Wright, John R., 188

Zaller, John R., 5, 7, 14, 15, 43, 46, 47, 48, 50, 51, 80, 122, 202, 205